The Love-Game Comedy

The Love-Game Comedy

By

DAVID LLOYD STEVENSON

AMS PRESS, INC.
NEW YORK
1966

Copyright 1946, Columbia University Press
New York

Reprinted 1966
with permission of Columbia University Press

AMS PRESS, INC.
New York, N.Y. 10003

Manufactured in the United States of America

To

Professor Oscar James Campbell

From women's eyes this doctrine I derive:
They sparkle still the right Promethean fire;
They are the books, the arts, the academes,
That show, contain, and nourish all the world;
Else none at all in aught proves excellent.
        Love's Labour's Lost, Act IV, scene iii

Acknowledgments

My mentor in this study has been Professor Oscar James Campbell, of Columbia University. Without his critical acumen, his encouragement, and his enthusiasm this study could never have been made. Other members of the English Department of Columbia University who have given me the benefit of their judgment and who have filled in the gaps where my knowledge was attenuated, sometimes almost to invisibility, are Professor Roger Sherman Loomis, Dr. Henry W. Wells, Professor Harry Morgan Ayres, Professor Jefferson Butler Fletcher, Professor Ernest Hunter Wright, and Professor Marjorie Nicolson.

I wish also to acknowledge the many courtesies extended me by Dr. Louis B. Wright, who, acting for the trustees of the Huntington Library at San Marino, California, made the resources of this library available to me. I should add that not the least of these resources is the stimulating interchange of ideas among the scholars who gather at the Huntington Library.

I am in debt to Professor Clinton K. Judy, Chairman of the Humanities, California Institute of Technology, for making the facilities of the institute and his personal library available to me, and to Professor Bertrand H. Bronson, University of California, for his help in matters of presentation of the material in this study. I am in debt to my mother, Mrs. Frank L. Lawrence, whose encouragement and assistance in this study have been invaluable. Finally, I am deeply in debt to my wife, Joan Stevenson, for the burdensome checking of footnotes and quoted material, and for many candid readings of the manuscript, which caused me to remove many phrases which seemed impressive when set down, but which turned out to be merely inchoate strivings.

I acknowledge with thanks the kind permission granted by the following publishers and writers to quote passages from the books which are listed below.

Kegan Paul, Trench, Trubner & Co. for *Giordano Bruno*, by William Boulting; Walter Wilson Greg, Esq., for *Pastoral Poetry and Pastoral Drama*; Oxford University Press, London, for *The Imperial Theme*, by G. Wilson Knight; Sidgwick & Jackson and Sir Edmund Chambers for the latter's *Sir Thomas Wyatt and Some Collected Studies*; University of London Press for *The Poems of Sir Thomas Wiat*, by A. K. Foxwell. Honoré Champion for *John Lyly and the Italian Renaissance*, by Violet Jeffery; *Mercure de France* for an article by Pierre Grasset, "Faillite de l'amour courtois." Thomas Y. Crowell Co. for *British Drama*, by Allardyce Nicoll; Harcourt, Brace and Co. for *Tudor Ideals*, by Lewis Einstein; Harvard University Press for *The Decline of Chivalry*, by R. L. Kilgour; The Johns Hopkins Press for *The Works of Edmund Spenser: a Variorum Edition*; Henry E. Huntington Library and Art Gallery for *Comicall Satyre and Shakespeare's "Troilus and Cressida,"* by Oscar James Campbell; Longmans, Green and Co. for *Edmund Spenser*, by W. L. Renwick; The Macmillan Co. for *Shakespearean Comedy*, by H. B. Charlton, *Medieval Panorama*, by G. G. Coulton, and *Shakespeare's Studies*, by E. E. Stoll; Oxford University Press for *The Enchanted Glass*, by Hardin Craig, and *Shakespeare's Sonnets*, by Tucker Brooke; G. P. Putnam's Sons for *Cambridge History of English Literature*; University of Minnesota Press for *Mythology and the Renaissance Tradition*, by Douglas Bush; The University of North Carolina Press for *The Romanesque Lyric*, by Allen and Jones; Yale University Press for *Harington and Ariosto*, by Townsend Rich.

David Lloyd Stevenson

BERKELEY, CALIF.
JANUARY 15, 1946

Contents

	Introduction	xi
I.	Shakespeare's Love-Game Comedies	1
	The Dramatic Method (2). - The Intellectual Substance (6). - The Significance of This New Comedy (10)	
II.	Ovid and Sixteenth-Century Amorous Controversy	18
	Ovid's Influence on *Hero and Leander* (22). - Chapman's and Marston's Use of Ovid (24). - Ovid's Influence on Shakespeare's *Venus and Adonis* and *The Rape of Lucrece* (26)	
III.	Amorous Controversy in Medieval Literature	32 ✓
	Ascetic and Misogynic Attitudes (35). - Realistic Attitudes toward Love (38). - Literary Expressions of Conflict (39)	
IV.	Chaucer's Presentation of Amorous Controversy	47
	The Three Conceptions of Love (47). - Chaucer's Use of Conflict (54). - Chaucer's Attempt to Resolve Conflicting Attitudes (60). - Amorous Controversy in the Middle Ages and in the Renaissance (65)	
V.	Romance in Fifteenth-Century Literature	69
	Traditional Attitudes in the Fifteenth Century (69). - The Re-examination of Courtly Love in Fifteenth-Century Literature (73)	
VI.	Renaissance Adaptations and Re-evaluations of Medieval Attitudes	82
	Theologians' Re-evaluations of Ascetic Doctrines (85).	

The Platonic Adaptation of Courtly Love (89). - The Marital Adaptation of Courtly Love (96). - Summary (101)

VII. RENAISSANCE ATTEMPTS TO ACTUALIZE THEORIES OF COURTLY LOVE 103
Conceptions of Courtly Love in Early Tudor Conduct Books (107). - The Analysis of Love in *The Courtier* (111)

VIII. AMOROUS CONFLICT IN ELIZABETHAN POETRY 123
Wyatt's Treatment of Lovers' Ideals (127). - Conflict in *Astrophel and Stella* (130). - Realistic Greville (132). - Minor Amorous Poets (135). - Satire in Drayton and Marston (137). - Donne's Solution to Lovers' Difficulties (141). - Conflicting Ideas in Elizabethan Poetry and Comedy (144)

IX. LYLY'S QUARRELING LOVERS 148
Contending Attitudes in Lyly's Comedies (156). - Lyly's Resolution of Controversy (164)

X. CONFLICT IN SHAKESPEARE'S SONNETS 174

XI. SHAKESPEARE'S COMEDIES OF COURTSHIP 185
Shakespeare's First Love-Game Comedy, *Love's Labour's Lost* (190). - *As You Like It* (198)

XII. COMEDY OF COURTSHIP IN *Much Ado about Nothing* AND SATIRE OF COURTSHIP IN *Troilus and Cressida* 208

XIII. THE RIGHT PROMETHEAN FIRE 223

BIBLIOGRAPHY 233

INDEX 247

Introduction

IN MATTERS of love, the Elizabethan world had declared for the life of the senses as against Christian ascetic restraint, and for the lady of courtly romance or Petrarchan sonnet as against humble Griselda. But not absolutely and with a clear conscience. Conflicting attitudes toward love pervade its literature. These attitudes had been in active opposition at least since the twelfth century, when troubadour lyrics and courtly romances, which celebrated love as the most important aspect of existence, had been challenged both by religious spokesmen for the Middle Ages and by the realistically minded. It was a quarrel over the nature of love, current in medieval literature, which survived to be expressed again in such sixteenth-century moral tracts as Elyot's *The Boke of the Governour*, in such conduct books as *The Courtier*, and in such love poetry as that written by Wyatt, Sidney, Spenser, and Donne. Further, the witty, dueling lovers in Shakespeare's comedies of courtship, or love-game comedies, are dramatized embodiments of this quarrel. The ultimate purpose of this study is to give historical perspective to the conflicting attitudes toward love which are dramatized by these comedies (*Love's Labour's Lost, As You Like It, Much Ado*), to examine them as a final literary product of four centuries of controversy over the reality of romantic love. The intermediate purpose is twofold: to show the origins of this controversy and to show the ways in which various writers preceding and contemporary with Shakespeare make literary use of it.

By way of caution, one must note that it is impossible to take all love for one's province. When one traces the main stream of literary tendency which culminates in certain of Shakespeare's comedies, much that is merely tributary must be omitted or be given casual treatment. For example, the general attitudes toward love expressed by troubadour poets are highly important for an understanding of sixteenth-century English sonnets; the individual lyrics of specific troubadours are not.

Moreover, one needs, perhaps, to defend the use of Shakespeare's comedies as the final focus of this study, since the writings of a number of other literary figures of the Renaissance illustrate a controversy over love. The explanation is simply that Shakespeare was more astute than his contemporaries. He was the only writer of his day who was able to resolve this controversy in a generally satisfactory fashion. He was able to turn a contemporary conflict of ideas into high comedy. In doing this, he produced one of the major aesthetic and psychological triumphs of his age.

· I ·

Shakespeare's
Love-Game Comedies

MEN OF the Renaissance were intensely interested in theories and problems of human conduct. This preoccupation with morality is illustrated by the Reformation itself and by the writings of its leaders: Luther, Calvin, John Knox. In England much of the secular literature produced during the sixteenth century is almost wholly concerned with some aspect of behavior. It may be the presentation of an individual's sensations and emotions as he experiences passion, as in the sonnets and lyrics of Wyatt, Sidney, and Donne. It may be a general discussion of moral concepts or of examples of such concepts, as in *The Mirrour for Magistrates*, Hoby's translation of Castiglione's *Il cortegiano*, the pamphlet war over the position of woman, Spenser's *Faerie Queene*, Francis Bacon's *Essays*. This sixteenth-century concern gave rise, in poetry, to the formal literary satires of Hall and Marston,[1] for example, and, in drama, to the beginnings of a comedy of manners or of "humours." In the latter those who had taken the conventions of deportment or the foibles and the morals of society too seriously or too literally were subjected to a witty and sometimes biting mockery. The comedy of manners, by appealing to the audience's sense of proportion, asked that the overly elegant Fastidious Briskes and Osrics, and the overly puritanical Zeal-of-the-land Busys and Malvolios be regarded as absurd or hypocritical pretenders. It is a special development of this kind of wit and mockery, applied to the conventions of ro-

[1] See Campbell, *"Comicall Satyre" and Shakespeare's "Troilus and Cressida,"* ch. ii, "The Prevailing Forms of English Satire, 1588–1599."

mance, which is found in Shakespeare's comedies of courtship, or "love-game" comedies.

The Dramatic Method

Shakespeare is indebted to John Lyly's comedies for a method by which to dramatize a controversy over the nature of romantic love, current both in the Renaissance and in the Middle Ages. The incongruities of a man's actions while in love had been expressed for comic purposes only slightly, if at all, in other sixteenth-century plays. In John Heywood's *A Play of Love* (1533), it is true, one can detect a certain skepticism of the elaborate sufferings traditional to those in love.[2] In *The Rare Triumphs of Love and Fortune* (c. 1582) a half-realistic, half-idealistic attitude toward love pervades the play, where Hermione's passion for Fidelia is depicted as the plaything of Venus and Fortune.[3] There is some wit at the expense of romance in Peele's *Arraignment of Paris* (1584),[4] in Greene's *A Looking Glasse, for London and England* (1589),[5] and in *George a'Greene, The Pinner of Wakefield* (c. 1593).[6] But the ardors and posturings of lovers are not presented as a comedy of the manners of love in any of these plays, and there is no reason to suppose that they influenced Shakespeare. The direct source for his three love-game comedies, *Love's Labour's Lost, As You Like It*, and *Much Ado*, is to be found in the plays of his contemporary John Lyly. Here is the beginning of a new dramatic pattern to which Shakespeare contributed his talent—a pattern

---

[2] Heywood, *A Play of Love*. That is, by the character in this play called the "Non lover, not loving."

[3] *The Rare Triumphs of Love and Fortune* (1589), ed. by W. W. Greg. Lentulo, a servant, falls in love with Fidelia and his appearance (Act IV, scene iii) mad for love is a parody of the romantic, Petrarchan lover. Note stage direction to this scene "Enter Lentulo with a Ring in his mouth, a Marigolde in his hand."

[4] Peele, *The Works*, ed. by A. H. Bullen, Act II, scene i.

[5] Greene, *The Plays and Poems*, ed. by J. Churton Collins, Vol. I, Act II, scene i, ll. 436–443.

[6] *Ibid.*, Vol. II, Act II, scene iii. Jenkin, servant to George a'Greene, makes sport of love.

which continued to appear in English drama at least until the very end of the seventeenth century, when Congreve's brilliant *The Way of the World* was produced.[7]

As Lyly conceived it, the love-game comedy is scarcely to be distinguished from the usual Elizabethan dramatized love idyll, until one perceives that here and there in the play the comic spirit is being served by a denial of the rites and the ideals of romance itself. Ramis, in the following scene from Lyly's *Love's Metamorphosis*, for example, indicates the new dramatic pattern.[8] He finds himself in the awkward position of one who would approach the mistress of his fancy, Nisa, in the ritual proper to romantic courtship, only to have this ritual scornfully rejected. Instead of giving proof of his fidelity to his mistress after the fashion of the lover in a courtly romance, Ramis must first prove the existence of "love" itself.

Ramis: Dost thou disdaine Love and his lawes?
Nisa: I doe not disdaine that which I thinke is not, yet laugh at those that honour it if it be.
Ramis: Time shall bring to passe that Nisa shall confesse there is love.
Nisa: Then also will love make me confess that Nisa is a foole.
Ramis: Is it folly to love, which the gods accompt honourable, and men esteeme holy?
Nisa: The gods make any thing lawfull, because they be gods, and

---

[7] Comedy of the manners of love does not cease in the year 1700. But Restoration drama exhibits for the last time comedy based upon attitudes derived directly from medieval tradition. After 1700 courtly love and Petrarchism are taken over by a different social class. Both the manners of love and the comedy built around these manners change.

[8] Many writers have suggested the novelty of Lyly's achievement. John Dover Wilson, *John Lyly*, suggests that the comedy which begins with *Campaspe* ends with Oscar Wilde (p. 131). R. Warwick Bond, in *The Complete Works of John Lyly*, goes back of *Campaspe* to *Euphues* and comments that here "we enter the path which leads to the Restoration dramatists" (I, 161). Felix E. Schelling, in his *Elizabethan Drama*, with an eye on the realistic minutiae of Restoration drama, suggests that Jonson and Middleton lead to a comedy of manners that ends with Goldsmith and Sheridan (I, xxxiii). Joseph Wood Krutch, *Comedy and Conscience after the Restoration*, suggests that there is continuity from Lyly to the Restoration and also a separation in the "constant tendency" of Elizabethan court comedy "to escape into the land of fancy" (p. 9).

>men honour shadowes for substance, because they are men.
> Ramis: Both gods and men agree that love is a consuming of the heart and restoring, a bitter death in a sweete life.
> Nisa: Gods doe know, and men should, that love is a consuming of wit, and restoring of folly, a staring blindnesse, and a blind gazing.
> Ramis: Wouldst thou allot me death?
> Nisa: No, but discretion.[9]

It is obviously a far cry from this thin sally of wit to the contention between Beatrice and Benedick, in *Much Ado*. But beginnings must be simple, and to appreciate the quality of Lyly's achievement, one must contrast his delicate mockery with the Plautine comedy of the Renaissance. In Latinate comedies the author presents an egregious dupe of love in order to laugh boisterously at him. Lyly's comic drama, created out of a conflict of ideas, demanded no mere ingenious farcing, but an imaginative astuteness of a high order.

The preoccupation of this love-game comedy is that of all Renaissance literature, the pursuit of love. But in this comedy of the manners of love the pursuit is lightly tempered with disbelief. Among Shakespeare's plays one can distinguish *Two Gentlemen of Verona* at once from *Love's Labour's Lost* because of the difference in the underlying attitude of each toward romantic ideals. In one, the ritual of Valentine's courtship is the supreme emotional expression of his existence. No skeptic challenges his conviction that his Silvia

> . . . excels each mortal thing
> Upon the dull earth dwelling.[10]

In the other, wooing is not much more than a game, the importance of which those who play it are not always willing to admit. When they finally do agree to love in good earnest, it is not after the fashion set by Troilus or Tristan. They accept their bondage, not as converts to romance, but as revelers at a masque.

---

[9] *The Complete Works of John Lyly*, Vol. III, Act III, scene i, l. 11 *et sqq.*
[10] *Two Gentlemen of Verona*, Act IV, scene ii, l. 52. Quotations from Shakespeare are from The Oxford Standard Edition, ed. by Craig.

Expediency rather than sober devotion sets the tone of their passion, where "rimes are guards on wanton Cupid's hose," [11] and

> ... revels, dances, masks, and merry hours,
> Forerun fair Love, strewing her way with flowers.[12]

The comedies of courtship are further distinguished from drama which presents love wholly as a romantic ritual of wooing. In the first type one or more of the characters questions the value of amorous pursuit even while coming closer and closer to overtaking the object pursued. As we have seen in Lyly's *Love's Metamorphosis,* Nisa lays bare the pretensions of the Elizabethan ideal courtship.[13] A similar skepticism is found in *Love's Labour's Lost,* when the three lords and the king deny idyllic romance by fleeing the courtly world where such love exists. But all of them, like Benedick, turn finally to love, leaving their doubts somewhat grudgingly for illusion.

This skepticism about love, in the love-game comedy, is dramatized as a sex duel, a bantering quarrel in which one character (for Lyly always the man) accepts the conventional exaggerations concerning love, and his opponent, the woman, rejects them. In Lyly's play *Endimion,* Eumenides defends love, but Semele is sharply antagonistic to it. In Shakespeare's farce *The Taming of the Shrew* this same disagreement is found in the battle between Petruchio and Kate. It must be added, however, that in the usual Shakespearean love-game, the sex duel is more complicated. Both protagonists may deny romance, as do Beatrice and Benedick; or the lovers may shift position from denial to acceptance, as does Berowne in *Love's Labour's Lost.*

This quarrel over the value and place of love, never serious, was always expressed in a style that the Elizabethans called "conceited," that is, witty.[14] The light touch of a conversational play

---

[11] *Love's Labour's Lost,* Act IV, scene iii, l. 58.

[12] *Ibid.,* Act IV, scene iii, l. 379.

[13] Bond, *op. cit.,* III, 566 (note to ll. 50 *et sqq.,* p. 307), notes "Nisa's exposé of poetic fictions" concerning love.

[14] Note title page, 1598 Quarto, *Love's Labour's Lost:* "A pleasant con-

of words was necessary to emphasize the fact that under the surface of the lovers' disagreement was actual or probable surrender. This wit is a teasing ridicule either of love itself, of the poetic ritual of courtship, or of the person one is wooing. Thus, Berowne ridicules all amorous experience and the sonneteering form of courtship, whereas Benedick laughs at love and at Beatrice. Rosalind's reply to Orlando, when he expresses a traditional wish to die for love, states the point of view of all the skeptics in the duels which form a large part of this comedy:

> The poor world is almost six thousand years old, and in all this time there was not any man died in his own person, *videlicet*, in a love-cause. Troilus had his brains dashed out with a Grecian club; yet he did what he could to die before, and he is one of the patterns of love. Leander, he would have lived many a fair year, though Hero had turned nun, if it had not been for a hot mid-summer night; for, good youth, he went but forth to wash him in the Hellespont, and being taken with the cramp was drowned; and the foolish coroners of that age found it was "Hero of Sestos." But these are all lies: men have died from time to time, and worms have eaten them, but not for love.[15]

The Intellectual Substance

The characters in Shakespeare's love-game comedies reflect a quarrel of attitudes not found in the usual Elizabethan play, properly called "romantic." In this second type emotions and points of view are presented without much analysis. Everyone is simply in love with love, and the chief purpose of each character is to find someone upon whom to bestow his emotions (as in *Twelfth Night* or, more extravagantly, in *A Midsummer Night's Dream*), or some means to overcome obstacles standing between him and the attainment of love (as in *Two Gentlemen of Verona* or in *The Merchant of Venice*). Such drama, in large measure, avoids the disagreeable aspects of passion found, for example, in *Measure for Measure*. It is "escape" literature. It substitutes a

---

ceited comedie." Also Blount calls Lyly's plays "conceipted," in his Introduction to the *Sixe Court Comedies* of Lyly, 1632.

[15] *As You Like It*, Act IV, scene i, ll. 97 *et sqq.*

satisfying aesthetic experience for the less ideal love, full of the dissonance of reality, known and practiced by the members of the audience. For the duration of the play, its characters represent, to borrow a phrase, "an enchanting and attainable perfection of the real." [16] In this sort of drama, therefore, lovers are not thwarted by any self-conscious skepticism. Bassanio and the Duke of Illyria are not allowed to complicate the plots of *The Merchant of Venice* and *Twelfth Night* by questioning the basis of their attachments. Their love comes to fruition when they have overcome a series of physical obstacles in the way: for Bassanio, a lack of money and the predicament it caused; for the Duke of Illyria, the events necessary to penetrate Viola's disguise.

Such romantic comedies as *The Merchant of Venice* and *Twelfth Night* are free from a reflection of the natural difficulties of love; the significance of Shakespeare's love-game comedies is that they are not. In them the chief interest lies in situations which arise from antagonistic attitudes toward love held by the would-be lovers (as with Beatrice and Benedick), not in the dramatic narrative. These comedies present romantic escape from reality seen in the light of its disavowal. Their criticism of the accepted behavior of lovers takes nourishment from all the humanistic forces working through Renaissance life. Elizabethan romance, with its Arcadias and Violas provides an easy formula for daydreaming; but harsh voices were raised against such indulgence, here and there, at the moment of its flourishing. Spenser expressed his disapproval by the destruction of his "Bowre of Blis"; Francis Bacon denied love categorically, in the name of reason; [17] Fulke Greville wished Sidney's *Arcadia* to be an end of all Arcadias; [18] Hall and Marston, in their satires, lashed

[16] Quoted from Murry by Elmer Edgar Stoll, *Shakespeare's Young Lovers*, p. 48. Cf. Stoll's *Art and Artifice in Shakespeare*; ch. viii, especially pp. 156–157 on "comic illusion."

[17] *Essays*, ed. by Wright, "Of Love," pp. 36–38.

[18] Brooke, Fulke Greville, *Life of Sir Philip Sidney*, pp. 223–224. Greville's reason is that no one could come up to the "excellent intended" moral pattern of Sidney.

out at stylized Petrarchan love; John Donne turned the differences between Petrarchan ideals and actual experience over and over in his verse, like bits of glass in a kaleidoscope, as if trying to see how many patterns these differences would form. Shakespeare's love-game comedies are part of the quarrel over the nature of love found in the writings of these contemporaries. The novelty of Shakespeare's plays lies, not in the fact that they point out the unreality of romantic conventions, but in the fact that they derive comedy from showing these conventions to be as delightful and necessary as they are illusionary and insubstantial.

No age easily avoids contradictions in amorous thought and feeling. Indeed, the controversy in regard to love which Shakespeare dramatized had been expressed at least since the lyrics of Catullus. The difficulty exists whenever one accepts the notion that desire is not the whole of sex experience and seeks to give love a dignity beyond that of an instinctive urge. In his poems to Lesbia, for example, Catullus shows himself to be torn between some pleasantly imagined evidence of his spiritual superiority to his instincts and his palpable physical subservience to them. But the quarrel in the verse of Catullus is personalized and individualized, whereas the quarrel as used by Shakespeare had itself become something of a literary convention.

Its particular form in Shakespeare's comedies comes from the literature of the Middle Ages which had expressed the general paradoxes of sex in a specific and well-defined fashion. In this period conflict revolves around three mutually incompatible attitudes. The first is found in the ritual of desire elaborated by the troubadours and called "courtly love." In this strange system woman was the embodiment of all good, the shrine of poetic worship, of ennobling adultery (since marriage and love were regarded as inconsistent with each other).[19] The second is the

---

[19] At least according to Andreas Capellanus's analysis, in his *The Art of Courtly Love* (ca. 1184–1185), with introduction, translation, and notes by John Jay Parry. Cf. especially Bk. I, ch. vi, seventh dialogue.

product of the ascetic philosophy of the church, the Pauline tradition, variously stated in moral tracts, in "exempla," and in clerical and secular expressions of misogyny. From the point of view of medieval moral theory, love had been perforce regarded in literal essence as mere desire. And since all desire was evil, so also was woman who provoked it. The third comes from a simple, realistic view of human behavior which accepted normal sensual experience as a pleasant end in itself, without need of idealizing or of vilification. Chaucer, for example, a typical expositor of medieval attitudes, idealizes passion as courtly sentiment in the *Troilus,* but describes it as cheerful lust in the *Miller's Tale.* He praises ascetic restraint in the story of Saint Cecilia and depicts robust physical pleasure, uncontaminated by romance, in the *Prologue to the Wife of Bath's Tale.*

By the sixteenth century the quarrel concerning these attitudes had taken on a significance which it does not seem to have had in the Middle Ages. Wyatt, Sidney, Spenser, and Donne are as much concerned with the complex nature of love as the troubadour poets were with idealizing it or misogynic writers with denouncing it. What Chaucer was generally content to describe as an interplay of contradictory ideas, the writers of the age of Shakespeare often portray as a vain seach for consistency. Moreover, the sentiments and ritual of *amour courtois,* if not always or in every aspect credible, were for Chaucer at least an acceptable characterization of erotic behavior. The romantic experience exalted in troubadour lyrics appealed to human vanity by lifting a man's desires above mere momentary impulse. Further, courtly love was especially important to the Middle Ages. It gave dignity to emotions which many, under Christian influence, felt to be degrading or ludicrously animal-like and absurd. However, for Wyatt, Sidney, and Donne romantic sentiment was never wholly acceptable. It was constantly being challenged by less exalted and more tangible notions of passion.

The intense interest of the Renaissance in the actual nature of love which pervades its literature (in contrast to the relatively amused unconcern with which Chaucer views contradictory attitudes toward love) [20] is part of what we would call a new rationalism. It is part of that general concern with mundane affairs which led to the Reformation. Ideally, at least, the older, medieval reference of thought had been to a stable, nonphysical world of the spirit. Beginning with the sixteenth century men began to express a greater degree of confidence in the world about them. Like the Wife of Bath, they tended to submit their ideals to correction by experience rather than by abstract moral theory. *The Book of the Courtier* (so important to the Elizabethan), for example, reflects all the controversial attitudes toward love found in Chaucer. But Castiglione's characters are interested in these attitudes largely because they hope to find some unifying, basic harmony among them. The speakers attempt to fit physical desire and its courtly (or Petrarchan) idealization, and the focus of both, woman, into a generally acceptable pattern of behavior. The character Britomart in the *Faerie Queene*, representing the union of passion and chastity under the banner of marriage,[21] is a result of Spenser's attempt to form a composite ideal from fragments of ascetic morality and from the courtly ritual of romantic love. It is this Renaissance interest in consistency—or possibly in eclecticism—its notion that it was possible to produce a kind of concord out of mutually contradictory attitudes toward love, which runs through the reflective literature of sixteenth-century England. It is this Renaissance interest which culminates in Shakespeare's comedies of courtship.

The Significance of This New Comedy

Critics have often described Lyly's and Shakespeare's witty, dueling lovers as the writers' mocking imitation of a contempo-

---

[20] *The Franklin's Tale* may be an exception. See G. L. Kittredge's "Chaucer's Discussion of Marriage," *Modern Philology*, IX, 435–467.
[21] Lewis, *The Allegory of Love*, p. 340, remarks: "Courtly Love is in Spenser's view the chief opponent of Chastity. But Chastity, for him, means Britomart, married love."

rary society. Schelling, for example, finds that a verisimilitude of character and conversation to Elizabethan life is employed by Lyly "as a running satirical commentary on the contemporary happenings of the inner court circle." His comedies give "a refined transcript of actual court life and dialogue." [22] Feuillerat would have realism completely triumphant over romantic ideals of love in Lyly's comedies. Lyly's intoxication with words [23] is a ridicule of "un amour fidèlement partagé." [24] He furnished Shakespeare a model for comedy "représentant l'homme et la femme dans leurs relations purement mondaines, dans leur oisiveté élégante et frivole." [25] That is to say, Lyly and Shakespeare wrote their love-game comedies like good Frenchmen, lashing out at the decorum of the *outré!*

In contrast to those who would find the origin of these plays in some kind of "realistic" imitation of Elizabethan life, commentators with an eye for literary borrowings have suggested Ariosto's *I suppositi* (or Gascoigne's sixteenth-century translation) as the model for Lyly's witty dialogue and comedy of love.[26] Professor Stoll, moreover, finds Ariosto's play merely a link in the history of a literary formula which goes back to Ovid's *ars amandi*.[27] There is a kind of shuttling back and forth between acceptance and rejection of love by hero and heroine in Ovid that he finds copied by Ariosto (and by Lope de Vega) and in Elizabethan drama by Lyly, Chapman, Marston, and Fletcher (he has another explanation for Shakespeare). The difficulty with this theory is that it overemphasizes the import of a literary device shared to some extent by all these writers. What is significant in these Elizabethan love-game comedies is a series of attitudes toward love quite foreign to Ovid and Ariosto. Ovid's lusty young men who pursue and his coy young women who resist with reluctance reflect the bargaining and haggling that always goes on over a purchasable commodity. For in Ovid, generally, "love"

---

[22] *Elizabethan Drama*, I, 133. [23] Albert Feuillerat, *John Lyly*, p. 368.
[24] *Ibid.*, p. 374. [25] *Ibid.*, p. 489.
[26] See J. D. Wilson, *John Lyly*, p. 126.
[27] *Shakespeare's Young Lovers*, p. 45.

means entering into possession.[28] Likewise, Ariosto's eagerly sensual lover, Dulipo, expresses sentiments beyond the scope of Lyly's and Shakespeare's comedies. Dulipo reproduces the delight of the antique Roman in a relationship uncomplicated by romance when he comments: "I have free libertie at al times to behold my desired, to talke with hir, to embrace hir, yea (be it spoken in secret) to lie with hir." [29] Moreover, there is no conflict over romantic ideals here, but only obstacles of plot; no awareness of any concept of love save the obvious one.

Though Professor Stoll accepts Ovid and Ariosto as the source for Lyly's court comedies, he has a special theory to explain the love game as it appears in Shakespeare's plays.[30] He finds that all Shakespeare's early comedies—romantic idylls as well as comedies of courtship—reflect an Elizabethan taste for supramundane romance. For this reason the lovers in these plays are not necessarily psychologically accurate. He notes, for example, that it is literary convention rather than fact that causes them to love at first sight. But they all create in dramatic form the highflown ideals of love poets. The witty verbal battles of Beatrice and Benedick, Stoll would regard as a device to keep a sense of reality from penetrating *Much Ado*. The Elizabethan audience, he points out, was unwilling to witness exhibitions of voluptuous love-making. Shakespeare therefore cleverly substituted an intellectual conflict of lovers. Not only Viola, but Rosalind and Beatrice as well, spring from the pastoral romances. They are "like the heroines of Greene and Sir Philip Sidney." [31] Viola represents selfless love, Rosalind exuberant love, and Beatrice spirited love. The fact that two of them are skeptics Stoll would see only as a dramatic build-up for surprise, for contrast, for the sudden release of transcendent romance. Their wit combats are

---

[28] Note Ovid's own statements concerning the kind of love involved: *Tristia*, Bk. II, l. 249: in *Tristia, Ex ponto*, with an English translation by Arthur Leslie Wheeler; *Ars amatoria*, Bk. I, l. 31: in *The Art of Love and Other Poems*, with an English translation by J. H. Mozley; *Remedia amoris*, ll. 385 et sqq., op. cit. See also *The Allegory of Love*, pp. 6 ff.

[29] *I suppositi*, Act I, scene i, l. 86.

[30] *Shakespeare's Young Lovers*, especially ch. II.   [31] *Ibid.*, p. 49.

a kind of "exhilaration of love," a substitute not only for unsavory erotic display but also for the "ordinary and natural difficulties and misunderstandings between lovers,"[32] or, as Stoll has phrased it elsewhere, for the ironies and paradoxes of sex.[33]

It is true that Viola and Orsino, for example, and Silvia and Valentine do not give a literally accurate description of human passion. Their reasons for love are, as Professor Stoll remarks, the traditional ones of "medieval epic poets and troubadours and the Renaissance sonneteers."[34] No doubt they appealed to an Elizabethan taste for idyllic pretense. But Rosalind and Orlando, Beatrice and Benedick, the quarreling couples in *Love's Labour's Lost*, and those of Lyly's court comedies never completely represent courtly love or its Petrarchan followers. Stoll ignores the fact that in the comedies in which these debates about love occur it is precisely the traditional reasons for love which are challenged. Shakespeare's characters who express their distaste for romance or their impatience with its conventions are critical realists. They exist in the plays of Shakespeare and in those of Lyly to deride Elizabethan taste for poetic love. Moreover, Shakespeare did not have to find a substitute for any kind of erotic exhibitionism. Sex was regarded as an almost transcendental experience in the romantic tradition out of which he created his comedies. If this witty lovers' contention is a "substitute," it is a substitute for romance itself.

The point of view which would see Lyly's or Shakespeare's love-game comedies as social satire gives them a purely local importance. They are of value only as a comment on the practices of the small group at the court of Elizabeth. Those who find these plays to be literary off-shoots of Ariosto and Ovid fail to take into account the attitudes which form the substance of their comedy. Professor Stoll's theory that Shakespeare devised a series of verbal battles to replace provocative love-making on the stage completely misses the import of these plays as part of a long tradition of amorous controversy. A few writers have

[32] *Ibid.*, p. 55.   [33] *Poets and Playwrights*, p. 95.
[34] *Shakespeare's Young Lovers*, p. 15.

expressed a rather indefinite awareness of their significance. Coleridge suggested that the Elizabethan audience would be prepared for this kind of comedy through its familiarity with the poetry of courtly love.[35] Dowden linked Shakespeare's general "realization of fact" to the Renaissance in its re-evaluation of the idealistic thought of the Middle Ages.[36] Allardyce Nicoll, in discussing a similarity between Lyly and Shakespeare, briefly hints at the interplay of ideas in this comedy: "prose . . . and verse Lyly frequently mingled in his comedies, and the interweaving of the two corresponds to the two worlds of reality and of the ideal. The same fusion is to be discovered in *As You Like It*."[37] Tucker Brooke points out that the "eccentric force of heroic and romantic aspiration" in Shakespeare's plays is balanced by Falstaff and Mercutio, by that "humorous or realistic tendency, which sees things as they are."[38] Further, he finds that Elizabethan drama reflected "rather the fundamental moral and intellectual content than the material superficialities of the epoch."[39] In *Love's Labour's Lost* and *Much Ado*, for example, the "realism is a matter of mood and character rather than of microscopic external detail."[40] But all such statements remain tantalizing generalities, seeds of ideas, vague clews to an explanation. The specific ways in which Lyly or Shakespeare reveals the moral and intellectual content of Elizabethan life are left undetermined.

The substance of love-game comedy is indeed complex when compared to that of such frankly romantic idylls as *The Merchant of Venice* or *Twelfth Night*. *Love's Labour's Lost*, *As You Like It*, and *Much Ado* not only reflect contradictory ideas of love familiar to the age, they also suggest a comic recognition and acceptance of the unresolvable conflict among them. These plays express an amused tolerance of the discrepancy existing between poetic fancy and crass human fact. As a comedy of manners, this type of play entertains, by exemplifying in terms of drama, con-

---

[35] Raysor, ed., *Coleridge's Shakespearean Criticism*, I, 93.
[36] Dowden, *Shakespere; a Critical Study of His Mind and Art*, pp. 9, 30.
[37] Nicoll, *British Drama*, pp. 93 et ante.
[38] Brooke, *The Tudor Drama*, p. 397.
[39] *Ibid.*, p. 390.   [40] *Ibid.*, p. 395.

cepts of amorous behavior familiar to the audience. A Nisa, a Beatrice, or a Benedick forms a sprightly contrast to the much more romantic way of wooing cherished by all who saw the play. Therefore, in a very limited sense, one must have disapproved the protagonists of this love-game to have enjoyed them. Social disapproval commonly acts in a more obvious way in comedies of manners. In Molière's *Bourgeois gentilhomme*, for example, the dramatist uses it as a lash to drive the chief character back into the norm of decorum. Shakespeare appeals to a much subtler level of perception, to that unexpressed recognition of fleeting incongruity which is one great source of laughter and delight. His audience had to accept a nice, almost exact, balancing of two incompatible attitudes for the duration of the play.

The dueling lovers in these plays do not dramatize the extreme position taken by Marston, for example, in some of his satires. There the conflict is often resolved by an ironic, biting recoil from an aesthetic abstraction (Petrarchism) in favor of simple physical release of desire. In Elizabethan drama a sharp emotional repulsion from idyllic love finds expression in Shakespeare's *Troilus and Cressida*. The controlling concept of the love-game comedy was delight, and it took a more nearly neutral position. It did not attempt to castigate an opposition, but to evaluate the opposed elements of a conflict. Its more imaginative touch, as has been noted by Krutch,[41] implies that love, though less than poets have wished, is ever more than desire. This much it concedes to illusion. Its teasing lovers direct their wit more toward a pretentious and traditional ritual of courtship than toward a denial of love. Beatrice and Benedick come to a final grudging admiration of romance, with all its trappings, though even at the end of their dueling their admiration is tempered by the fact that they have been taken in by love despite themselves.

These love-game comedies are significant from a psychological point of view for the way in which they illumine the inherent despair common to all love poetry written in the courtly or Petrarchan tradition. The young men and women of these plays

[41] Krutch, *Comedy and Conscience after the Restoration*, p. 9.

who quarrel about the function and value of love, only to accept it in the end, are dramatizing in terms of a particular play a fundamental paradox in the very nature of love itself. Their wit combats, their sex duels carry the burden of a conflict often hidden in the subconscious. The struggling representatives of poetic ideals who are checked at every turn by a consciousness of pretense (as with Berowne) or by a realistic mistress (as with Orlando) portray a very natural desire for the unattainable loveliness of Arcadia. These comedies appeal to the fundamentally skeptical, ironic thinker who sees love as a paradoxical state in which imagination races ahead of reason or lingers behind to make of a given moment of passion, as it is reflected in literature, something neither wholly ideal nor wholly real. They appeal because they suggest that there is an essentially comic unity to be found in inherent opposites, that the basic incongruity between what is possible in love and what is desired is amusing and therefore can be endured.

The origin of this equivocal and comic approach to poetic ideals is to be found in the controversy between imagined enchantments and less presumptuous reality which had been going on since the twelfth century. The significance of this comedy, historically, lies in the fact that it re-estimates a conception of love that first comes to light in the lyrics of Provence. Its reconsideration of lovers' ideals is a partial illustration of a general reevaluation of existence. It is a literary product of humanistic thought, and a study of the individual's growing preoccupation with the character of his own emotions. It is the contrast, expressed succinctly by Francis Bacon, between the lover "speaking in a perpetuall Hyperbole" and the sober man; between the lover kneeling before his "little Idoll," making himself subject to shadowy illusion, and his examination of this idol under the glare of Renaissance "reason" so that the shrine of love might be seen (as it was in the love-game comedy) bereft of its misty aura.[42]

Since it is in the plays of John Lyly that this particular kind

[42] Bacon, *Essays*, p. 37.

of comedy first appears, Lyly has a considerable place in the history of English literature. He transferred to the stage something quite new for his day and thereby established one great tradition of English drama. He portrayed love as a game of conflicting attitudes, when elsewhere in literature lovers' desires were generally pictured as the old ritual of suffering and adoration. Castiglione in *Il cortegiano* and Spenser in *The Faerie Queene* had tried to rationalize romantic illusions and had fled into the greater abstraction of Platonism;[43] Elizabethan prose romances maintained the level of their Italian sources and kept the lovers' ritual painless by making it pretty. Sonneteers continued to write of love as a serious and grave pursuit, a confusion of idolatry and reality from which one withdrew in despair. But Lyly changed all this. He did not flee, and he did not deny. He wrote a comedy in which old antagonisms began to dissolve under the glance of the comic spirit.

Shakespeare brought subtlety and consummate art to the kind of comedy which Lyly had created. The skirmishes of Beatrice and Benedick are not important because they are like something in Ariosto or because a clever dramatist thought them up as a literary trick. They are significant because their comedy begins and ends *in medias res*, in the dramatization of a conflict in contemporary attitudes toward love. The solution to this conflict reaches its sharpest expression, probably, in the final speech of Benedick before he accepts the bondage of marriage. His words exhibit complete awareness of the romantic desires of his age. The suggestion of their comic incongruity as a transcript of experience hovers, beats through the words: "Prince, thou art sad; get thee a wife, get thee a wife: there is no staff more reverend than one tipped with horn."[44]

---

[43] As it will be seen, some of the wit at the expense of love in *The Courtier* foreshadows the love-game drama.

[44] *Much Ado*, Act V, scene iv, l. 125.

· II ·

OVID AND SIXTEENTH-CENTURY AMOROUS CONTROVERSY

THE GENERAL controversy, which was described in the preceding chapter as Shakespeare made use of it, is intelligible largely in the light of its medieval origins. For Spenser, for Sidney, for John Donne (as well as for Shakespeare) the very connotations of the word "love," the aura of implications which surround it, go back to Provençal lyrics and to the tradition of courtly romance. At the same time, whatever feelings of insecurity in these writers check their wholehearted acceptance of romance come also from the immediate medieval past, from its ascetic idealism, and from its common sense denial of idyllic passion. Yet many Elizabethans might have given casual acceptance to Gosson's remark that the "amorous schoolmaster"[1] of the age was the disenchanted Ovid. The phrases of this sophisticated libertine are scattered widely throughout sixteenth-century literature.[2] A glance at the fifty-four printings of his writings listed in the *Short Title Catalogue* is a good gauge of his popularity. A critic such as Meres, seeking to praise Shakespeare's two long narrative poems, goes naturally to Ovid for comparison.[3] The Middle Ages had transformed Ovid until they idealized his eroticism into a system of courtly love (Chau-

---

[1] Gosson, "Schoole of Abuse," in Smith, ed., *Elizabethan Critical Essays*, I, 367 (note to 75, 22).

[2] See Bush, *Mythology and the Renaissance Tradition in English Poetry*, p. 74: "concrete testimony of imitation proclaims Ovid the favorite of the Renaissance." See references to Ovid in Index, *Elizabethan Critical Essays*; Cooper, *Some Elizabethan Opinions of the Poetry and Character of Ovid*, pp. 3 ff.

[3] *Elizabethan Critical Essays*, II, 317.

cer calls him "Venus clerk" [4]). The Renaissance, in its different fashion, also translated his direct and simple way of regarding passion into something rich and strange. The Roman poet obviously strengthened the natural skepticism of the realistic English in their revolt from their own conventions and illusions. The problem provoked by this sixteenth-century delight in Ovid, however, is to discover in what ways his libertine conception of love served the Renaissance in its attempt to synthesize conflicting attitudes toward romance.

In Ovid's two witty discussions of the subject he denies all transcendental notions of sex. Desire is all, and its purpose is served by formulating techniques of seduction and capture (as in the *Ars amatoria*), and techniques of escape (as in the *Remedia amoris*). *Amor* is not an emotional experience deeply rooted in the personality, as it was to the Renaissance Petrarchan, but an affair of the nerves.[5] Hence, for Ovid it is most naturally reflected in poetry of flippantly erotic import. A lover's mistress is in the position of a merchant with a commodity to sell,[6] and Ovid's advice to the connoisseur in erotic pleasure is to be sure that he gets a good bargain. He warns against avarice: "Magna superstitio tibi sit natalis amicae." [7] The old hag Dipsas, who instructs Ovid's Corinna in the arts of desire (she reappears as the Duenna in the *Roman de la Rose* and in caricature under her own name in Lyly's *Endimion*), reduces this libertine's notion of love to the single phrase "casta est quam nemo rogavit," [8] which Marlowe, less subtly, translated for his own age, "she's chaste whom none will have." [9]

Perhaps it is not literally accurate to label Ovid "disenchanted" or, with Douglas Bush, to designate him the creator

[4] *House of Fame*, Bk. III, l. 1488. All citations from Chaucer are from *The Complete Works of Geoffrey Chaucer*, ed. by F. N. Robinson (Cambridge, Mass., 1933).
[5] Lewis, *The Allegory of Love*, pp. 5 ff.
[6] *Ars amatoria*, Bk. II, ll. 261 *et sqq.*   [7] *Ibid.*, Bk. I, l. 417.
[8] *Amores*, Bk. I, Elegy viii, l. 43: in *Heroides* and *Amores*, with an English translation by Grant Showerman, 1914.
[9] *Marlowe's Poems*, ed. by L. C. Martin, p. 161, l. 43.

of "soulless subject matter."[10] Only in his two poems on the art of love does he show himself this sort of realist. His *Heroides*, if they do "invite the romantic into the light of common day,"[11] are devoted not so much to banishment of romance as to the study of the minds of lovers. A pastoral, mythological haze of fancy drifts through much of the *Metamorphoses*. But if Ovid has a rather matter-of-fact notion of love, he does not stand alone. It would be difficult to find anything like courtly love in the writings of any Roman other than Catullus.[12] Vergil does present Aeneas' passion for Dido. But it is a hazard to be overcome. Lucretius concludes the fourth book of *De rerum natura* with an analysis of a relationship between lovers in which their passion becomes the most important aspect of their existence. But he views such a relationship with alarm, because lovers who ask for more than physical sensation find their desires dismally frustrated. Ovid, because of his wit and grace in writing, was merely the leading exemplar for the sixteenth century of a tradition in which love "seldom rises above the levels of merry sensuality or domestic comfort."[13] In his two poems on the art of love Ovid had gathered up, systematized, and added to the collection of erotic precepts which, in the words of one of his editors, "had gradually been developed (largely under Greek influence) by the Roman poets, especially Gallus, Tibullus, Propertius."[14] Ovid's amorous thoughts may occasionally be shadowed by something less mundane than the simple pleasures of sex. But in gen-

---

[10] *Mythology and the Renaissance Tradition in English Poetry*, p. 75.

[11] Rand, *Ovid and His Influence*, p. 20.

[12] Rand (*ibid.*, p. 9) remarks that Catullus wrote "poetry of a love that none of his successors could feel." He points out that Ovid, in listing his precursors, quite properly fails to mention Catullus.

[13] C. S. Lewis, *The Allegory of Love*, p. 4. Cf. Jones, Howard Mumford, and Philip Schuyler Allen, *The Romanesque Lyric*, pp. 77, 302n; "The literary treatment of the passion of love is one of the matters in which the ancient world stands farthest apart from the modern world. Perhaps the action of love on human lives differs but little from one age to another, but the form in which it was expressed was altered in western Europe in the Middle Ages, and ever since we have spoken a different language."

[14] Arthur Leslie Wheeler in the Introduction to *Tristia, Ex ponto*, The "Loeb Classical Library," p. xix.

Ovid

eral he represents an attitude of complete and cynical detachment from love.

Certainly Ovid ought to have served as a model for the sixteenth-century English poets who attempted to make a medieval system of romance conform to the facts of experience. But an examination of the most obvious imitations of Ovid in Elizabethan poetry will show that there never was a rebirth, in a literal sense, of the classical libertine tradition. The Elizabethan who wrote in this tradition merely invaded an exotic sentiment with a Renaissance ideal. In Marlowe's *Hero and Leander,* for example, romance is colored by an erotic lushness out of Ovid. But Marlowe does not transcend the moral convictions or the romantic ideals of his age. He uses the Roman's point of view as a kind of piquant embellishment of the sixteenth-century idea that love was a half-mystical experience, an escape through sexuality into a realm of perfected desire. Ovidian *amor* has little radical connection, wherever transplanted, with Elizabethan thought, where sex for its own sake represented the very nadir of all emotion.

Sometimes an Elizabethan writer turned to erotic and provocative phrases as a substitute for those expressing his courtly or Petrarchan ideal. In such instances he abandoned himself to Ovid for an entirely different purpose. He sought then, not to clarify conflicting Renaissance attitudes toward love, but to blight or ridicule his own romantic concepts. He used Ovid's emphasis on desire to express a savage recognition of the imperfect nature of an actual and passionate attachment. For example, Shakespeare sometimes reduces love to an experience appropriately expressed in phallic metaphors.[15] Such display does not show him accepting a grossly realistic point of view, but retreating, grim and chastened, from romance. The Elizabethan poet surrenders his standards to the libertine, not in pleasure or release, but in caustic satire of his own illusions. When he thought in terms of his romantic ideal, it was impossible for the Elizabethan to accept the simplicity of Ovid's conviction, "Successore

---

[15] *Sonnet CXXXV* or *CLI.*

novo vincitur omnis amor." [16] When he thought in terms of his morality, he denied even the gay, cheerful side of Ovid, the glorification of the warm heat of all animal life and vegetation in the spring.

Spenser, as an example of the second point of view, cannot agree with Ovid's April motto, in the *Fasti*, "et formosa Venus formoso tempore digna est." [17] In the Elizabethan poet's calendar the quickened world is greeted in quite another fashion. The spirit of the pagan is glimpsed by the Renaissance darkly, through medieval eyes, where Willye's motto for spring is:

> To be wise and eke to love
> Is graunted scarce to God above.

And Spenser's explanation (Ovid, one notes, did not offer any) presents a strange confusion of "amor" and "love," where

> all the delights of love, wherein wanton youth walloweth, be but follye mixt with bitterness, and sorrow sawced with repentaunce. For besides that the very affection of Love it selfe tormenteth the mynde, and vexeth the body many wayes, with unrestfulnesse all night, and wearines all day, seeking for that we can not have, and finding that we would not have.[18]

Ovid's Influence on
Hero and Leander

Despite the fact that Ovid's reduction of all the ties between a man and a woman to mere sex irked the Elizabethan, Ovid's verse did form a different and new "genre" of erotic poetry in Elizabethan literature. It is represented, perhaps, most memorably in the work of Marlowe, Chapman, Marston, and Shakespeare. When these writers turned from translating and adapting Ovid's phrases to adapting his legends, they effected a curious transformation. Marlowe's *Hero and Leander*, for example, is Ovid's matter written in the spirit of a romantic idyll. Ovid's

---

[16] *Remedia amoris*, l. 462.
[17] *Ovid's Fasti*, with an English translation by Sir James George Frazer, "Loeb Classical Library" (1931), Bk. IV, l. 129.
[18] Spenser's *Shepherd's Calendar*, ed. by W. L. Renwick, p. 42 and pp. 44–45.

Ovid

psychologically realistic interpretation of the legend, in the *Heroides*, gives way to the mood of "Come live with me and be my love." [19] Marlowe's Hero, who

> Ware no gloves, for neither sun nor wind
> Would burn or parch her hands,[20]

is hardly recognizable as a daughter of the Hero of Ovid, who could cry in anger to her lover, "me miseram! brevis est haec et non vera voluptas; nam tu cum somno semper abire soles." [21]

In Marlowe's poem medieval Provençal tradition is not corrupted by that derived from Ovid, but assimilates it. Here idealized desire has replaced the antique libertine attitude, for Marlowe's Hero, like his Zenocrate, is a creature of the Renaissance. Thus, in a curious marriage of the two worlds the Elizabethan mistress of Leander, twice referred to as "Venus' nun," [22] yields to her lover in chaste regret: "And fain by stealth away she would have crept." [23] Leander displays, in symbolic devotion to a medieval and Christian idea, "love's holy fire, with words, with sighs and tears." [24]

Even the convention of love at first sight, which had trapped Chaucer's Troilus, and which Shakespeare (probably quoting Marlowe's poem) puts into the mouth of the surprised Phoebe in *As You Like It*, is there. It is grafted onto the Ovidian story in the lines:

> Where both deliberate, the love is slight;
> Who ever lov'd, that lov'd not at first sight? [25]

And finally, Leander's plea to Hero for the surrender of her chastity removes the spirit of this poem about as far from the Roman world as it would be possible to go. He offers her, in ex-

---

[19] "The Passionate Shepherd to His Love," in Marlowe, *The Works*, ed. by A. H. Bullen. London, 1885, Vol. 3, p. 283. Bush (*Mythology and the Renaissance Tradition*, p. 138) contrasts Marlowe's "sensuous rapture" with the "fleshliness of the *Amores*." L. C. Martin, in *Marlowe's Poems*, p. 7, calls the poem "baroque-romantic."

[20] *Hero and Leander*, Sestiad I, l. 27.
[21] *Heroides*, Bk. xix, l. 65.
[22] *Hero and Leander*, Sestiad I, ll. 45, 319.
[23] *Ibid.*, II, l. 310.   [24] *Ibid.*, I, l. 193.   [25] *Ibid.*, I, l. 175.

change for her virginity, the Elizabethan romance of marriage.

> Virginity, albeit some highly prize it,
> Compar'd with marriage, had you tried them both,
> Differs as much as wine and water doth.[26]

Thus, Marlowe prepared for the moral conclusion which Chapman wrote to the poem. Leander is actually guilty of a "plain neglect of nuptial rites." The desires of the lovers, illegally gratified, bring a tragic penalty.

> Joy graven in sense, like snow in water wastes,
> Without preserve of virtue, nothing lasts.[27]

Chapman's and Marston's Use of Ovid

Like the authors of *Hero and Leander,* the Elizabethan poet may often have plucked, in Holofernes's words, Ovid's "odiferous flowers of fancy," yet he was strangely and invariably remote from the cool sophistication of his original. Ovid, an acknowledged favorite (even with so late a Renaissance poet as Milton), was sometimes justified to the Elizabethans by the kind of analogy that a medieval monk might have made. In a phrase, it was that of the bee which extracts honey "out of the bitterest flowers and the sharpest thistles." [28] There was very general agreement, when Elizabethans cared to express themselves directly on the subject, that Ovid was in need either of interpretation or of oblivion. And Chapman, in his use of Ovid, clings to the ethical interpretation of the Roman poet.[29] He suggests to Matthew Royden that, like the poetry of Ovid, his own must not be understood too quickly, since, in his opinion, that "which being with a

---

[26] *Hero and Leander,* I, l. 262.

[27] *Ibid.,* III, l. 157. See Bush, *Mythology and the Renaissance Tradition,* p. 206: "In Musaeus the personal integrity of the lovers is full justification, as, though to a less degree, it is in Marlowe . . . Yet Chapman's seriousness, here and elsewhere in his work, is not quite that of a mere precisian."

[28] Quoted from Nashe by Cooper (in *Some Elizabethan Opinions of the Poetry and Character of Ovid,* p. 20). Cf. William Webbe, "A Discourse of English Poetrie" (1586), in *Elizabethan Critical Essays,* I, 238, 252–254.

[29] Bush (*op. cit.*), pp. 68–72.

little endevour serched, ads a kinde of majestie to Poesie." [30]

Unlike Marlowe, who attempted to combine disparate attitudes of two very different ages, Chapman frankly contrasts them. This is seen in the theme of his *Coronet for His Mistresse Philosophie*, which is the "majestie and riches of the mind" opposed by "loves sensuall Emperie." [31] This same contrast is used as the framework for his poetic discussion of Ovid's conception of *amor*, in the *Banquet of Sence*. Here each of the five senses, in turn, makes its appeal for Chapman's Corinna. They urge him to "let rude sence subdue" his "reasons skill." [32] But love, in terms of sensual appeal, is the libertines' delight, not really love at all:

> This beauties fayre is an enchantment made
> By natures witchcraft, tempting men to buy
> With endles showes, what endlesly will fade
> Yet promise chapmen all eternitie.[33]

But even a careful Elizabethan imitation of Ovid's cynical eroticism, such as Marston's *Pigmalion's Image*, shows its "Gothic" heritage. In Ovid's own verse an amused skepticism of anything beyond momentary enchantment partly checks lush descriptions. Ovid voices the sentiment, crystallized for Roman thought in the doings of the deity himself, "Iuppiter ad veteres supplex heroïdas ibat." [34] But a Jupiter who was incorruptibly fickle, since "Iuppiter ex alto periuria ridet amantum." [35] Hence the Roman poet's description of the seductive Corinna, in the fifth elegy of the *Amores*, does not disintegrate into mere sensual titillation. His mistress comes to make endurable the warm summer afternoon as he lies restless, tossing on his couch. The episode is graceful, swift, touches just the right details for poetic evocation of *amor* as fulfillment of desire.

The late Elizabethan imitation of this incident, however, is

---

[30] Chapman in the Introduction to *Ovids Banquet of Sence* (1595), sig. A2.
[31] "Coronet for his Mistresse Philosophie," sig. E4 verso., in *Ovids Banquet of Sence*.
[32] *Ibid.*, sig. D4 verso.   [33] *Ibid.*, sig. C3 verso.
[34] *Ars amatoria*, Bk. I, l. 713.   [35] *Ibid.*, Bk. I, l. 633.

not at all like Ovid in spirit. John Marston's *Pigmalion* recalls the Roman poet's erotic suggestiveness, but without his restraint. Marston's hero is a ludicrous, not a satisfied lover. The Renaissance poet, with a medieval asceticism lurking in his consciousness, plunges ahead into poetic exaggeration of provocative details to prove his unfettered individualism—a medieval monk in reverse—where his

> . . . wanton Muse lasciviously doth sing
> Of sportive love, of lovely dallying.[36]

In a specific reference to Ovid's elegy Marston transforms his own Pigmalion into a caricature of a libertine's desires.

> But when the fair proportion of her thigh
> Began appeare, O Ovid, would he cry,
> Did ere Corinna show such Ivorie
> When she appear'd in Venus livorie? [37]

This kind of provocative description says too much, and its significance is subjected to the law of diminishing returns. Marston, as an Elizabethan, has pushed the other-world quality of love too far aside, and has made the Roman's attitude unpleasant. His gloating conclusion concerning his poem altogether misses the unconcern of Ovid.

> Come come Luxurio, crowne my head with Bayes,
> Which like a Paphian, wantonly displayes
> The Salaminian titillations,
> Which tickle up our leud Priapians.[38]

Ovid's Influence on Shakespeare's
Venus and Adonis and
The Rape of Lucrece

Marlowe incorporated an antique, libertine conception of love into a traditional, romantic idyll; Chapman sought to rationalize and to moralize this conception; and Marston used it to give

---
[36] *The Metamorphosis of Pigmalions Image and Certaine Satyres* (1598), dedicatory poem, "To his Mistres."

[37] *Op. cit.*, stanza 12.

[38] "The Author in prayse of his precedent poem," p. 23.

substance to a gloating cynicism. But even the most thoughtful Elizabethan poet who went to Ovid for inspiration and story did not capture his urbane disenchantment. Thus, in Shakespeare's *Venus and Adonis* and *The Rape of Lucrece*, derived ultimately from Ovid,[39] the attitude toward sex is in part a realistic one, in part a romantic one. In the first-named, the Roman poet's delighted praise of sexual desire is contrasted with an idealized love.[40] In the second, Shakespeare joins the Renaissance in its questioning, its critical examination of romantic passion. The story of the rape of a Roman matron is used as the basis for a description of the despairing retreat of a man caught in a revolt from a romantic ideal under the tremendous pressure of reality.

The lubricous character of individual figures of speech, rather than the use to which they are put, has often given rise to an erroneous conception of *Venus and Adonis*. For example, the editor C. Knox Pooler regrets "the presence of certain lines which offend equally against good manners and good taste. . . . They cannot be wholly explained either by the character of the subject or by the coarseness of the age." [41] Obviously the question is one of the author's intent. In Shakespeare's narrative, as in Marlowe's *Hero and Leander* or in Marston's *Pigmalion*, there are many enticing and provocative lines. Shakespeare transferred to the Venus of his poem the violent desire which Ovid had described for Salamacis.[42] The relationship between Shakespeare's pair of lovers, sustained throughout the poem, is suggested by Venus's metaphor of the park and the grazing deer. But Shakespeare's intent is not entirely to stimulate a sensual reverie in his readers' minds. He wrote the erotic passages partly to suggest the incongruity between an unrestrained desire and romantic, amorous pretensions.[43] The succinctness of Ovid is lacking in

---

[39] C. Knox Pooler makes this fact plain in his "Introduction" to *Shakespeare's Poems*, "The Arden Shakespeare."

[40] Cf. Adonis's speech, ll. 769–810.

[41] *Shakespeare's Poems*, p. xxiv.   [42] *Ibid.*, pp. xxx, xxxiv–xxxix.

[43] Bush (*Mythology and the Renaissance Tradition*, p. 146) contrasts Marlowe's *Hero and Leander* with Shakespeare's *Venus and Adonis* in this fashion: "Shakespeare, dealing with an unattractive pair who are more remote from

Shakespeare's method, to be sure, because his purpose is different. It was not to portray the joys of fruition. Ovid's short sketch of Venus's love for Adonis is confined to the episode of the two lovers stretched out under the shade of a poplar tree, while Venus related the story of Atalanta's race. Ovid does not describe frustrated love, but suggests the fulfillment of desire. Adonis is not a child, Ovid makes plain, but an adult, "iam vir, iam se formosior ipso est." [44] Shakespeare's Venus seems to seek something more than the possession of Adonis's body. She is ill with a frantic passion that appears to need much more than a physical release to be assuaged.[45] Her conception of lovers' rites is nearer that found in Elizabethan amorous poetry than in the verse of Ovid.

Certainly the Roman poet treated the theme of Shakespeare's story quite differently. Salamacis's thwarted desire for Hermaphroditus is merely an erotic episode in the *Metamorphoses*. On the other hand, Ovid makes the impotent young lover of the *Amores* the subject of hilarious farce.[46] Shakespeare was writing in quite another tradition, and one should not take offense because he used the materials of the antique Roman as a man of the Renaissance. In his poem the contrast to *amor* is the understood background of courtly and Petrarchan sentiment. He suggests that the sexuality which Ovid praised is incompatible with the dignity of a human being. "Sick-thoughted" Venus is not languorous and seductive, but hovers constantly on the verge of the absurd. In her amorous frenzy she seeks to experience "love" by violent means. Her exaggerated ardors frighten Adonis, and she fails to realize that which she seeks. The nearest approach in this poem to the emotional level of Ovid is in the scene between the stallion and the mare. Venus suggests that this encounter should be their model, but she is quickly reproved. She cries out,

---

humanity, fiddles on the strings of sensuality . . . without even being robustly sensual."

[44] *Metamorphoses*, with an English translation by Frank Justus Miller, Bk. X, l. 523.

[45] See Venus's speech, ll. 720–769, and Adonis's chiding reply, ll. 770–810.

[46] *Amores*, Bk. III, Elegy vii.

> ". . . Thy palfrey, as he should,
> Welcomes the warm approach of sweet desire." [47]

Adonis's reply, in phrases suggesting the Elizabethan tradition of suffering love, describes passion as more than a mere animal impulse:

> ". . . it is a life in death,
> That laughs and weeps, and all but with a breath!" [48]

The erotic scenes in this poem fail to produce the disillusioned amusement of Ovid; and this failure enables them to keep the spirit of Shakespeare's *Venus and Adonis* faithful to Elizabethan conventions. The poem represents the sixteenth century again, in its metamorphosis of Ovid. But Shakespeare's final comment on Venus neither wholly renounces nor wholly accepts romance. He merely states the Elizabethan's realistic irritation with intrusions of traditional ideas into simple passion:

> O hard-believing love! how strange it seems
> Not to believe, and yet too credulous;
> Thy weal and woe are both of them extremes;
> Despair and hope makes thee ridiculous. [49]

In Shakespeare's *Lucrece* one finds that even the eroticism of Ovid has disappeared. Here the entire atmosphere is utterly different from that of the Roman world. *Lucrece* presents a psychological study of desire, not a poetic description of it. The poem is an objectified, exaggerated example of the sort of study the Elizabethan sonneteer was making of his own emotions or a Castiglione was transcribing for Renaissance society. It is a poetic treatment of the contrasting relationship between romantic attitudes toward love and that of unchecked lust. There is a kind of unshakable awareness of an emotional conflict important to the Elizabethan behind every line of this poem. Tarquin's long searchings of heart show him trapped between ideal promptings and intensely real physical instincts. Ideally, he could not touch Lucrece; actually, he could do nothing else. And the despairing

---

[47] *Venus and Adonis*, l. 385.   [48] *Ibid.*, l. 413.
[49] *Ibid.*, l. 985.

conflict between "love" and *amor* is presented as entirely within the mind of the protagonist. He is in the distracting position of one watching his own fate. His will is paralyzed, unable to check his desire, which moves insatiably forward toward consummation. Two sentiments fuse in this poem: a cynical note concerning "love," the deluding idealized passion, and a jaded one concerning desire. Love is "An expir'd date, cancell'd ere well begun," [50] from which Tarquin is driven by the "lightless fire" [51] of lust.

The source of the poem's emotional power is that Tarquin cannot escape being what he most abhors, "soft fancy's slave." [52] The impetus to his desire is precisely the exalted concept of Lucrece that he has formed from hearing her virtue discussed. He is driven by instinct to try to capture this illusion, this image of Lucrece that by his very course of action, he knows, prevents such capture. His realization of what he is doing is omnipresent. Shakespeare states for Tarquin what he states in "Sonnet CXXIX"—the transitory quality of the libertine's delight.

> "What win I if I gain the thing I seek?
> A dream, a breath, a froth of fleeting joy.
> Who buys a minute's mirth to wail a week?
> Or sells eternity to get a toy?" [53]

But "brain-sick rude desire" [54] is "past reason's weak removing." [55] Tarquin explains his conflict and dilemma even to Lucrece—that he repents and reviles what he is forced to do.

> "I have debated, even in my soul,
> What wrong, what shame, what sorrow I shall breed;
> But nothing can affection's course control,
> Or stop the headlong fury of his speed.
> I know repentant tears ensue the deed,
>   Reproach, disdain, and deadly enmity;
>   Yet strive I to embrace mine infamy." [56]

Thus, the shocking disparity between what Tarquin seeks and what he is to receive has been prepared for. Recoil follows ful-

---

[50] *Lucrece*, l. 26.   [51] *Ibid.*, l. 4.   [52] *Ibid.*, l. 200.
[53] *Ibid.*, l. 211.   [54] *Ibid.*, l. 175.   [55] *Ibid.*, l. 243.
[56] *Ibid.*, l. 498.

Ovid

fillment. The figures of speech connected with it, that point the emotion, are those of surfeit, of vomit, of cold, of shuddering withdrawal.[57] Once the sought-for illusion is lost through his futile and desperate possession of Lucrece, Tarquin is so changed that he asks the "spotted princess how she fares."[58] And as he leaves her, he portrays the terror and pain of retreat from the intolerable triumph of physical fact over ideal satisfactions.

> He faintly flies, sweating with guilty fear,
> She stays, exclaiming on the direful night;
> He runs, and chides his vanish'd, loath'd delight.[59]

The contrast here is between the disenchantment of Ovid and the romantic idealism of Shakespeare.[60] The contrast is made even more striking when one recalls Ovid's advice to the retreating lover in his *Remedia amoris* concerning the function of this "post coetum triste" period.[61] One should seize the moment when desire is at ebb tide to take inventory of the charms of one's mistress. One should open the windows and let in the light. But he was not writing in terms of the Elizabethan's inherited poetry in which one experienced an unearthly translation in possession. Shakespeare's presentation of emotional recoil from mere sex impulses emphasizes here, as in his sonnets, not the boredom of a libertine, but a romantic's sense of degradation. The psychology of attack and retreat governs Ovid's amorous poetry; that of internal conflict governs the treatment of physical love in the Elizabethan Renaissance. In Shakespeare's *Rape of Lucrece* the medieval literary code which had ennobled passion is shown in conflict with the cynical disenchantment of the old world, but not in surrender to it.

[57] *Ibid.*, ll. 694 *et sqq.*   [58] *Ibid.*, l. 721.
[59] *Ibid.*, l. 740.
[60] See Bush (*Mythology and the Renaissance Tradition*, p. 150): "The brief reflections in Chaucer on Tarquin's violation of chivalry might have suggested a text for the long debate in Shakespeare."
[61] *Remedia amoris*, ll. 411 *et sqq.*

· III ·
Amorous Controversy in Medieval Literature

THE ELIZABETHAN's essentially romantic love poetry has been described as "a 'Gothic' and edifying tapestry into which are woven more and more silver threads from Ovid." [1] The figure may suggest a more steady process of infusion from the *Ars amatoria* than actually occurred. But the intense interest with which sixteenth-century writers regarded Ovid had called attention to a sophisticated and mannered realism. Marlowe decorating his *Hero and Leander* with provocative phrases, Shakespeare seeking an extreme contrast for traditional ideals in *Lucrece*, no doubt suggested to their age that in Ovid was a mighty opposite to the kind of love described in Petrarch's sonnets or in Chaucer's *Troilus*. Nevertheless, such triumph as libertine notions of sex enjoyed temporarily in sixteenth-century literature was, from the point of view of romantic ideal, a dismal one. The central and basic factor, as far as passion was concerned, was the courtly ideal of love. The troubadours attached to the courts of southern France in the twelfth century gave this concept of love to western Europe. The ways in which a medieval knight or a Renaissance courtier was supposed to woo his lady, as well as the values the experience would bring him, are all implicit in the writings of these poets. They wrote to such effect, indeed, that as late as 1600 both the natural common sense of the English and the cynicism of Ovid had failed to conquer wholly the tradition they established.[2]

[1] Bush, *Mythology and the Renaissance Tradition*, p. 6.
[2] C. S. Lewis (*The Allegory of Love*, p. 11) describes courtly love as one of the three or four actual and recorded changes in human sentiment.

Lewis Freeman Mott has suggested that there were three stages in the development of the theory of courtly love.[3] The lyrics of Bernart de Ventadorn, the poet attached to the twelfth-century court of Eleanor of Aquitaine, illustrate the formative stage.[4] Here the stereotyped thoughts and feelings of later courtly poets are fresh and new. The writings of Chrestien de Troyes and of Andreas Capellanus mark the second period in the history of courtly love. Both men were under the patronage of Marie de Champagne, the daughter of Eleanor of Aquitaine. In Chrestien's romance *Cligès* (*ca.* 1162),[5] the ideas of the troubadours were turned into a system or art of love. In this writer's *Chevalier de la Charrette* (*ca.* 1164) a single aspect of the courtly system was emphasized: the complete submission of the lover to the lady's will.[6] In Andreas Capellanus's treatise *De arte honeste amandi* (1184–1185) [7] these ideas were given the status of laws. The final stage is illustrated by Guillaume de Lorris's allegory the *Roman de la Rose* (*ca.* 1225–1239). Here the amorous conceptions of court poets are in "complete possession of literature." [8] In most love poems which follow the *Roman de la Rose*, "the traits of one answer for the traits of all." [9]

Medieval courtly love theories, whether found in poetry or

---

[3] Mott, *The System of Courtly Love Studied as an Introduction to the "Vita nuova" of Dante*, pp. 6–21, 82–108.

[4] One should compare Mott's treatment with more recent studies which give a somewhat more detailed analysis: Jeanroy, *La Poésie lyrique des troubadours;* Cross and Nitze, *Lancelot and Guenevere;* Kirby, *Chaucer's "Troilus,"* ch. i–v. The lives, works, and influence of the troubadours are presented in Anglade, *Les Troubadours.* Such books as the following suggest the routes that medieval love-sentiment followed from twelfth-century France to sixteenth-century England: Einstein, *The Italian Renaissance in England;* Lee, *The French Renaissance in England;* Pearson, *Elizabethan Love Conventions.*

[5] For dates see Holmes, *A History of Old French Literature.*

[6] Mott, *The System of Courtly Love*, pp. 29 ff., pp. 37–38. Cf. Voretzsch, *Introduction to the Study of Old French Literature*, pp. 39 ff., for discussion of spread of these courtly ideals.

[7] Andreas Capellanus, *The Art of Courtly Love.* For the date of Andreas's treatise see Arpad Steiner, "The Identity of the Italian 'Count' in Andreas Capellanus' *De Amore*," *Speculum*, XIII, 308.

[8] Mott, *The System of Courtly Love*, p. 61.

[9] *Ibid.*

in treatises, prescribed a ritual of courtship and a system of emotional values. Love was personified as a god with irresistible power over his victims. Love was borne by the glance of a woman's eyes [10] and pierced like an arrow the heart of a gentle lover. There the shaft remained, a perpetual incentive to desire. The first effect of this wound was to awaken in the victim such fear of his lady as to endanger his health. He should be so afraid to disclose his passion that he would grow faint in her presence. The second effect of this seizure by love was to ennoble the lover and to increase his chivalric virtues. As a result of his surrender to the will of his mistress, he became a more courageous fighter, a more generous and courteous knight. The desired end of this love was physical consummation. The woman who was the object of passion was idealized in every way (this was necessary, of course, to make the lover's worship plausible). The lover's humble submission of his will to that of his mistress parallels that of a penitent prostrate before the Virgin.[11]

This love sentiment which delighted the courtly society of the twelfth century demanded a ritualized and refined sex experience.[12] But, paradoxically, the conventions of courtly love are in part a revivifying of a pagan sensualism.[13] Troubadour poets exalted Venus and Cupid and drew heavily upon Ovid. From Ovid comes the personification of Love, the concept of his irresistible power, the physical symptoms of the lover while endur-

---

[10] See p. 124.

[11] See Mott, *The System of Courtly Love*, p. 13; Lewis (*The Allegory of Love*, p. 29) notes that the Lancelot of Chrestien de Troyes "makes a genuflexion as if he were before a shrine," as he leaves the chamber of Guinevere. Cf. Francis Bacon's discussion of love as an idol in his essay "Of Love."

[12] Mott, *The System of Courtly Love*, pp. 6 ff.

[13] Anglade (*Les Troubadours*, p. 196) remarks that a "fonds ineffable de paganisme caractérise les origines de la poésie des troubadours et la première périod de la littérature provençale." Cf. William Allen Neilson, *The Origins and Sources of the "Court of Love,"* p. 176: "The ascetic ideal upheld by the medieval church could not in the nature of things appeal permanently to a fashionable society, so that, when the reaction came, the pendulum not only swung away from celibacy, but passing the point of married chastity, went to the other extreme, and a system of conduct grew up in which the central point was adulterous love."

ing the tyranny of the god. From the *Amores* comes the picture of "Love as a god who wounds his victims with his arrows."[14] The *Heroides* provided the Provençal poet with a language of love and with lovers' *suasoria*,[15] while the love psychology of Ovid's *Ars amatoria* underlies all courtly romance. But it is "Ovid misunderstood."[16] Andreas Capellanus and the Middle Ages generally mistook, perhaps by design, Ovid's mockingly solemn treatment of a frivolous subject for a serious treatment of a serious subject. Courtly poets allowed their imaginations to flirt with a pagan sexuality, but idealized it beyond anything that its Roman spokesman would have recognized.

Ascetic and Misogynic Attitudes

The Pauline tradition formed the second of the three general attitudes toward love current in the Middle Ages.[17] St. Paul's repudiation of the life of the senses was the basis for both the ascetic idealism and the misogynic scorn expressed all during this period by clerical and secular writers alike. As Plato's *Symposium* indicates, a nonphysical love was scarcely the invention of the church fathers. A misogynic attitude is also quite ancient. The antifeminism of Juvenal's sixth satire, for example, is itself not new, but merely a summary, at about the end of the first century, of much older materials.[18] The peculiarity of the medieval writings which express these attitudes is that they are not intellectual theorizing on the one hand or mere comedy and satire on the other. They are didactic and uphold very real moral tenets of the

[14] Mott, *The System of Courtly Love*, p. 57 (*Amores* I, Elegy i). See also Bush, *Mythology and the Renaissance Tradition*, p. 77; Rand, *Ovid and His Influence*, pp. 150–153.

[15] Bush, *Mythology and the Renaissance Tradition*, p. 77.

[16] Lewis, *The Allegory of Love*, p. 7.

[17] See St. Paul's Epistle to the Ephesians 5: 22; cf. Dow, *The Varying Attitudes toward Women in French Literature of the Fifteenth Century: The Opening Years*, pp. 49 ff.

[18] Jerome draws upon the lost "golden book" of Theophrastus, the literary executor of Aristotle, for much of his misogynic material. Jerome is, of course, merely the most important medieval exponent of the Pauline tradition. See F. A. Wright, *Fathers of the Church*, for a discussion of such other antifeminists as Tertullian, Lactantius, and Ambrose.

period. Indeed, as late as the sixteenth century, when John Calvin wished to defend marriage of the clergy, he found it necessary first to reinterpret St. Paul.[19]

The theory advanced by the church fathers to explain their revulsion from sex was that an absence of carnal pleasure represented the uncontaminated state of man before his fall. St. Augustine gave succeeding centuries a restrained and philosophic treatment of this ascetic idealism. His writings exhibit a rationalist's revolt from the pagan excesses of the Roman civilization in which he had grown up.[20] The Garden of Eden, in Augustine's analysis in his *City of God*,[21] was the "golden age" of man, his supreme moment of good. St. Jerome gave this Pauline tradition its most violently emotional and misogynic expression. Throughout his writings runs an almost feverish antipathy to woman and to all erotic behavior.[22] His disdain for sensual pleasure and for woman as amorous temptress led him to see only three possible degrees of chastity for her. The virgin stood highest, next came a chaste widow (a recreated virgin), lowest came a married woman.[23] It was Eve who had led Adam and the human race out of the golden age.[24] In misogynic treatises which followed the pattern set by Jerome woman was described as a constant temptation to be with-

---

[19] John Calvin, *Commentary on the Epistles of Paul the Apostle to the Corinthians*, I, 222–223.

[20] Jerome had been brought up as an adept in the new religion of Rome, whereas Augustine had been converted to it. Hence the latter's ascetic idealism was inevitably tempered by remembrance of his own pagan youth. "Et quid erat, quod me delectabat, nisi amare et amari," Augustine remarks of his own youth, though in scorn (*St. Augustine's Confessions*, with English translation by William Watts, Vol. I, Bk. II, ch. ii, p. 64). Cf. Augustine's analysis of marriage, *De civitate Dei*, Bk. XIV (ed. by John Grant).

[21] Books XII–XIII.

[22] The most concentrated statements of Jerome's attitude are found in the following tracts, published in *Nicene and Post-Nicene Fathers*, second series, ed. Philip Schaff and Henry Wace (New York, 1893), Vol. VI: *The Perpetual Virginity of the Blessed Mary*, written against Helvetius A.D. 383; *Contra Jovinianum*, A.D. 393 (to which Chaucer refers, *Wife of Bath's Prologue*, l. 673); Letter CXXX, "to Demetrius," A.D. 414. See also Saint Jerome, *Select Letters*, ed. F. A. Wright,, "To Eustochium," No. XXII, A.D. 384, concerning the virgin's profession. [23] *Select Letters*, pp. xiv, 386n.

[24] Jerome remarks that Adam was ejected "de paradiso virginitatis," *ibid.*, Letter CXXVIII, p. 471.

stood, for she had continued to seduce men out of their individual Edens of chastity.

The austere, spiritualized love which St. Augustine had praised found medieval expression not only in church dogma but in secular literature as well. In the lives of the saints, narrated in the *Golden Legend,* for example, stern repudiation of all sexual experience is regarded as a necessary ideal for which even martyrdom is not too high a price to pay. There exists a vast body of medieval lyrics devoted to the praise of chastity.[25] The asceticism advocated by the church is no doubt responsible, in part, for Dante's spiritualized desires for Beatrice. The penetration of such an attitude into romance, itself, is indicated by the fact that Lancelot's sensual experiences kept him from succeeding in his quest for the Grail in some versions of the story. In Malory's *Morte d'Arthur* it is Galahad, the son of Lancelot, who successfully represents the ideal of virginity.

Writers who imitated Jerome, however, instead of praising the ascetic life for its own sake, turned to defaming women as instigators of unchastity. Vicious satires elaborating a misogynic point of view may represent an effort to popularize the church's official attitude toward sexual indulgence. Whatever the source of its strength, such a satiric attitude is found in treatises by secular and clerical moralists and in the *exempla* of preachers; it is everywhere alike, from the writings of St. Jerome in the fourth century down to the fourteenth-century sermons of John of Bromyard.[26] Walter Map's twelfth-century tract *Dissuasio Valerii ad Rufinum philosophum ne uxorem ducat* [27] does little more than

---

[25] See Brown, ed., *Religious Lyrics of the XIVth Century.* Also Anglade, *Les Troubadours,* ch. ix, "La Poésie religieuse."

[26] John Bromyard, the English Dominican, professor of theology at Cambridge, opponent of Wyclif, d. 1418. See G. R. Owst, *Literature and the Pulpit in Medieval England,* pp. 24 ff., for illustrations from Bromyard's *Summa predicantium.* See Thomas Wright, ed., *A Selection of Latin Stories,* Vol. VIII. See also Jaques de Vitry, *The Exempla or Illustrative Stories from the 'Sermones Vulgares,'* ed. by Thomas Frederick Crane. For a conventional, late fourteenth-century expression of the church's attitude toward sex, see Ross, ed., *Middle English Sermons,* pp. 234–237. For probable date, see pp. xxxiv–xxxviii.

[27] In *De nugis curialium,* tr. by Frederick Tupper and Marbury Bladen Ogle (London, 1921), p. 183.

repeat St. Jerome's *Contra Jovinianum*. Chaucer, in his "Wife of Bath's Prologue," refers both to Jerome and to Map and makes use of such later redactions of antifeminine materials as those found in Jean de Meung's portion of the *Roman de la Rose*, and in Deschamps's *Miroir de mariage*.[28] Medieval moralists, taking illustrations from all sources available to them, sought to prove first of all that the carnal desires of woman were insatiable. In the second place, as wife, she would commit any act of folly or indecency to betray her husband and to gain sovereignty over him. From this point of view, love and its representative, woman, were the perdition of mankind.

Realistic Attitudes toward Love

Courtly love was the product of the aristocratic class of the Middle Ages. Asceticism was inherently a Christian ideal and espoused by the medieval church. It is difficult to localize, socially, the attitude which accepted sensual pleasure as an end in itself, divorced from all theory. One assumes, a priori, that both courtly love and monkish chastity represent ways of conduct neither tempting nor practicable for the mass of men, regardless of class or creed. But the literary expression of this sensual attitude is somewhat localized in the Middle Ages. It does find its way into aristocratic literature from time to time, perhaps most notably in Jean de Meung's portion of the *Roman de la Rose* and in Chaucer's *Canterbury Tales*. It appears in clerical writings only at the end of the medieval period, when the movement within the church itself away from the harsh idealism of Jerome culminates in Erasmus's effective attack on the monastic way of life. For the most part, however, it is given voice in writings meant to appeal to the uneducated and the socially inferior.

A coarse realism appears here and there in medieval drama. French farces were almost wholly cynical regarding love and woman.[29] The comic treatment of Joseph as a cuckold and the

---

[28] See references in Robinson's *Chaucer*, pp. 801–802.

[29] See Petit de Julleville, ed., *Histoire de la langue et de la littérature française*, II, 435.

set quarrels between Noah and his wife in the English mystery cycles are examples of a lively sense of unadorned sexual behavior. The most important medieval literary examples of consistent sensualism, however, are found in the *fabliaux* and in goliardic verse. In both these literary forms love was presented sometimes grossly and obscenely, sometimes merely joyously and simply, but always with emphasis on the act of coition. Chaucer indicates that he is aware of this fact when he describes the Miller, who is to tell a *fabliau*, as

> . . . a janglere and a goliardeys,
> And that was moost of synne and harlotries.[30]

Goliardic poetry, "satirical and convivial verse, chiefly in Latin," [31] was written in the twelfth and thirteenth centuries by vagabond clerics. The *fabliaux*, short tales in verse, disappear as a genre with the writings of Jehan de Condé in the first half of the fourteenth century.[32] The latter are related in part to an ancient tradition of storytelling which comes from the Orient.[33] Both literary forms may also make use of attitudes and events imitated from the rough-and-tumble of everyday living. But the importance of goliardic poetry and *fabliaux*, in the history of romantic thought is that they picture woman as an engaging and direct source of physical pleasure. They show that a conscious awareness of passion not only as *fine amor* and as ascetic restraint but also as an unsophisticated and wholly natural delight was part of medieval literature.

Literary Expressions of Conflict

The three ways in which men of the Middle Ages chose to regard love were mutually incompatible. Each one represented an attitude which could be justified only by evading, for the mo-

---

[30] See Robinson's note to line 560, "The General Prologue," in *Chaucer*, pp. 766–767. Cf. Symonds, *Wine, Women and Song; Medieval Latin Student Songs*, pp. 1–48, 190–197.   [31] Robinson, p. 766.

[32] Voretzsch, *Introduction to the Study of Old French Literature*, pp. 369 ff., 477.

[33] Joseph Bédier, *Les Fabliaux*, pp. 67 ff.

ment, consideration of the other two.[34] The courtly romances expressed a refined eroticism which contradicted by implication all writings which exalted the austere behavior advocated by the church. Lovers' pleasures, idyllically portrayed by troubadours, were frowned upon even in marriage by strict moralists.[35] From the point of view of a realistic critic, however, both the attitude of the church fathers and that held by court poets was questionable. According to Jean de Meung, some compromise with romantic and spiritual perfection is necessary for average human beings. As early certainly as the second half of the *Roman de la Rose* (*ca.* 1275) the mutually opposed ethics of monk and courtier were themselves challenged by a simple, naturalistic view of erotic behavior.

The clash between the sensuality which was idealized for the Middle Ages in a Tristan or a Troilus and that for which St. Cecilia and Jerome stood was made articulate in various ways. For example, the great twelfth-century patroness of poets, Eleanor of Aquitaine, is praised by Bernart de Ventadorn as the object of his amorous devotion. To Walter Map, another contemporary writer, she is a mere wanton. She is not the arbiter of a court of love, but a notorious woman who "cast glances of unholy love"[36] on the man who was to be the English king, Henry II. Andreas Capellanus, the man who reduced this courtly love to a system, wrote a palinode in which he confesses the love of God to be more important. Troubadours of the thirteenth century often turned from describing earthly mistresses to sing the joys of worshiping an unchanging lady, the Virgin.[37] In the fourteenth-century conduct book, the *Book of the Knight of La Tour-Landry*, the Knight and his Lady discuss the values belonging to the courtly

---

[34] As Lewis has phrased it (*The Allegory of Love*, p. 41), ". . . the whole world of courtesy exists only by 'leaving the religious side of the question out for a moment.'"

[35] Saint Jerome, *Contra Jovinianum*, p. 385. *The Parson's Tale*, l. 860.

[36] *De nugis curialium*, p. 297. Giraldis Cambrensis, the skeptical critic of Geoffrey of Monmouth's Arthurian tales, makes an even more damning comment on Eleanor. See *Rerum Britannicarum medii aevi scriptores*, No. 21, Vol. VIII (London, 1891), pp. 298 ff.

[37] See Joseph Anglade, *Les Troubadours*, ch. ix.

code and to that of the church, and find them far apart and irreconcilable.[38]

An indirect reflection of this clash is found in the medieval quarrel over sex superiority. From the point of view of the troubadours, a lover was ennobled because he had surrendered himself and was completely controlled by his lady. Chrestien de Troyes's *Chevalier de la Charrette*, for example, is "exclusively devoted to setting forth and heightening by every device of exaggeration, the submissive devotion of the lover and the absolute authority of the lady beloved." [39] In the medieval Griselda story, on the other hand, the man's domination of his lady is the main theme. Likewise, in the misanthropic *fabliaux*, as Bedier remarks, "les femmes sont des êtres inférieurs et malfaisants." [40] Such literature expresses the persistent belief advocated by the clergy that a man should rule his wife as he himself was ruled by the church. No doubt the origins of this conception of masculine sovereignty were in part secular and dependent upon long established folkways (as in the *fabliaux*). But this conception was not only incompatible with courtly love, but was also highly praised by spokesmen for the church.[41] Indeed, this contest over sex superiority is a common medieval way of expressing the basic antagonism between philogynic and misogynic points of view. It reached most memorable expression, probably, in the tale told by Chaucer's Wife of Bath.

A very direct illustration of the conflict between heavenly and earthly love may be found in medieval poems which present this conflict as a debate. In the late twelfth- or early thirteenth-century poem *The Owl and the Nightingale*, for example, these two birds quarrel over the relative values of carnal and spiritual desire.[42] In the *Thrush and the Nightingale*, of the thirteenth

---

[38] La Tour-Landry, *Book of the Knight of La Tour-Landry; Compiled for the Instruction of His Daughters.* Cf. Kilgour, *The Decline of Chivalry as Shown in French Literature of the Late Middle Ages*, pp. 108–122.
[39] Mott, *The System of Courtly Love*, p. 39.
[40] Bédier, *Les Fabliaux*, p. 321.
[41] Dow, *The Varying Attitudes toward Women*, pp. 49 ff.
[42] *The Owl and the Nightingale*, ed. by J. W. H. Atkins, pp. xlvii–lvii.

century, opposing points of view are expressed in the lines,

> That on hereth wimmen that hoe beth hende,
> That other hem wole with migte shende.[43]

The nightingale defends the courtly mistress by remarking that

> Hit is shome to blame levedy
> For hy beth hende of corteisy.[44]

She is "swettoust thing in armes to wre."[45] The thrush denounces troubadour love, however, by pointing out that woman is essentially vile because of her guilt in the fall of mankind.[46] A similar antipathy to romantic courtesy appears, in slightly different fashion, in another medieval poem, the *Quatrefoil of Love* (*ca.* 1350). Here a lovesick maiden is found in the conventional setting of medieval amorous allegories—a meadow on a May morning. But she is advised to flee her lover and to seek God. Gollancz has described this poem as an attempt "at the sublimation of the sex instinct." It is "linked to the great medieval debate between Sacred and Profane love."[47]

Direct conflict between the Christian ascetic philosophy and a realistic criticism is rare in medieval literature. The point of view of the church fathers in regard to sex had gathered a con-

---

[43] Brown, ed., *English Lyrics of the XIIIth Century*, No. 52, l. 10.
[44] *Ibid.*, l. 25.   [45] *Ibid.*, l. 58.
[46] *Ibid.*, ll. 70 *et sqq.*
[47] *The Quatrefoil of Love*, ed. by Sir Israel Gollancz and Magdalene M. Weale, p. xxii. For other poems illustrating this debate see Brown, ed., *English Lyrics of the XIIIth Century*, No. 43, "Friar Thomas de Hales' Love Ron," and No. 79, "I Repent of Blaming Women"; John Edwin Wells (*Manual of Writings in Middle English*, pp. 496 ff.) cites this as an ironic attack on women: No. 90, "The Way of Christ's Love"; No. 91, "The Way of Woman's Love."

See also Wright, ed., *The Latin Poems Commonly Attributed to Walter Mapes*, pp. 331–349, for three debates between the body and the soul.

See also Brown, ed., *Religious Lyrics of the XIVth Century*, No. 110, "Of Women cometh this Worldes Weal"; and No. 121, "The Bird with Four Feathers" (ll. 93–96), in which courtly love is denounced by name:

> "This fedir me bare ful ofte to synne,
> And principally to leccherye;
> Clipping and kessing cowth I not blynne,
> me thought it craft of curteseye."

siderable momentum by the twelfth century, and no individual writer could easily attempt to arrest it. Authors of goliardic verse and of *fabliaux* show a spontaneous hostility to the monkish way of life. The comic treatment of Joseph in the mystery cycles is incompatible with reverence for the Virgin and a solemn renunciation of fleshly delight. When one compares the interest which the Middle Ages had for the austere behavior of the saints described in the *Golden Legend* with medieval cynicism as to the actual practices of men and women, one perceives the inevitable conflict between ascetic ideals and reality.[48] But all these examples are indirect and not a sharp intellectual challenge to the position of the church. Jean de Meung, who challenged not only the attitude of the church but also that of court poets, seems to have been one of the few men before the Reformation with a sufficiently courageous grasp of the world he inhabited to advocate a frank acceptance of the life of the senses.

The erotic precepts and sentiments of courtly love, however, were easier prey for the skeptic than was the asceticism advocated by the church. Obviously these precepts were not accepted by everyone. They were more than literary substitutes for an unattainable ideal. The lyrics of Provence, the treatise of Andreas, the *Charrette* of Chrestien de Troyes suggested a manner of living one's emotional life that some medieval courtiers no doubt emulated.[49] But, perhaps for this very reason, the system of courtly love conflicted not only with Christian moral theories but also with mundane and realistic notions of sex. As a recent critic has remarked, the "goût de la perfection est au dedans et le désire de le voir, à la rigueur, suivi de quelque effet. Mais, comme règle de vie pratique, l'amour courtois n'est que faillite fleu-

---

[48] See Bédier, *Les Fabliaux* (pp. 326–340), for a discussion of the treatment of monk and cleric in these tales. See also Wood, *The Spirit of Protest in Old French Literature*, ch. v, for a discussion of medieval realistic attitudes toward sex. See Furnivall's account of literary reflections in the Middle Ages of monkish lubricity: Furnivall, ed., *Ballads from Manuscripts*, pp. 59–88, 313–314 (comment on the ballad "A godlye sayng").

[49] Kilgour, in *The Decline of Chivalry*, discusses courtly love theories in relation to the life of the Middle Ages, ch. iv, "The Status of Courtly Love."

rie." [50] That is to say, the longing for some earthly apotheosis of desire that is evoked by *fine amor* is real enough. The lover's quest in the *Roman de la Rose* is true to the aspirations of young men seeking perfect consummation of their passions. But after a little experience the lover might come to regard the object of his desire as a mortal, with the irritating potentialities of a human being.

Hence the contrast of the poet's own experience of love with the formal, courtly ideal (which is a commonplace of Elizabethan poetry) is found as early as the thirteenth century in the lyrics of the troubadour Peire Cardenal. He presents a point-by-point repudiation of the doctrines of courtesy by stating that not one of the supposed physical symptoms of lovers has been present in his own amorous affairs:

Maintenant je puis me louer d'amour, car il ne m'enlève ni le manger, ni le dormir, je ne sens ni la froidure, ni la chaleur; il ne me fait soupirer, ni errer la nuit à l'aventure . . . je ne fais point de folie héroïque, je ne suis point frappé, je ne suis pris ni volé, je ne connais pas les longues attentes, je ne prétends pas être vaincu par amour.[51]

Furthermore, he challenges the courtly dogma that one is ennobled by submitting oneself to passion. "Je tiens pour fou l'homme qui fait alliance avec Amour," he remarks. He states that he has never gained more than when he lost his lady ("ma mie"), "car en la perdant je me gagnai moi-même que j'avais perdu." [52]

The most memorable literary expression of conflicting points of view, however, until we come to Chaucer, is probably to be found in the *Roman de la Rose*. Indeed, beginning with Christine de Pisan's criticism of this poem in her *Epistre au Dieu d'Amours* (1399), the *Roman de la Rose* became the focal point for an acrimonious debate as to the nature of love, which was kept alive in French literature for a century. The first portion, written by

---

[50] Pierre Grasset, "Faillite de l'amour courtois," *Mercure de France*, CCXCII (June, 1939), 346.
[51] Anglade, *Les Troubadours*, p. 182.   [52] *Ibid.*, p. 183.

Guillaume de Lorris early in the thirteenth century, is of course (along with Chrestien's *Chevalier de la Charrette* and Andreas Capellanus's *Art of Love*) one of the most influential medieval poems in the courtly tradition. On the other hand, Jean de Meung's portion (before 1277) expresses a critical, realistic attitude toward both courtier and monk. Jean de Meung makes an attempt to find a theory of love more practicable than that described by either Guillaume de Lorris or the church fathers. As Ernest Langlois has remarked, Jean's "instruction sérieuse et son bon sens lui donnent une idée plus réelle des choses de la vie, et en particulier de l'amour et de la galanterie." [53]

What Jean de Meung does is to take the romantic lover of the first portion of the poem and open his eyes to the reality of the world in which he hopes to realize his passion. He is taught by a series of skeptics. The character Reason emphasizes the incongruous mixture of pleasure and pain prescribed by troubadours.[54] He suggests that love between friends or love of mankind is more agreeable than romantic bondage to one's lady.[55] The Friend accepts love between a man and his mistress, but raises the very real problem of how one should keep love alive when once it has been conjured into being. He suggests that love and masculine domination are incompatible and illustrates the fact by depicting the misfortunes that overwhelmed a husband who sought to coerce his wife.[56] He advises the Lover to maintain by simulation his position as humble servant of his mistress and to overlook all her infidelities to him. In this way he may maintain her as the instrument of his desires.[57] The Duenna in this poem is equally matter of fact. She is highly derisive of the lady eulogized by romantic idealists. This character notes that the modest

---

[53] Petit de Julleville, ed., *Histoire de la langue et de la littérature française*, II, 122.

[54] *The Romance of the Rose*, tr. F. S. Ellis, ll. 4560–4638. In Guillaume de Lorris's portion, Reason is an enemy of the Lover; cf. ll. 3207 *et sqq.*

[55] *Ibid.*, ll. 4977 *et sqq.*, 5742 *et sqq.*

[56] *Ibid.*, ll. 8673 *et sqq.*; 8863 *et sqq.*; 8870–10464.

[57] *Ibid.*, ll. 10147–10348.

behavior and slow yielding of the courtly mistress is actually mere coquetry.[58] Genius concludes his speech with a plea for a simple yielding to passion. He suggests that such behavior is more suitable to human nature than either the chastity advocated by the church or the sensual ritual of adoration described by courtly love poets.

[58] *Ibid.*, ll. 13457 *et sqq.*; especially, ll. 14369–14416.

·IV·

Chaucer's Presentation of Amorous Controversy

As we have seen, the opposed ways of regarding love represented by the courtier, the monk, and the realist are scattered throughout medieval literature. Their inherent incompatibility is made artfully explicit for French literature in the *Roman de la Rose*. For English literature a similar service is rendered in the fourteenth century by Chaucer. He is particularly important in the history of romantic ideas because his century in England represents a final crystallization of medieval culture. The relationship between conceptions familiar both to the Middle Ages and to the Renaissance can be illustrated by a study of his writings. One can perceive specific literary conventions which survived the first period and can see how far a realistic criticism both of ascetic theory and of courtly ideals had ventured in each age. Moreover, one can compare the literary use made of conflicting and paradoxical conceptions of love in the fourteenth century with that made in the sixteenth and can thereby discover in what direction these conflicting notions of love had to go before men of Shakespeare's day could accept their romantic heritage as pure comedy.

The Three Conceptions of Love

Jean de Meung's portion of the *Roman de la Rose* is not only critical but also didactic. Guillaume de Lorris, for his part, if not seeking converts, is at least engaged in analyzing and explaining the nature of courtly love. Chaucer, however, seems to take no side, or all sides. A wholehearted presentation of the world as he found it, including all its paradoxes and incongruities, appears to be fundamental to his art. He may present characters who believe in romance, or in chaste devotion to God, or in simple sensuality. But their beliefs characterize them and make them seem real. Their attitudes are part of Chaucer's artistry, not necessarily personal tenets of his own. In the *Book of the Duchess*, the "Knight's Tale," *Troilus and Criseyde,* and a number of minor lyrics Chaucer invokes the conventions of courtly love as a way of depicting men and women in love. He shows little or no concern (as had Jean de Meung) for the accuracy with which troubadour ideals describe actual behavior. Even in his own love lyrics, where he writes as if he were describing personal experience, there is little distinguishing individuality in his treatment of love. In the *Complaint unto Pity* and the *Complaint to His Lady,* for example, Chaucer is content to reiterate the usual thoughts and feelings of a courtly lover: his desires have been unassuaged, he is in agony, he protests his amorous servitude and devotion. As Professor Robinson points out, the "individual 'lyric' cry was not characteristic of his age." [1]

In his two long romances, the "Knight's Tale" and *Troilus and Criseyde,* Chaucer explores the psychology of lovers. But the exploration is almost entirely after the pattern of courtship and surrender given authenticity by Chrestien de Troyes and by Guillaume de Lorris.[2] In both of Chaucer's romances love is a sensual experience and captures the lover, as was customary, through the eye. He grows sick and languishes until he finally wins his lady. In the first of these tales, however, the plot is emphasized, and the courtly element is not given the elaborate treatment it receives in the *Troilus.* In the latter the emphasis is upon the characters and their reactions to love. The *Troilus,* indeed, is one of the great medieval poems in the courtly tradi-

---

[1] Chaucer, *Complete Works,* ed. by Robinson, p. 612.
[2] See Fansler, *Chaucer and the Roman de la Rose,* p. 150: "Troilus fulfils practically all the requirements which are codified, as it were, in Guillaume de Lorris' 'art d'amor.'" Langlois remarks that Guillaume is "un élève de Chrétien de Troyes, tout imbu des théories quintessenciées de l'amour courtois." (Petit de Julleville, ed., *Histoire,* II, 122.)

tion, because in it Chaucer explores the predicaments in which a pair of lovers become involved by their adherence to troubadour ideals.[3]

The lovers in this poem meet in the spring, the traditional season for passion in medieval romance,

> . . . whan clothed is the mede
> With newe grene, of lusty Veer the pryme.[4]

Criseyde, quite properly, is the most beautiful woman in Troy,[5] and yet modest:

> Simple of atir and debonaire of chere
> With ful assured lokyng and manere.[6]

Her future lover, Troilus, is temporarily skeptical and lightly scornful of passion. He teases friends who are its victims, crying to them, if he finds them sighing or languishing,

> . . . God woot, she slepeth softe
> For love of thee, whan thow turnest ful ofte.[7]

But Troilus's cynicism merely emphasizes the irresistible power of the God of Love. The mocker becomes the victim of that which he has mocked:

> . . . with a look his herte wax a-fere,
> That he that now was moost in pride above,
> Wax sodeynly moost subgit unto love.[8]

He sees Criseyde for the first time among a crowd of worshipers at the temple of Palladion. Immediately he is caught by love:

> Therewith his herte gan to sprede and rise,
> And softe sighed, lest men myghte hym here.[9]

The shaft has gone to his heart, and his emotions are kindled:

> And of hire look in him ther gan to quyken
> So gret desir and such affeccioun,

---

[3] See Thomas A. Kirby's *Chaucer's Troilus; a Study in Courtly Love.*
[4] *Troilus and Criseyde*, Bk. I, l. 156. [5] *Ibid.*, Bk. I, ll. 102–105.
[6] *Ibid.*, Bk. I, l. 180. [7] *Ibid.*, Bk. I, l. 195; see also ll. 183–205.
[8] *Ibid.*, Bk. I, l. 229; see ll. 206 *et sqq.* for Troilus's conversion.
[9] *Ibid.*, Bk. I, l. 278.

> That in his hertes botme gan to stiken
> Of hir his fixe and depe impressioun.[10]

Troilus enters upon the second stage described in the courtly system of love. He begins to languish, and finally takes to his bed in an agony of sick passion, crying out:

> ". . . now wolde God, Criseyde,
> Ye wolden on me rewe, er that I deyde!"[11]

Fear of his lady becomes an obsession.

> Ne of his wo ne dorste he nat bygynne
> To tellen hir, for al this world to wynne.[12]

It is only after his friend Pandarus has agreed to sue for him that Troilus begins to be ennobled by his experience. He then becomes

> . . . the friendliest wighte,
> The gentilest, and ek the mooste fre.[13]

Criseyde is not won immediately, Chaucer makes plain.[14] Love at first sight was for the man; the lady's role was to yield slowly. But the desires of the hero are encouraged by an exchange of letters and then a meeting. The climax of the affair is reached when Troilus is permitted to possess Criseyde. Thereafter, until she is forced to leave Troy, he becomes the embodiment of courage, gentleness, and courtesy.[15]

In the *Troilus* the formal conventions of romance are given more vitality and carry more conviction (at least for us today) than they do elsewhere in Chaucer's writings. There are a number of reasons for this fact. Troilus and Criseyde are made so real that their thoughts and feelings transcend the formal code from which they spring. The lovers' personalities triumph over literary traditions of courtly poets. Pandarus's gently derisive acceptance of Troilus's passions also serves to lend them credence. Further, Chaucer gives a seductively literal picture of Troilus's carnal delights. But for all his art, the experiences which Chaucer

---

[10] *Ibid.*, Bk. I, l. 295.
[11] *Ibid.*, Bk. I, l. 459.
[12] *Ibid.*, Bk. I, l. 503.
[13] *Ibid.*, Bk. I, l. 1079.
[14] *Ibid.*, Bk. II, ll. 666–679.
[15] *Ibid.*, Bk. III, ll. 1772–1820.

describes in this romance and in his other love poems are limited by a literary and an aristocratic code. His characters do not seek release from romantic bondage, but surrender to it.

Chaucer reveals the catholicity of his imagination by the fact that when it serves his purpose to mirror the life of the senses as it was regarded by the church, he can follow St. Jerome and St. Augustine as well as Chrestien and Guillaume de Lorris. In his portrait of St. Cecilia, in the "Second Nun's Tale," for example, he depicts the orthodox and sincere contempt for physical love which was one of the basic attitudes of his age. The religious tone is in keeping with the piety of the speaker. The "Prologue" contains an invocation to the Virgin and a brief sermon on the perils of idleness. The tale concerns the life of St. Cecilia from a period just before her marriage to Valerian, to her martyrdom. As a maiden, she was a devout Christian, always praying to be kept in the purity of her sexual innocence.[16] Under her wedding garments she wears a hair shirt, symbolic of her scorn for fleshly indulgence.[17] After her marriage she convinces her husband of the sincerity of her desire to remain a virgin. He respects her wishes, and the two abstain from normal relations while they remain alive.

Likewise, when Chaucer has occasion to refer directly to the tenets of the church, he makes use of specific phrases by which the church fathers expressed their attitude toward the relations of the sexes. In the prologue to the *Legend of Good Women*, for example, Chaucer defines a "good" woman as one who retains that degree of chastity demanded by Jerome's measurement of virtue:

> For alle keped they here maydenhed
> Or elles wedlok, or here widwehed.[18]

The Parson's discussion of "luxuria," in the *Canterbury Tales*, is an accurate résumé of both fourth- and fourteenth-century theology. Commenting on chastity in marriage, the Parson states

---

[16] "Second Nun's Tale," ll. 125–126. [17] *Ibid.*, ll. 132–133.
[18] Text G, l. 294. (For St. Jerome's statement see *Select Letters of St. Jerome*, pp. xiv, 386*n*.)

that man "sholde loven hys wyf by discrecioun, paciently and atemprely; and thanne is she as though it were his suster." [19] This is Jerome's rationalization of St. Paul, that "a man ought to love his wife with judgment, not passion." [20] For to the strict moralist of the Middle Ages, pleasure of the marriage bed, though venial, was a sin. The Parson exclaims, "God woot, a man may sleen hymself with his owene knyf." [21] The purpose of marriage, as Jerome had phrased it, was to beget virgins.[22] The Parson was only repeating what everyone should know, that it was a sin

> When a man list dele in bed
> With his wyf that he has wed
> His lust anly to fulfille
> And to gette a child is noght in wille.[23]

Chaucer's poetry includes not only a Troilus and a St. Cecilia but also characters who are aware of their passions as naturally and simply as they are aware that they are alive. From the point of view of either Guillaume de Lorris or of John Bromyard such characters would seem to exist in a neutral limbo beyond the reach of the two systematized conceptions of love. Alice of Bath, for example, is presented as a woman whose desires do not go beyond a cunning libidinousness. The Host, likewise, reacts easily and unintellectually to love as it is found in the world about him. In the "Prologue of the Monk's Tale" he jocularly teases the Monk as an exemplar of chastity. He notes the plump,

---

[19] "Parson's Tale," l. 860.
[20] Saint Jerome, *Contra Jovinianum*, p. 385.
[21] "Parson's Tale," l. 858. Cf. Dan Michel's *Ayenbite of Inwit* (1340), p. 48:
        And mid owene zuord:
        Man may him-zelve sle.

Seven kinds of unchastity are listed in Mannyng, Robert of Brunne's *Handlyng Synne* (1303), ed. F. J. Furnivall, E.E.T.S. (1901), pp. 234 ff. Dan Michel swells the number to fourteen (*Ayenbite of Inwit*, pp. 48 ff.).

[22] Saint Jerome, *Select Letters*, XXII, 95: "I praise marriage, but it is because it produces me virgins. I gather the rose from the thorn, the gold from the earth, the pearl from the oyster."

[23] *The Pricke of Conscience*, ed. by Richard Morris, Bk. IV, l. 3460.

well-fed look of the man and remarks that it is a pity he is a member of a religious order. Abstinence seems ill-suited to one of such vigor. The Host says, slyly, "Thou woldest han been a tredefowel aright!" [24]

In the stories of the Miller, the Reeve, and the Merchant in the *Canterbury Tales* Chaucer vividly depicts the attitudes of the *fabliaux*. These misanthropic tales present amusing portraits of women's unstable desires and ingenious depravity. They express a popular cynicism toward sex, as witnessed by the Miller's remark:

> ". . . Leve brother Osewold,
> Who hath no wyf, he is no cokewold." [25]

The Cook's amused, involuntary recognition of the faithfulness of the Reeve's tale to his own view of the way of the world is expressed by an unconscious gesture. He scratches in sheer delight: "For joye him thoughte he clawed him on the bak." [26]

The asceticism of the church and the elaborate ritual of courtly passion are entirely absent from these popular stories. The women of the *fabliaux* do not deny their lovers after the fashion of St. Cecilia and are not slow and cautious in accepting them as was Criseyde. Indeed, the way in which the husband shall be fooled is the only restraint put upon lust. Alisoun's husband, in the "Miller's Tale," is made to believe that a second flood is coming, and his preparations for this event keep him out of her way. May's husband, in the "Merchant's Tale," actually witnesses her seduction, but is convinced by her that he has imperfect vision. And the wife in the "Reeve's Tale" is the cheerful victim of circumstances. These examples of uninhibited sensuality are about as far from the court lady's pageant of love as one could go. Where Emelye, of the "Knight's Tale," is the modest, reluctant woman of courtly romance and Criseyde's passion is the product of artistry in love, May is an illustration of unmannered lubricity, and Alisoun yields to desire as easily as a young cat.

---

[24] "Prologue of the Monk's Tale," l. 1945.
[25] "Miller's Prologue," l. 3150.   [26] "Cook's Prologue," l. 4326.

Chaucer's Use of Conflict

Chaucer's literary artistry is nowhere more apparent than in his use of the conflicts among the three conceptions of love current in his age. The focus is almost always on the conflict as evoking laughter and revealing character, not as pressing some private conviction of the poet. Unlike Jean de Meung, who felt impelled to take sides, Chaucer remains for the most part objective and impartial. He seems content (except perhaps in the "marriage group" of the *Canterbury Tales*) to make purely literary use of tensions existing among these opposed attitudes. In the prologue to the "Second Nun's Tale," for example, he uses the speaker's revulsion from courtly love as a natural way of characterizing a woman who represents a religious order, not as an attack on romance itself. Indirectly and appropriately she disparages the whole world of medieval courtesy in her denunciation of "ydlenesse," "That porter of the gate is of delices." [27] This is the porter at the entrance to the Garden in the *Roman de la Rose* and the figure chosen elsewhere by Chaucer to preside in the Garden of Venus in the "Knight's Tale." In the "Nun's Priest's Tale," on the other hand, Chaucer makes a direct appeal to his audience's awareness of conflict to evoke humor. In Chauntecleer's compliment to Pertelote he places *vis-à-vis* a common medieval phrase [28] embodying clerical antifeminism and one suggesting the courtier's exaltation of woman. Alisoun and Emelye and Alice of Bath and Criseyde are neatly and amusingly balanced in these lines:

> For al so siker as 'In principio,
> Mulier est hominis confusio,'
> Madame, the sentence of this Latyn is
> Womman is mannes joye and al his blis.[29]

[27] "Second Nun's Prologue," l. 3. See Brown, "The Prologue of Chaucer's 'Lyf of Seint Cecile,'" *Modern Philology*, IX (July, 1912), 2.

[28] Carleton Brown cites many appearances of this phrase in the Middle Ages: "Mulier est hominis confusio," *Modern Language Notes*, XXXV (1920), 479 ff.

[29] "Nun's Priest's Tale," ll. 4353 *et sqq*.

In the conclusion to the *Troilus* Chaucer makes literary use of the opposition between earthly and heavenly love in still another way. He had revealed the pleasure and the beauty of human passion in the main portion of the poem. The concluding verses suggest a different point of view. Troilus is made to look down, after his death, on those weeping his loss and to laugh at them because they follow, as he had followed, the "blynde lust, the which that may nat laste." [30] Here Chaucer seems to be indicating that from the religious point of view Troilus and Criseyde have fought against their mortal destiny and have lost. They have pursued an evanescent pleasure, and its disappearance illustrates this "false worldes brotelnesse." [31] The last few stanzas of the poem imply that their tragedy is not merely their separation through unfortunate circumstances. They have moved toward tragedy because they sought happiness through sensuality, through what was regarded by the orthodox as transitory and fragile. The conclusion to the *Troilus* is not a narrow didactic attack on courtly love. Rather, Chaucer relates Troilus's personal grief to a general conflict of medieval attitudes toward passion in order to heighten the significance of his lovers' downfall.

Chaucer had characterized the Second Nun, as we have seen, by revealing her attitude toward courtly love. Reversing this process, he characterizes both the Host and the Wife of Bath by showing their reaction to the ideal abstinence sponsored by the church. In the "Prologue of the Monk's Tale," the Host indicates his lighthearted, amused skepticism toward a man who professes virginity. He argues that the world is getting a poor crop of children because the church has

> . . . take up al the corn
> Of tredyng, and we borel men been shrympes.[32]

If he were pope, not only this particular monk, but

> . . . every myghty man,
> Though he were shorn ful hye upon his pan,
> Sholde have a wyf.[33]

---

[30] *Troilus and Criseyde*, Bk. V, l. 1824.   [31] *Ibid.*, Bk. V, l. 1832.
[32] "Prologue of the Monk's Tale," l. 1954.   [33] *Ibid.*, l. 1951.

The Host makes the same sort of remarks to the Nun's Priest. If he had been secular, he too would have been a "trede-foul":

> For if thou have corage as thou hast myght,
> Thee were nede of hennes.[34]

Alice of Bath is somewhat more aggressive in her reaction. She is not content merely to tease representatives of the ideal of celibacy. Chaucer provokes laughter by making her defend her own unascetic conduct. Having enjoyed herself so fully, she who has been married five times wonders why Christ reproved the Samaritan:

> . . . I axe, why that the fifthe man
> Was noon housbonde to the Samaritan?
> How manye myghte she have in mariage? [35]

She prefers to think about the polygamous men of the Old Testament,[36] and the Biblical command to "wexe and multiplye." [37] Also, she quibbles over church dogma. Men may advise a woman to be chaste, but she points out that "conseillyng is no comandement." [38] The supreme comic moment in her conflict with the ideals of the church is reached when she paraphrases St. Jerome. He had grudgingly accepted marriage because it produced virgins. Alice uses this argument to defend her own outrageously robust appetite:

> . . . certes, if ther were no seed y-sowe,
> Virginitee, thanne wherof sholde it growe? [39]

Chaucer is as willing to make use of a realistic attitude toward courtly love in order to reveal the nature of a character in his writings as he is to portray men and women by their acceptance or rejection of the ideals of the church. Thus Chaucer characterizes the Miller, in part, by his down-to-earth scorn for the refinements of courtly romance. His attitude conforms to his social position. The gentlefolk, Chaucer tells us, particularly enjoyed the conventionally romantic wooing of Emelye:

---

[34] "Epilogue to the Nun's Priest's Tale," l. 3452.
[35] "Wife of Bath's Prologue," ll. 21 *et sqq.*
[36] *Ibid.*, ll. 35 *et sqq.*   [37] *Ibid.*, l. 28.
[38] *Ibid.*, l. 67; see also ll. 59–70.   [39] *Ibid.*, ll. 71–72.

> Whan that the Knyght had thus his tale ytoold,
> In al the route nas ther yong ne oold
> That he ne seyde it was a noble storie,
> And worthy for to drawen to memorie;
> And namely the gentils everichon.[40]

But the drunken Miller seems to have been irritated by this elaborate romance. He could "abyde no man for his curteisie," and, perhaps with conscious irony on Chaucer's part, the Miller remarks that he also knows a "noble tale for the nones." [41] Before this character retaliates with his own ribald version of love, to "quite the Knyghtes tale," [42] Chaucer further emphasizes the conflicting points of view of these two pilgrims by stating that if the Miller's story to come be too bold for any "gentil wight," he may

> Turne over the leef and chese another tale.
> For he shal fynde ynowe, grete and smale,
> Of storial thyng that toucheth gentillesse,
> And eek moralitee and hoolynesse.[43]

The "Prologue to the Legend of Good Women" is Chaucer's most self-conscious revelation of his awareness of the conflict between courtly love as an ideal and the somewhat less exalted nature of those who attempt to follow it. He walks into the fields on a May morning, he tells us, to pay his devotion to the flower which symbolizes his mistress.[44] He hears birds singing love lays and acting out the ritual of desire praised by troubadours:

> Yelding honour and humble obeysaunces
> To love . . .[45]

But Chaucer arraigns himself for his skepticism of courtly love. He falls asleep and dreams that the God of Love, who enters the field with a train of court ladies, at once challenges the poet's right to worship this flower. Chaucer has been guilty of heresy against the whole courtly system. He has translated the *Roman*

---

[40] "Miller's Prologue," ll. 3109 *et sqq*.   [41] See *ibid.*, ll. 3120–3127.
[42] *Ibid.*, l. 3127.   [43] *Ibid.*, ll. 3171 *et sqq*.
[44] "Prologue to the Legend of Good Women," Text F, ll. 103 *et sqq*.
[45] *Ibid.*, ll. 149–150; see also 160–163.

de la Rose (Jean de Meung's portion is probably meant) and has described Criseyde's betrayal of her lover. Since he has portrayed the courtier's mistress to be less than perfect, he is the "mortal fo" of Love, "And lettest folk from hire devocyoun." [46] He is further reviled, for, as the God of Love remarks, Chaucer has shown himself to think

> That he nys but a verray propre fol
> That loveth paramours, to harde and hote.[47]

The ostensible purpose of this "Prologue" is the celebration by Chaucer of the woman he loves. Actually, it is both a joke at the expense of a romantic convention and the poet's gentle apostrophe to the whole troubadour ritual. The curious paradox here is that Chaucer, who has acknowledged mutually contradictory attitudes toward love, at the same time courts the unadulterated ideal itself.

There is an obviously realistic simile at the expense of romantic convention in the short lyric *To Rosemounde* in which Chaucer says of his sufferings as a courtly lover:

> Nas never pyk walwed in galauntyne
> As I in love am walwed and ywounde.[48]

The very fabric of Pandarus as a literary creation is built out of his somewhat mocking insistence that Troilus and Criseyde cut through the ritual of wooing prescribed by the troubadour system and achieve the consummation of their passion. But Chaucer occasionally describes the submissive, emotionally tortured wooer in a harsher fashion. In a passage in the "Knight's Tale," for example, the Duke of Athens is made to comment satirically on the disastrous folly of courtiers who make a romantic passion the sole purpose of existence. As the desperate sufferings of Palamoun and Arcite and their final bloody quarrel illustrate, such devotion to one's lady is a kind of madness:

> Who may been a fool, but if he love?
> Bihoold, for Goddes sake that sit above,

---

[46] *Ibid.*, l. 325.   [47] *Ibid.*, Text G, l. 259.
[48] *To Rosemounde*, l. 17.

> Se how they blede! be they noght wel arrayed?
> Thus hath hir lord, the god of love, ypayed
> Hir wages and hir fees for hir servyse! [49]

In the opening stanzas of the *Complaint of Mars* Chaucer chooses to regard the exquisite pleasures of a courtier's love-making from the point of view of the work-a-day world in which most of life is lived. They are described, therefore, as transient and variable. They cannot survive the strong light of day. When the flowers unfold in the warm sun, the lover's night is over. The poet cautions,

> . . . ye lovers, that lye in any drede,
> Fleeth, lest wikked tonges yow espye!
> Lo! yond the sunne, the candel of jelosye!

Later on in this poem there is a more vehement diatribe against the anguished fate of the traditional amorist. Mars asks,

> To what fyn made the God that sit so hye,
> Benethen him, love other companye,
> And streyneth folk to love, malgre her hed? [50]

Experience shows that the joys of passion are as transitory as the "twynkelyng of an ye." Hence, whether

> . . . love breke or elles dure,
> Algates he that hath with love to done
> Hath ofter wo then changed is the mone.[51]

Chaucer again depicts the unstable nature of love, as a skeptic would see it, in the opening lines of the *Parliament of Fowls*. Courtiers' passion is described as incongruously fleeting:

> The lyf so short, the craft so long to lerne,
> Th' assay so hard, so sharp the conquerynge,
> The dredful joye, alwey that slit so yerne:
> Al this mene I by Love, that my felynge
> Astonyeth with his wonderful werkynge

---

[49] "The Knight's Tale," l. 1798. Cf. ll. 1785–1868. Robinson remarks (Chaucer, *The Complete Works*, p. 778): ". . . the humor, even flippancy of tone, is Chaucer's. . . . Such mockery of love is common in Old French Poetry."

[50] *Complaint of Mars*, l. 218.   [51] *Ibid.*, l. 222.

> So sore iwis, that whan I on hym thynke,
> Nat wot I wel wher that I flete or synke.

Finally, in the last book of the *Troilus*, Chaucer reduces the inexorable fragility of all men's desires, of which romantic love is one, to four pensive lines:

> Criseyde loveth the sone of Tideus
> And Troilus moot wepe in cares colde.
> Swich is this world, whoso it kan byholde:
> In ech estat is litel hertes reste.[52]

Chaucer's Attempt to Resolve Conflicting Attitudes

In the sequence of poems in the *Canterbury Tales* usually referred to as the "Marriage Group" (from the Wife's "Prologue" through the "Franklin's Tale" [53]) the subject discussed directly or by implication is the proper relationship between husband and wife or between courtier and lady. It is difficult to decide whether Chaucer is putting to further literary use these conflicting attitudes toward love current in his age or whether he is displaying didactic concern somewhat after the fashion of Jean de Meung and is using these poems to advocate his own solution to lovers' difficulties.[54] At any rate, a series of solutions are suggested by a number of spokesmen, and the final one, suggested by the Franklin (the romance of marriage), makes its appeal to all romantics who wish to domesticate passion.

The first of these suggested ways to bring harmony out of discord is described by the Wife of Bath. In her "Prologue" she remarks that the obvious result of attempts, in the name of morality, to keep a woman humble and submissive is to make her instead the shrewish, libidinous creature described by misog-

---

[52] *Troilus*, Bk. V, ll. 1746–1749.

[53] "The tales and links in the sequence mentioned, from the 'Wife's Prologue' through the 'Franklin's Tale,' are usually referred to as the Marriage Group" (Robinson, in *Chaucer, The Complete Works*, p. 801).

[54] See Kittredge's "Chaucer's Discussion of Marriage," *Modern Philology*, IX (1912), 435–467.

ynists.⁵⁵ Therefore women should rule men. She illustrates her solution to amorous difficulties in the tale which she tells. A lover is asked to choose either a foul, old, but humble and faithful wife, or one young and fair and possibly fickle.⁵⁶ Because he refuses to make a decision between conventional piety and natural desire (which is also a choice between a quiet life and a tormented one), but leaves the decision to the woman, he thereby achieves both. The latter cries that she will be "bothe fair and good," since he has surrendered to her "maistrie." ⁵⁷ All the complex problems of love disappear. Husbands who permit themselves to be ruled by their wives will live

> . . . unto hir lyves ende
> In parfit joye.⁵⁸

In opposition to the theory of the Wife, the Clerk advocates the traditional supremacy of the husband. His story of Griselda illustrates the benefits which follow such a "proper" relationship. Griselda's husband has tested her by pretending to kill their children, by turning her out of the palace, and finally by calling her back to prepare the palace for a new bride. Through all her trials, she has acted

> As glad, as humble, as bisy in servyse,
> And eek in love, as she was wont to be.⁵⁹

Her reward is that she proved worthy in her husband's eyes and lived out her days with him "in concord and in reste." ⁶⁰

The Clerk himself, however, is sadly aware that the humility and obedience which he has described is merely an ideal and finds no actual counterpart in the behavior of such creatures as the Wife of Bath. By implication, then, his solution is not very practicable. In the closing stanzas of the poem he notes, first, that it would be difficult to find two or three such paragons as Griselda in "al a toun." ⁶¹ Then he forces the contrast between

---

[55] "Wife of Bath's Prologue," ll. 321–322; 517–518.
[56] "Wife of Bath's Tale," ll. 1219–1227.   [57] Ibid., ll. 1236–1241.
[58] Ibid., l. 1257.   [59] "Clerk's Tale," l. 603.
[60] Ibid., l. 1128.   [61] Ibid., l. 1165.

the ideal he has described and the palpable actions of the Wife and those like her. He concludes by arguing, ironically, the advantages accruing to shrewish, domineering women.[62]

His derisive comment on the unpleasant nature of married "love" is agreed to both by the Host [63] and by the Merchant, the latter crying out:

> Ther is a long and large difference
> Bitwix Grisildis grete pacience
> And of my wyf the passing crueltee.[64]

And the *fabliau* that the Merchant tells forces a violent contrast between a desire to find a kind of sensual paradise of peace in married love and the actual finding of the earthly hell described by clerical misogynists. The old dotard January, in the "Merchant's Tale," carps incessantly against the conception that women are evil and thinks to have in his marriage his "hevene in erthe heere." [65] But as he relates his story, the Merchant constantly interrupts to point out the absurdity of January's point of view. The Merchant makes use of the sayings of Theophrastus, whose "Golden Book" was known to the Middle Ages through its incorporation in Jerome's treatise *Contra Jovinianum*. "Who is so obedient as a wife?" the Merchant exclaims sardonically.

> Who is so trewe, and eek so ententyf
> To kepe hym, syk and hool, as is his make? [66]

Some clerks, of which Theophrastus is one, indicate that women are vile creatures. But the Merchant, unfolding a tale of a wife's betrayal of her husband, remarks with bitterness:

> . . . take no kep of al swich vanytee;
> Deffie Theofraste, and herke me.[67]

---

[62] *Ibid.*, ll. 1183 *et sqq.*

[63] See the remarks of the Host, following the "Clerk's Tale," l. 1212a *et sqq.*; also in the Epilogue to the "Merchant's Tale," ll. 2419–2440.

[64] "Merchant's Prologue," l. 1223.

[65] "Merchant's Tale," l. 1647. See John Livingston Lowes, "Chaucer and the 'Miroir de Mariage,'" *Modern Philology*, VIII (1910), 176: ". . . the cynical implications of the panegyric are alike in both."

[66] "Merchant's Tale," l. 1288.   [67] *Ibid.*, l. 1309.

The Wife, the Clerk, the Host, and the Merchant have agreed that love in reality may be an unpleasant affair. The Wife and the Clerk have advanced contradictory theories for altering such a state. But the Franklin is not content with either plan. He points out that

> Wommen, of kynde, desiren libertee,
> And nat to been constreyned as a thral;
> And so doon men, if I sooth seyen shal.[68]

The Franklin proposes to tell a story in which two lovers are bound to each other by marriage, and yet in which neither one dominates the other.

His plan is simple enough. A knight, Arveragus, woos Dorigen in the traditional manner of suffering lover.[69] But he promises that after marriage he will take "no maistrie" upon himself. He will

> . . . hire obeye, and folwe hir wyl in al
> As any lovere to his lady shal,
> Save that the name of soveraynetee,
> That wolde he have for shame of his degree.[70]

Dorigen, for her part, promises that she will not take advantage of his "gentillesse." She will be to him the "humble trewe wyf" [71] prescribed by the moral conventions of the time. The Franklin calls this pact a "humble, wys accord." [72] He has indicated a way in which the antagonistic conceptions of troubadour poets and the church fathers can be brought into harmony. Dorigen's husband is both

> . . . hir servant and hir lord.
> Servant in love and lord in mariage.[73]

Likewise, Arveragus has found in marriage both his "lady, certes, and his wyf also." [74]

The Franklin wishes to have the best of both the courtly world and the Christian. His tale shows the way in which these con-

[68] "Franklin's Tale," l. 768.
[69] Ibid., ll. 729 et sqq.
[70] Ibid., l. 749.
[71] Ibid., l. 758.
[72] Ibid., l. 791.
[73] Ibid., l. 792.
[74] Ibid., l. 797.

tradictory spheres can be united. Dorigen and her husband live together "in blisse and in solas." [75] On the one hand they are lovers in the pagan-courtly sense of the word and are not concerned with the sexual restraints praised by the church. This fact is made plain when Dorigen remarks to her suitor, Aurelius, that Arveragus "hath hir body whan so that hym liketh." [76] When Arveragus returns from his voyage to England, the Franklin says of Dorigen, "O blisful artow now,"

> That hast thy lusty housbonde in thyne armes
> The fresshe knyght, the worthy man of armes,
> That loveth thee as his owene hertes lyf.[77]

On the other hand, Dorigen remains faithful to her husband even though solicited by the languishing courtier Aurelius. She has the attitude of a Christian martyr toward desire not legalized by marriage.[78] She would prefer death to this "dishonor" praised by courtly love.

According to Professor Kittredge,[79] this story of married, courtly lovers represents Chaucer's solution of the amorous problems raised by conflicting medieval theories of love. Chrestien de Troyes, at the end of his romance *Cligès*, had advanced the same solution.[80] It cuts across both the Christian ideal of ascetic restraint and the courtly ideal of adulterous passion. Whether or not the Franklin speaks for Chaucer, in this tale of Dorigen and Arveragus the humble wife of the Griselda tradition and the worshiped lady of troubadour poets are fused. But the romance of marriage, from a realistic point of view, merely substitutes a legal union of lovers for an adulterous one. The Franklin's portrait of love in marriage gives no very tangible clew as to how the idyllic passions envisaged by courtly poets are to be kept alive in the reality of daily living together. The Franklin attempts to justify his theory by calling upon experience:

---

[75] *Ibid.*, l. 802.　　　　[76] *Ibid.*, l. 1005.
[77] *Ibid.*, l. 1091.　　　　[78] *Ibid.*, ll. 1355–1456.
[79] "Chaucer's Discussion of Marriage," *Modern Philology*, IX, 467.
[80] See Kirby, *Chaucer's "Troilus,"* p. 38.

>Who koude telle, but he hadde wedded be,
>The joye, the ese, and the prosperitee
>That is bitwixe an housbonde and his wyf? [81]

But the experience of the Host, the Wife, and the Merchant stands as proof of the rather theoretical solution suggested by the Franklin.[82]

Amorous Controversy in the Middle Ages and in the Renaissance

The controversy over the nature of love which thrived in medieval and Renaissance literature had a certain inevitability about it, due to the importance of the philosophies at stake. In medieval literature, as we have seen, expressions of conflict range all the way from the rather obvious weighing of courtly love against religious ideals in Walter Map's reaction to Eleanor of Aquitaine, in Andreas's palinode to his *Art of Love*, in "debate" poems like the *Owl and the Nightingale*, to the self-conscious irony of Chaucer's *Prologue to the Legend of Good Women*, and to the comic contrasts of the "Marriage Group" of the *Canterbury Tales*. Courtly love found its most bitter critic in Jean de Meung, who wished to abandon the system completely, and its most subtle foe in the Franklin, who wished to tame passion by marrying it. The one thing the medieval writer did not do to any appreciable extent was to examine such love in the light of his personal experience. He balanced and opposed conflicting theories of behavior. But his imagination was not caught up by the problem as to whether or not the system described that which actually took place when an individual experienced passion. This aspect was left to the probing of the Renaissance poet and thinker, who turned the controversy in a new direction in which the individual was greater than the system. But the system itself

---

[81] "Franklin's Tale," l. 803.
[82] For disagreement with Kittredge's interpretation of the "Franklin's Tale" see Hinckley, "The Debate on Marriage in the *Canterbury Tales*," PMLA, XXXII (1917), 292–305.

flourished in the Middle Ages (and with modifications in the Renaissance), despite its most formidable adversaries. Indeed, for most readers its most persuasive treatment in English literature is to be found in Chaucer's *Troilus and Criseyde*, where the lovers' tragedy, by being linked to Christian tradition, makes courtly love stand for the fundamental, if mortal, beauty of human experience.

It is true that Jean de Meung's plea for an artless delight in sex somewhat anticipates a Renaissance point of view. But the effects of Jean's challenge were delayed until the fifteenth century, when Christine de Pisan's rejoinder (1399), *Epistre au Dieu d'Amour*, provoked a re-examination by French writers of the whole nature of courtly love. But for Chaucer's century and in Chaucer's poetry there is little evidence of interest in the aspect of the problem which two centuries later was to evolve into a comedy of the manners of love: whether a romantic ideal of love could be attained in fact. Moreover, this comparative lack of personal reaction lends a certain objectivity and neutrality to some medieval treatments of conflict. Chaucer, for example, can present the philosophy of those outside the circle where courtly love could exist, as in the "Prologue to the Wife of Bath's Tale," with vigor and understanding. But he makes no effort to reconcile the incongruity that Criseyde makes an art of that which was simple appetite to Alice. In the Marriage Group, he does not praise the naturalism of the Wife at the expense of either the Clerk or the Franklin. When Chaucer is personal, as in the "Prologue to the Legend of Good Women" and in the lyric *To Rosemounde*, he may evince the inevitable restlessness of an alert intelligence in the presence of improbable or fanciful descriptions of human behavior. But he does not set up his lightly derisive, private reactions as standards by which to judge the whole tradition of courtly love.

Possibly in the "Franklin's Tale" Chaucer makes a concession and attempts to resolve these conflicts of his age. Elsewhere his writings reflect a counterpoint of themes. The Wife of Bath is amusing because her philosophy is incompatible with Christian ascetic ideals. But Chaucer does not seem to be making out a case for her [83] and against the church fathers. He is scarcely holding up to ridicule the morality of his time. The contrasts between the courtly idealism of the Knight and the natural vulgarity of the Miller is amusing in much the same fashion: the effect depends upon the willingness of Chaucer's audience to be interested in inconsistency for its own sake. There is little to show that Chaucer intends more. Likewise, the conclusion to the *Troilus* links it with the general medieval concern over the relationship between temporal and eternal affairs. But Troilus's final laughter at his earthly predicament scarcely makes this romance an "exemplum," a moral warning.[84] Rather, his laughter appeals to the audience's sense of irony and paradox, a simple aesthetic pleasure.

The sixteenth-century Englishman who inherited this controversy over love tended to be both less objective and more individualistic. The aspect of conflict which was to prove so disturbing, from the poetry of Wyatt to that of Donne, was whether a secularized, practicable version of courtly love was possible. After the Reformation the quarrel between the points of view of monk and courtier was of less importance. At the same time, under the specific influence of the Petrarchan sonnet and under the general influence of the new humanism, it seemed important

---

[83] It has been suggested that Chaucer's portrait of the Wife is an attack on the medieval ideal of chastity. See Lounsbury, *Studies in Chaucer*, II, 522–530; see also Root, *The Poetry of Chaucer*, pp. 231–238. The opposite point of view is expressed by Owst, *Literature and the Pulpit in Medieval England*, p. 386n: "The whole of the *Wife of Bath's Prologue* is nothing but a series of brilliant literary variations upon . . . pulpit themes." As Professor Tatlock has expressed it, irreverence in Chaucer is "largely an optical illusion"; "Chaucer and Wyclif," *Modern Philology*, XIV (1916–1917), 276.

[84] But cf. J. S. P. Tatlock's comment, "The Epilog of Chaucer's *Troilus*," *Modern Philology*, XVIII (April, 1921), 636: "Here we see Catholic tradition and classic-Renascence tradition in combat, and the victory for the time with the Catholic . . ." See also p. 658: ". . . it is difficult to doubt that the Epilog consciously reflects the age-long dispute as to the right attitude for a Christian man toward pagan poetry. Such a poem could have been written only when it was. Earlier it would not have been so classic, and later its classicism would not have been retracted."

to explore in literature private, individual worlds of feeling and sentiment and to compare these with a codified system of what one ought to feel. In the sixteenth-century sonnet sequences, for this reason, the fundamental conflict was between a romantic theory of love as an art and a ritual and an individual's difficulty in realizing this theory in his own experiences. Almost every important Elizabethan poet who wrote of love suggests that courtly (or Petrarchan) love describes that which should be or that which ought to be, but that which in fact is not.

The medieval scholar G. G. Coulton, in analyzing the difference between the mind of the Middle Ages and that of the Renaissance or the present, has described for all phases of life what is illustrated specifically in the reaction of two ages to a controversy over love:

> Men of the Middle Ages often held conflicting ideals; they did homage, as men must in every age, to things which in strict logic seem ultimately almost irreconcilable; but their conception of harmony between those opposites differed greatly from ours. We ourselves generally aim, as Aristotle taught, at the Golden Mean, striving by all sorts of concessions and compromises to temper one ideal with the other. They, on the other hand, strove far less to be all things at all times.[85]

This difference is important in the history of the literary use of amorous conflict. For the new effort to achieve harmony and a practicable decorum of love out of an old quarrel gave rise, in Shakespeare's century, to a comedy of manners which kept the idealizing spirit of *fine amor*, but shuffled off the outworn conventions which had expressed this ideal for four centuries.

---

[85] Coulton, *Medieval Panorama; the English Scene from Conquest to Reformation*, p. 254.

·V·

ROMANCE IN FIFTEENTH-CENTURY LITERATURE

THERE is a rather sharp break in English literature between Chaucer as literary representative of the Middle Ages and Sir Thomas Wyatt as herald of the Renaissance. Wyatt's lyrics, written in the third decade of the sixteenth century, serve conveniently to mark the shift from ascetic idealism to practicability as the chief opponent of courtly love. They are the first artistic manifestations of the new humanism. The "individual lyric cry" of Wyatt's love sonnets is the first important literary product of the Renaissance concern for the conflict between its inherited theories of behavior and individual thought and feeling. In the century intervening between Chaucer and Wyatt much of the writing continued to treat lovers' problems in the literary patterns which have been described for the Middle Ages. The arbitrary conventions of courtly love were unquestioned; its romantic conception of love, when opposed, was challenged by the medieval ideal of chastity. The fifteenth-century writings that do indicate a general shift of interest toward the kind of conflict which was to occupy the minds of the Elizabethans are often inconclusive. They do not line up in any rigidly chronological fashion to form stepping stones between the literary habits of two ages. Rather, they form a background of discontent with formal romance from which the pattern of conflict in Wyatt's verse suddenly crystallized.

Traditional Attitudes in the Fifteenth Century

A graceful example of a fifteenth-century poem which keeps alive, unblemished, the decorum of romance is the *Kingis Quair*, written by James I of Scotland (*ca.* 1424) to Lady Jane Beaufort, granddaughter of Chaucer's patron, John of Gaunt. As two centuries of tradition demanded, love is at first sight, is borne by the lover's glance, pierces to his heart, causing him to languish.[1] As in the *Troilus*, the lover exists solely to endure his passion. Stephen Hawes's *Passetyme of Pleasure*[2] is also (in part [3]) a reflection of courtly romance. On a day in spring the poet wanders through a meadow, falls asleep, and dreams of the love which La Graunde Amoure suffers for La Bell Pucell. The austere conceptions of the church, which were opposed to such amorous writings, are given traditional and highly imagined portrayal in the version of the Grail story found in Malory's *Morte d'Arthur* (printed by Caxton, 1485). Further indication of the prevalence of medieval ways of thought in this century lies in the fact that the most popular book to come from Caxton's press was a translation of the *Golden Legend*.[4]

The inevitable clash between sacred and profane love, reflected with solemnity at the conclusion of the *Troilus*, also continued to be voiced directly in fifteenth-century writings. It is found, for example, in the first stanza of Lydgate's *A Balade: In Commendation of Our Lady* (*ca.* 1415).[5] The servants of cupid end their lives in woe, we are told; therefore one should cling to the love of the Virgin, which is unfailing. In the *Flower and the Leaf*, a poem written in the first quarter of this century, idleness and worldly pleasure are opposed to the virtues of

---

[1] James I of Scotland, *The Kingis Quair*, in *The Kingis Quair* and *The Quare of Jelusy*, ed. by Alexander Lawson, stanzas XL–LXXI. For debt of *Kingis Quair* to Chaucer see stanza I and Introduction, pp. lx ff.

[2] Hawes's *The Passetyme of Pleasure*, ed. by William Edward Mead, p. xxix; first printed by Wynkyn de Worde in 1509.

[3] The courtly romance is given largely in ll. 2031–2548, 5187–5298. The rest discusses the utility of the "Seven Arts" in medieval education, the feats of *Graunde amoure*, the advice given him by various pagan deities.

[4] Legouis and Cazamian, *A History of English Literature*, p. 200. That is, "popularity" judged by the number of copies circulated. John Skelton, for example, devotes more space in his *Philip Sparrow* (before 1508) to *Troilus and Criseyde* than to any other single work from the Middle Ages.

[5] In Skeat, ed., *Chaucerian and Other Pieces*, p. 275.

chastity, constancy, and perseverance.[6] Henryson's *Testament of Cresseid* (after 1450) depicts a cruel earthly punishment overtaking Chaucer's gentle heroine as a reward for her unchastity. William Dunbar, in his early sixteenth-century imitation of a medieval quarrel of birds, presents another version of this same conflict of attitudes. A poet, in the amorous month of May, overhears the debate between a merle and a nightingale. The merle suggests that not to experience physical passion is against the "law of kynd";[7] God made women beautiful for the sake of earthly desire,[8] and a man is purified in his mistress' service.[9] But the merle finally accepts the religious point of view expressed by the nightingale, that women are beautiful to reflect heavenly love,[10] that carnal pleasure is a "frustir [i.e., frustrating] love" and blinds man to God.[11]

There are many short lyrics in the fifteenth century which present conventional philogynic and misogynic arguments.[12] E. K. Chambers remarks that such controversial poems "were the outcome of a skeptical 'bourgeois' reaction against the rigorous idealism of *'amour courtois.'* "[13] It is true that by the last decade of the sixteenth century, with Shakespeare's *Taming of the Shrew*, this reaction was at full tide. But it is difficult to see any clear advance over the quarrel between the Wife of Bath and the Clerk in most of these lyrics of the following century. Thomas Hoccleve's "Woman's Superiority,"[14] for example, is a mocking defense of woman against her detractors. With ironic gravity he presents arguments, ostensibly to prove that women should

---

[6] *Ibid.*, p. 361.
[7] Dunbar, *The Poems*, ed. by John Small, l. 37.
[8] *Ibid.*, ll. 49–56.   [9] *Ibid.*, ll. 81–88.
[10] *Ibid.*, ll. 57–64.   [11] *Ibid.*, ll. 89–96.
[12] See Chambers and Sidgwick, comps., *Early English Lyrics*, Nos. CXIII, CXIV, CXVII–CXXII.
[13] *Ibid.*, p. 276.
[14] From the *Regement of Princes* (1412), in Neilson and Webster, eds., *Chief British Poets of the Fourteenth and Fifteenth Centuries*, p. 201. (For a summary of the conventional arguments for and against woman see Barbara Matulka, *The Novels of Juan de Flores and Their European Diffusion*, pp. 138–157.)

rule their husbands. Woman comes from Adam's rib, not as men do, of "slyme of eerthe," he notes. Philosophers say that a circle is the most perfect figure, and this rib from which woman comes, is part of a circle.[15] Moreover, Christ's mother was a woman and was trusted to care for her son until he was twelve years old. Contemporary women, Hoccleve suggests, are therefore to be trusted to exercise equal care in their control of husbands.[16] Indeed, women are not shrews, since they take offense only at the vices of their husbands. Hoccleve asks slyly,

> Thogh a woman hir housbonde contrairie
> In his oppynyoun erroneous
> Shul men for that deme hir his adversarie? [17]

John Lydgate's *Mumming at Hertford* [18] likewise treats traditional denunciations of woman in a mocking, flippant fashion. His poem was presented as a dramatic skit for a Royal Christmas entertainment at Hertford in the first quarter of the fifteenth century. A group of husbands enter and complain of maltreatment. The wives reply by holding up the Wife of Bath as an example of proper feminine virtue. They are proud to do battle with their husbands for supremacy, they say, because they

> . . . clayme maystrye by prescripcyoun,
> Be long tytle of successyoun
> From wyff to wyff . . .[19]

In keeping with the spirit of burlesque, here, Lydgate offers no decision between warring couples,

> Til man may fynde some processe oute by lawe
> That they should by nature in theyre lyves
> Have soverayntee on theyre prudent wyves.[20]

More serious in tone and more clearly a reaction against unreasoned vilifications of woman is the poem the *Nut Brown Maid*. Here there is a reversal of the usual ritual of courtship in the

---
[15] *Ibid.*, ll. 28 *et sqq.* [16] *Ibid.*, ll. 87–88.
[17] *Ibid.*, l. 99.
[18] In Neilson and Webster, eds., *Chief British Poets*, p. 223.
[19] *Ibid.*, l. 203. [20] *Ibid.*, l. 241.

romances. The hero offers nothing to the maid but a life of outlawry. Only when she agrees to follow him out of pure affection does he reveal that he is an earl's son. The poem begins with a reference to the antifeminist attitudes found all through the Middle Ages:

> Be it right or wrong, these men among
> On women do complaine.[21]

E. K. Chambers aptly remarks that the "professed purpose of the poem connects itself with the old dispute as to the qualities of woman which the *amour courtois* had provoked." [22] The conclusion to the *Nut Brown Maid* shows woman to be worthy a natural, human affection, not mere masculine contempt:

> Here may ye see that wimen be
> In love, meke, kinde, and stable.
> Late never man repreve them than,
> Or calle them variable.[23]

The Re-examination of Courtly Love in Fifteenth-Century Literature

The transitional character of fifteenth-century literature is revealed in a series of poems in which there is an increasing emphasis on the unreality of courtly love conventions and a changing manner of expressing this sense of unreality. The amorous sentiments and decorum of the troubadours and of Guillaume de Lorris were a generally satisfactory means of portraying love in Chaucer's age. In this next century there are signs that interest is shifting. First in France, then in England, writers show concern for the contradictions between romantic concepts and the deviations therefrom by actual human beings. The traditional ritual of wooing becomes the subject of critical analysis based on observed experience. Such poetry is suggestive of the sixteenth-century effort to discover a psychology and theory of love more practicable than that presented by courtly or Petrarchan ideals.

[21] Chambers and Sidgwick, comps., *Early English Lyrics*, p. 34.
[22] *Ibid.*, p. 279.   [23] *Ibid.*, l. 349.

Christine de Pisan's *Epistre au Dieu d'Amours* (1399) is one of the first writings to show this new direction of interest. Her poem signalizes the fact that the conceptions of romance needed to be defended and that a debate over the nature of courtly love was under way. She sought to defend the position given to woman by courtly love against the cynical disregard of her eminence expressed by courtiers of the day. The focus of Christine's attack is Jean de Meung and his century-old treatment of the court lady as a wanton coquette, one who simply uses the ritual of courtesy as a shield for vile and lascivious passions. Christine states that in actual practice it is men who observe the mere forms of courtship in order to seduce ladies of the court and afterward brag of such conquests. This poem stimulated a debate [24] over Jean de Meung's conception of love, and Christine attracted to her side Jean Gerson, chancellor of the University of Paris; Guillaume de Tignonville, Prévôt of Paris; and Marshall Boucicault, who had founded an order of knighthood, in 1399, for the defense of women.[25]

Christine de Pisan's analysis of love in the *Epistre* is important because she concerned herself with the degree to which the ritual of courtesy could be embodied in the experiences of men and women. As a recent critic remarks, her "point of view is very significant, for it gives evidence of the sturdy growth of the rationalistic spirit which was stripping some of the more poetic elements from the knightly ideal." [26] In her poem *Le Débat de deux amans* the realistic, skeptical court lady, who was elaborated into a literary type in the first quarter of the fifteenth century by Chartier in *La Belle Dame sans Merci*,[27] makes her appearance.

---

[24] See Ward, *The Epistles on the Romance of the Rose and Other Documents in the Debate*; Petit de Julleville, *Histoire*, II, 153; Kilgour, *The Decline of Chivalry*, pp. 181–182; Voretzsch, *Introduction to the Study of Old French Literature*, p. 487; Dow, *The Varying Attitude toward Women in French Literature of the Fifteenth Century*, ch. iv, "La Querelle de la Rose."

[25] "La Dame blanche à l'écu vert." See Kilgour, *The Decline of Chivalry*, p. 130.

[26] Kilgour, *op. cit.*, p. 137.

[27] See A. Piaget's study of the "Parlement d'Amour" by Baudet Herenc, a fifteenth-century reply to Alain Chartier's *Belle Dame*, *Romania*, XXX (1901),

Fifteenth-Century Literature

In Christine's poem the woman treats as sheer pretense her wooer's assertion that he is languishing from passion, suggesting to him that she has not been informed of the graveyards set aside for those dying of love. Despite what many say, she adds, she herself believes that no man in good health will be sick because of love.[28]

A similar skepticism is expressed by the Bastard of Coucy in verses he contributed to the *Cents ballades* of the late fourteenth century. In each of three stanzas he describes some aspect of the formal romantic code of love, and he ends each stanza with the sardonic refrain, "Ainsi dit-on, maiz il n'en sera riens." [29] Discussing this poem, Kilgour states that the game of courtly love "had ended by boring the players, and some of the bolder ones, not necessarily the most depraved, either, loved to poke fun at it.... We find now and then in late medieval literature a gay and cynical laugh at all the fuss made over loyalty and inconstancy." [30] Indeed, after the middle of the fifteenth century appeared Antoine de la Salle's *Petit Jehan de Saintré* to carry the realistic analysis of troubadour ideals found in the verse of Christine de Pisan, Coucy, and Chartier into a parody of Provençal traditions.[31]

In English poetry of the fifteenth century, some of it translated or adapted from Christine de Pisan and Alain Chartier, a

---

317–320. Piaget remarks, p. 319, "Baudet reprend point par point le poème d'Alain Chartier et s'efforce de réfuter, sans le moindre esprit d'ailleurs, les arguments mis dans la bouche de la jeune dame." Cf. also Piaget's analysis of the poem, "Erreurs des judgement de la Belle Dame sans Merci," *Romania*, XXXIII (1904), 179–183. See Siciliano, *François Villon et les thèmes poétiques du moyen âge*, Bk. II, ch. iv, "L'Amant martyr et la Dame sans Merci," for Villon's part in this fifteenth century realistic treatment of love.

[28] Cf. quotation from *Le Débat de deux Amans* in Dow, *The Varying Attitudes toward Women*, p. 193.

[29] Quoted by Kilgour, *The Decline of Chivalry*, pp. 127–128.

[30] *Ibid.*, p. 127.

[31] See Petit de Julleville, ed., *Histoire*, II, 396, for the following comment on this work, "Ainsi le moyen âge vieilli brûle de ces propres mains ce qu'il avait adoré." Cf. Kilgour, *op. cit.*, ch. viii, pp. 279 ff., 309. For an analysis of the skeptical spirit which invades fifteenth-century French literature see *ibid.*, chs. iv–ix; Neilson, *The Origins and Sources of the "Court of Love,"* pp. 83 ff.

similar realistic irritation with romantic theories is in evidence. For example, John Lydgate's *Complaint of the Black Knight; or, The Complaint of a Loveres Lyfe*, early in this century, presents an attack on *amour courtois* by a courtier who is languishing in traditional manner. The speaker elaborates the criticism, found earlier in the *Knight's Tale*, that all true lovers have fared badly. He lists as proof Pyramus, Tristan, Achilles, Antony, and Arcite and Palamoun, crying:

> What was the ende of hir passioun
> But, after sorowe, deeth, and than hir grave?
> Lo, here the guerdon tha these lovers have! [32]

Those who win in love are those who merely counterfeit the proper symptoms of passion. Troubadour doctrines are but tricks of wooing. By his very fidelity to the courtly ritual the true lover purchases only anguish:

> The whiche thing I bye now al to dere,
> Thanked be Venus and the god Cupyde! [33]

But the speaker, for all his derision, remains ready to die of his passion. Lydgate illustrates the new interest in a critical examination of courtly ideals, which did not repudiate them, but sought to understand them.

Thomas Hoccleve translated, as the *Letter of Cupid*, Christine de Pisan's *Epistre au Dieu d'Amour*, thus making her poem part of the English critical appraisal of romance. The *Letter of Cupid* is in the form of a reproof sent by Cupid to all masculine lovers. It appears to be an attempt to describe the actual practices of courtiers in love in order that such practices may be discontinued. Gentlemen behave in an unscrupulous fashion, acting out the role of suffering, anguished suitor until the woman sought has yielded. Then they step out of their simulated courtly passion and cynically boast of their conquests.[34] Or, perhaps, the woman

---

[32] In Skeat, *Chaucerian and Other Pieces*, ll. 365 *et sqq*. For sixteenth-century printings of this poem and those which follow see Skeat, *Chaucerian and Other Pieces*, Introduction.

[33] *Complaint of the Black Knight*, l. 435.

[34] *Letter of Cupid*, in Skeat, *Chaucerian and Other Pieces*, p. 217, ll. 15 *et sqq*.

Fifteenth-Century Literature

is adamantine. In this case her suitors slander her virtue in revenge for their lack of success:

> For he him-selve her ne winne may,
> He speketh her repreef and vileinye.[35]

But this poem, like Lydgate's *Complaint,* is not an attack on courtly love. The ideal is accepted, even though the author points out its distance from known behavior. Indeed, Christine's epistle turns from criticizing courtly lovers to defending the lady of the court with traditional philogynic arguments.[36] There are many good women for every bad one, she states.[37] Since all men are descended from woman, she remarks,

> Lat thy moder be mirour unto thee.
> Honoure her, if thou wolt honoured be! [38]

Eve did not cause the fall of man, as traditional antifeminists argued, but the Devil. God himself chose the Virgin, thus recognizing that a woman could be free from sin.[39] But Christine does not dwell on this last point, because she is defending the essentially sensual ideals of romance.

> For ever I werry ayein chastitee
> And ever shal . . .[40]

she says. Finally, the "real" nature which she ascribes to her own sex is inconsistent with the rationalism (or pique) which has guided her portrayal of the fifteenth-century gentleman. Her conception of woman is more like Chaucer's initial picture of Criseyde than actuality might justify:

> Wommannes herte un-to no crueltee
> Enclyned is, but they ben charitable,
> Pitous, devout, fulle of humilitee,
> Shamfaste, debonaire, and amiable,

---

[35] *Ibid.,* l. 114.
[36] See Matulka, *The Novels of Juan de Flores,* pp. 138–157.
[37] *Letter of Cupid,* ll. 148–154, 302 *et sqq.* This is Chaucer's argument in the "Prologue to the Legend of Good Women."
[38] *Ibid.,* l. 179. [39] *Ibid.,* ll. 400 *et sqq.* [40] *Ibid.,* l. 431.

> Dredful, and of hir wordes mesurable:
> What womman thise hath not, peraventure,
> Ne folweth nat the wey of her nature.[41]

Clanvowe's *The Cuckoo and the Nightingale; or, The Book of Cupid, God of Love* is another of these early fifteenth-century poems questioning, if not rejecting, courtly love. A poet dreams that a cuckoo challenges the arguments of a nightingale who asserts the romantic's conviction:

> For who that wol the god of love not serve,
> I dar wel say, is worthy for to sterve.[42]

The cuckoo emphasizes the fact that lovers, with their usual sorrows, are the most unhappy creatures alive.[43] The nightingale replies by listing the supposed chivalric effects of love. But the poet finds the caustic criticism of the cuckoo intolerable and drives it away by flinging rocks at it. The bird flies off, leaving the field to the nightingale. But the cuckoo's skepticism of romantic traditions has not been answered.

Sir Richard Ros translated Chartier's *La Belle Dame sans Merci* into English about the middle of the fifteenth century. As has been stated, this poem is an important reflection of the new interest in detailed criticism of *amour courtois* because from it emerge, as literary types, the skeptical woman and the idealistic, uncritical wooer. The poet overhears a debate between a courtier pleading his passion and an adamantine lady who simultaneously refuses him and suggests that his courtship is mere pretense. For example, when the lover states the conventional notion that his mistress' eyes have made him worship her,[44] she replies,

> To live in wo he hath gret fantasy
> And of his hert also hath slipper hold,
> That, only for beholding of an y,
> Can nat abyde in pees, as reson wolde.[45]

---

[41] *Ibid.*, l. 344.
[42] *Cuckoo and the Nightingale*, in Skeat, *Chaucerian and Other Pieces*, p. 347, l. 133.
[43] *Ibid.*, ll. 136 *et sqq.*, 164 *et sqq.*
[44] *La Belle Dame sans Merci*, in Skeat, *Chaucerian and Other Pieces*, p. 299, l. 255.
[45] *Ibid.*, l. 261.

Fifteenth-Century Literature

That is to say, La Belle Dame insists upon taking literally (after the fashion of Phebe in Shakespeare's *As You Like It*) [46] the symbols of courtly love. She destroys its sentiments by over-emphasizing the unrealistic, traditional phrases by which these sentiments were described.

Chartier's court lady comments on the physical suffering of her wooer much as had the mistress in Christine de Pisan's *Débat* and as Rosalind was to do to Orlando in *As You Like It*:

> This sicknesse is right esy to endure,
> But fewe people it causeth for to dy.[47]

La Dame argues that because a lover chooses to follow tradition and worship her, she need not also follow the ritual and accept him. Pandarus had suggested to Criseyde that "love for love is skilful guerdonynge." [48] Chartier's heroine remarks,

> Guerdon constrayned, a gift don thankfully,
> These twayn may not accord, ne never shal.[49]

The lady of Chartier's poem denies one of the fundamental tenets of the courtly code, that the lover must be humble and self-effacing. She cries:

> Who loveth not himself, what-ever he be
> In love, he stant forgete in every place;
> And of your wo if ye have no pitè,
> Others pitè bileve not to purchace.[50]

Moreover, pity for a distressed lover

> . . . ought to be resonable,
> And to no wight of greet disavantage.[51]

Two poems at the very beginning of the sixteenth century are, finally, important illustrations of this increased preoccupation with the unreality of courtly love ideals. One is William Dunbar's *The Golden Targe*, in which the unreasonableness of romantic doctrines is allegorized. Reason carries a "golden targe"

---

[46] See p. 201.
[47] *La Belle Dame sans Merci*, l. 293.
[48] *Troilus*, Bk. II, l. 392.
[49] *La Belle Dame sans Merci*, l. 443.
[50] *Ibid.*, l. 661.
[51] *Ibid.*, l. 693.

which protects the poet from the attack of Venus and her supporters. But Presence casts powder in the eyes of this guard,[52] and the poet is taken prisoner by Beauty. The second of these poems is the anonymous *Court of Love*. This is a partial burlesque of *fine amor* and the practices of its adepts and praise of simple carnal pleasure. Here the mockery is especially effective because the poem is, ostensibly, simply a collection of thoroughly stereotyped romantic materials.[53]

In this poem the traditional sentiments and decorum of courtly love are ridiculed in a number of different ways. In one instance courtiers are solemnly advised to obey their ladies in all things. But the advice is actually a satire on the submissive lover of romance in the form of a *reductio ad absurdum* of the Wife of Bath's argument:

> Sey as she seith, than shalt thou not be shent
> The crow is whyte; ye, truly, so I rede:
> And ay what thing that she thee will forbede
> Eschew all that, and give her sovereintee
> Her appetyt folow in all degree.[54]

In the twentieth statute of love suitors are told in mock seriousness to follow the traditional routine of suffering (much as Orlando is by Rosalind),

> To wring and wail, to turn, and sigh and grone
> When thy lady absent is from thee . . .[55]

In another part of the poem the poet accepts all the duties imposed by custom on the courtier, but is curious to learn what rules of love are imposed on the court lady. Rigor denounces such prying inquisitiveness by the satiric suggestion that

> . . . it paraventure may right so befall
> That they be bound by nature to disceive.[56]

---

[52] *Golden Targe*, l. 201.

[53] The famous study of this poem is *The Origins and Sources of the "Court of Love,"* by William Allan Neilson. He traces the relationships between this poem and all other medieval amorous writings.

[54] *Court of Love*, in Skeat, *Chaucerian and Other Pieces*, l. 430.

[55] *Ibid.*, l. 491.   [56] *Ibid.*, l. 540.

Fifteenth-Century Literature

And the poem closes with the bitter complaints of both men and women, members of religious orders, against their enforced chastity. The monks complain:

> We serve and honour, sore ayenst our will
> Of chastite the goddes and the queen;
> Us leffer were with Venus byden still
> And have rewards for love, and soget been
> Unto these women courtly, fressh and shene.[57]

This is sensuality for its own sake superseding any idealism in love, sacred or profane.

[57] *Ibid.*, ll. 1128 *et sqq.*

·VI·

Renaissance Adaptations and Re-evaluations of Medieval Attitudes

Traditional literary formulas found in medieval romances of courtesy were both adopted and changed by Renaissance writers to suit a new way of presenting amorous controversy. The lady who is so difficult to win in Chaucer's *Troilus and Criseyde* becomes difficult in a different way in the sonnets of Sidney, in Lyly's *Euphues,* and in Shakespeare's comedies. Like Chartier's "Belle Dame," she turns critic and seeks to destroy the ideals of love envisaged by her wooer. Another piece of romantic machinery that survives, but in an altered form, is the convention of presenting the lover, a Troilus, for example, as at first and briefly scorning love, only to become enslaved, thereby proving its power. In the Renaissance comedies *Love's Labour's Lost* and *Much Ado* this lover's scorn is prolonged almost for the duration of the story. When Berowne and Benedick finally become amorously involved, they do so by compromising the ideal conceptions found in Chaucer, not by dying for them.

The "love question" which is everywhere in the Middle Ages an integral part of courtly tales of desire is also made to serve the purposes of the Renaissance skeptic. These "questions" were originally, perhaps, part of a perpetual debate within the bounds of courtly love theory itself. In Andreas's treatise, for example, they implied no criticism of the idyllic nature of love, but were attempts to interpret lovers' rites and codes. A part of Chaucer's "Knight's Tale" is a kind of love question,[1] an endeavor to

---

[1] See *The Complete Works of Chaucer,* ed. by Robinson, p. 774, l. 1347n. Neilson discusses these debates in troubadour lyrics, in *Origins and Sources of*

determine which lover suffered most, and the "Franklin's Tale" raises the question of generosity in love. The Wife of Bath joins this courtly debate to the more general one of the Middle Ages, between ascetic desire and carnal desire, when she has the lover of her story asked to choose between fidelity and beauty.[2]

In the sixteenth century, however, this debate over details of amorous decorum is turned against the improbabilities of the ideal itself. Castiglione's *Il cortegiano,* the book of courtly manners adopted by the Elizabethans, which has been described as "only an elaborate 'dubbio' discussion,"[3] illustrates this new use of old literary tradition. And most of Lyly's comedies might be described as dramatized love questions used to portray Elizabethan criticisms of idealized desire. It is this medieval interest in amorous quibbles that survives in new, realistic vein in Shakespeare's *Two Gentlemen of Verona* and is glimpsed briefly in Benedick's decision to side with romance and to slight Claudio in *Much Ado*.[4]

The misogynic attitude current in medieval *fabliaux* in set quarrels over the position of woman survived in Shakespeare's period in a popular war of prose tracts for and against women.[5] The theologians of the Reformation, though they had objected to abstinence for its own sake, kept alive some of the righteous antifeminism of the church fathers to lend vigor to this sixteenth-century controversy. They stood firm on the "natural" inferiority of woman to man. Calvin, for example, annoyed by

---

the "Court of Love," pp. 241 ff.; and as familiar courtly exercises in wit in the Italian Renaissance, *ibid.,* pp. 247 ff.; and in Andreas Capellanus, *ibid.,* pp. 181 ff. See also Karl Voretzsch, *Introduction to the Study of Old French Literature,* pp. 325 ff.

[2] "Wife of Bath's Tale," ll. 1219 *et sqq.*

[3] Neilson, *Origins and Sources of the "Court of Love,"* p. 247.

[4] See *ibid.,* p. 262. Kilgour discusses the realism penetrating "love question" debates in fifteenth-century French literature, in *The Decline of Chivalry,* ch. iv and ch. vi (*Les Cents Ballades* of Jean le Seneschal and *Le Livre des Quatres Dames* of Alain Chartier).

[5] For the extent of this controversy see Hazlitt, ed., *Remains of the Early Popular Poetry of England,* IV, 147. See also Wright, *Middle-Class Culture in Elizabethan England,* ch. xiii.

the profound silence with which the young Elizabeth had greeted the dedication of his *Commentaries on Isaiah* (1559) to her, wrote Sir William Cecil that government by woman was "among the punishments consequent upon the fall of man." [6] At the same time, this controversy expressed on its own level the same forces of rationalism that were moving through all Renaissance thought, and the source of its realism was, at least in part, from its own time. Vituperative analysis of woman had progressed to the point where it was used to express an astringent, puritan dislike for the emotional waste of romantic love pursuits.

The complaint of most of the tracts in this controversy, from *The Pain and Sorrow of Evil Marriage* (*ca.* 1530) to Gosson's *Pleasant Quippes for Upstart Newfangled Gentlewomen* (*ca.* 1595) or to the translation called *The Batchelars Banquet* (1603), is not Jerome's complaint, that Venus tempts one to perdition. It is that a wife, through inordinate pride in her dress or her body, may make one bankrupt in emotion as well as in purse. That is to say, the ethics of the Elizabethan puritan-merchant world, for which this quarrel was important, were now determined less by dogma than by practicability. A "new note of respect" for women "was creeping into popular literature." [7] But it was chiefly respect for thrifty husbandry. The abject Griselda (in Boccaccio, Petrarch, and Chaucer an idealization of the virtue of patient humility) turns up in this Elizabethan discussion as a kind of forerunner of Pamela. She illustrates, now, the secular rewards of chastity, "shewing how maides, by her example, in their good behavior may marrie rich husbands." [8]

This controversy kept alive a traditional antagonism toward love and toward its object, woman, that is reflected in Shakespeare's comedies. G. R. Owst points out that Noah's wife in the mystery plays, the Wife of Bath, and Kate in *The Taming of*

---

[6] John Knox, *The First Blast of the Trumpet*, ed. by Edward Arber, p. xvii. Knox called Elizabeth herself a "weak instrument," *ibid.*, p. 60.

[7] Wright, *Middle-Class Culture in Elizabethan England*, p. 465.

[8] *The History of Patient Grissel*, supplementary title.

the Shrew are literary representatives of the vast body of fourteenth-century misogynic invective.[9] But in Shakespeare's *Taming of the Shrew*, antifeminism is used neither to exhibit the unrestrained appetites ascribed to woman by popular *fabliaux* nor to illustrate clerical satire "de malitia filiarum Evae." Comedy is achieved by bringing together the ritual of courtly love and the fury of the conventional shrew. When Petruchio woos Kate, it is almost as if Troilus should turn realist and pay court to the well-to-do Wife of Bath. Moreover, Katharina, who is the embodiment of attitudes similar to ones found in *exempla* and *fabliaux*, exists in her own right and apart from these attitudes. In a Renaissance comedy she must be tamed, and her character turned inside out. Her final capitulation illustrates, in a comic fashion, that which the writer of the *Nut Brown Maid* had sought to prove by a more solemn consideration of complaints against women.

Theologians' Re-evaluations of Ascetic Doctrines

Antiromantic literary traditions, which originated in a religious contempt for sensual pleasure, survive in Elizabethan literature often without religious significance. A divorcing of lovers' difficulties from theology, which is apparent in occasional fifteenth-century writings, had become the rule by the time John Donne wrote his amorous satires. This secularization of controversy was possible because humanists within the church, such as Erasmus and More, and reformers who broke with the established church, such as Luther and Calvin, categorically denied Jerome's and Augustine's contempt for the delights of sex.

There was never unanimity of opinion on the part of medieval writers, to be sure, that sensual experience was either fatal or undesirable. Indeed, Chaucer's contemporary John Wyclif, in his tract *Of Weddid Men and Wifis*, advocates marriage of the clergy "sith fornicaciuon is so perilous." He argues that since "this bodily matrimoyne is a sacrament . . . therefore he that

[9] Owst, *Literature and Pulpit in Medieval England*, pp. 386–390.

forbedith or letiith verrey matrimonye, is enemye of God." [10] In early fifteenth-century Italy, Lorenzo Valla was not only advocating the life of the five senses, but wishing for more than five.[11] But these early reactions from medieval ascetic ideology were largely immature and ineffective as far as the amorous literature of England is concerned. It was only during the last decades of the fifteenth and the early decades of the sixteenth century, under the combined attacks of exponents of the new learning and theologians of the Reformation, that medieval ethics, "as supremely represented in monastic asceticism with its poverty," [12] began to yield place.

The humanists' recreation of the pagan learning that Augustine [13] had turned from and Jerome had fought, started in the quiet of scholars' studies [14] and reached, perhaps, its most influential expression in the writings of Erasmus. By the aid of the recently discovered art of printing, his works were now available to all who could both read and think. His *Colloquies*, for example, became one of the most popular books of the sixteenth century and went through ninety-nine editions before 1546.[15] It was condemned by the Sorbonne in 1526 "as dangerous to the morals of the young." [16] Even Luther disapproved the book, calling it a subtle poison for youth.[17] Ostensibly a text for the study of grammar and rhetoric, actually the *Colloquies* contains a critical analysis of traditional ethics written in vivid dialogue. Throughout the book runs Erasmus's virulent scorn of the monastic system of morality and a concomitant hatred of carnal

---

[10] Wyclif, *Select English Works*, ed. by Thomas Arnold, III, 189.

[11] See Fletcher, *Literature of the Italian Renaissance*, pp. 98–99.

[12] Niebuhr, *The Social Sources of Denominationalism*, p. 91.

[13] See Saint Augustine, *Select Letters*, No. 24 (to the Decurion of Calama, a pagan).

[14] See *Cambridge History of English Literature*, Vol. III, ch. i, "Englishmen and the Classical Renascence," by Rev. T. M. Lindsay. See also introductions by J. H. Lupton to Colet's *Letters to Radulphus on the Mosaic Account of Creation, An Exposition of St. Paul's Epistle to the Romans, Two Treatises on the Hierarchies of Dionysius*.

[15] *Cambridge History of English Literature*, III, 20.

[16] Emerton, *Desiderius Erasmus*, p. 424.   [17] *Ibid.*, p. 424.

pleasures. In dramatizing a model courtship, for example, Erasmus suggests that a husband may not be refused by his wife, even though procreation is not in mind.[18] In his dialogue concerning the young girl who wishes to enter a convent, he concludes that her place is in the world, that marriage is preferable to chastity, and that her soul will be safer outside than inside a nunnery.[19]

Erasmus, like Wyclif, advocated marriage of the clergy, since it would be better to turn "concubyns into wyves."[20] But Wyclif had viewed such marriage as merely an expedient. Calling upon "Seynt Austin and Jerom" as witnesses, he concluded that "though matrimonye be good and gretly comendid of God, yit clene virgynite is moche betre."[21] Erasmus, on the contrary, was able to push his thought beyond the limits set by the church fathers and to achieve historical perspective. Of Jerome's contempt for wedlock he writes, "let this heate be graunted to those tymes."[22] The sexual impulse is not sinful. "And as touchyng the fowlnes/ surely we make that by our imaginacion to be fowle, which of the selfe nature [i.e., in itself] is fayre and holy."[23]

Erasmus states that he was influenced by Sir Thomas More to depart from the traditional antifeminist attitude of clerics.[24] Indeed, More's own daughters were excellent adepts of a new feminine erudition. More's most popular book, *Utopia*, contains many direct disavowals of conventional misogyny. For example, divorce is granted in Utopia for mere incompatibility, and the innocent party is allowed to remarry. Punishment for sexual

---

[18] Erasmus, *The Colloquies*, ed. by Rev. E. Johnson, "A Lover and Maiden," I, 210 ff.

[19] *Ibid.*, "The Virgin Averse to Matrimony," I, 225; and "The Penitent Virgin," I, 237.

[20] Erasmus, *A Ryght Frutefull Epystle . . . in Laude and Prayse of Matrymony*, tr. by Rychard Taverner, sig. C 3, verso [dated 1536–1537 by C. R. Baskerville, *Studies in Philology*, XXIX (1932), 149–150].

[21] Wyclif, *Select English Works*, III, 120.

[22] Erasmus, *A Ryght Frutefull Epystle*, sig. C 4, verso.

[23] *Ibid.*, sig. B 8.

[24] See Woodward, *Desiderius Erasmus concerning the Aim and Method of Education*, p. 149.

immorality is as severe for men as for women. And that lovers may prepare intelligently for the delights of the marriage bed, they are required to see and approve each other naked before they become husband and wife.[25] This is, then, a candid acknowledgment of the physical basis of a valid and happy marriage.

When Luther and Calvin sought to lessen the severity of the asceticism advocated by the church fathers, they not only criticized, as had Erasmus, but also acted in a forthright fashion.[26] In 1525 Martin Luther, the former Augustinian friar, took a wife, as he says, "thereby to upbraid the devil and to confound the practice of popedom."[27] To forbid marriage, he repeats again and again, is "as though we were forbidden to eat, to drink, to sleep."[28] One finds in a letter written by Luther in 1525 a curious reversal of the stereotyped invective against marriage found, earlier, in Walter Map's tract or in the words of Chaucer's Merchant. Marriage, says Luther to his friend, conducts a man "out of the stormy billows into the haven, and from the world into Paradise."[29]

Calvin, by his marriage, went one step beyond Luther and committed the double mistake, according to Jerome, of taking to wife that recreated virgin, a widow. But Calvin denied Jerome's misogyny not only in practice but also in theory. In a commentary on St. Paul (who had aroused Jerome to his stubborn defense of the ascetic life) Calvin brushes aside Jerome's conclusions by saying that the church father mistook suggestion for divine command.[30] As to those "profane jests which are commonly in vogue with a view to bring it [marriage] into discredit, such as the following: that a wife is a necessary evil," Calvin states, "they are out of Satan's workshop."[31]

---

[25] More, *Utopia*, tr. by Ralph Robinson, pp. 179 ff.
[26] See Jacobs, *A Study in Comparative Symbolics*, pp. 4 ff.
[27] Luther, *Autobiography*; comp. by John Parker Lawson, p. 262.
[28] Luther, *The Table Talk*, tr. by William Hazlitt, p. 300.
[29] Luther, *Letters*, selected and tr. by Margaret Currie (letter dated January 17, 1525).
[30] Calvin, *Commentary on the Epistles of Paul the Apostle to the Corinthians*, tr. by John Pringle, I, 222–223.
[31] *Ibid.*, p. 224.

The Platonic Adaptation of Courtly Love

The sixteenth century had inherited a traditional ascetic revulsion from courtly love, the religious authority for which had been challenged. But the austere idealism of the church was not entirely a spent force, merely continuing under the lessening momentum of inertia into the Renaissance. As Sidney's sonnet "Leave me ô Love which reachest but to dust" indicates, the attitude which held sexual abstinence to be nobler than consummated desire lingered on, even in amorous verse. Indeed, this attitude which had been partly cut off from its original impetus, remained of sufficient importance to some Renaissance writers to be used to justify the sentiments and decorum of courtly love itself.[32] Edmund Spenser, for example, writing in a period of intense interest in man and his emotions, infused his *Amoretti* with asceticism derived from the Platonic philosophy of love. In the final one of his *Fowre Hymnes; an Hymn of Heavenly Beautie* the worship of love is vindicated, since carnal experience is described as merely the first, frustrating introduction to perfect, heavenly love.

It is true that earlier, in the thirteenth century, the romantic conventions of courtesy had supplied a convenient pattern and language for Dante's spiritual devotion to Beatrice.[33] This singular transformation of troubadour ideals was also made articulate by poets of this century other than Dante and by his avowed master, Guinizelli. The lyrics in praise of the Virgin written by the poet Peire Cardenal [34] illustrate this supplanting of the

---

[32] See Harrison, *Platonism in English Poetry of the Sixteenth and Seventeenth Centuries* (p. 104); Platonism in sixteenth-century England, he remarks, was "used to explain and dignify the conception of love as a passion having its source in a desire for the enjoyment of beauty."

[33] Mott, in *The System of Courtly Love*, presents a detailed account of Dante's transformation of the ritual of troubadours. Individual sonnets are analyzed pp. 130–134; ideas pp. 146–151.

[34] See Anglade, *Les Troubadours*, p. 182. But Cardenal fled from one extreme to the other, from profane to sacred love. He isolates himself from the usual accommodation of sensual and spiritual love either as "Petrarchism" or as "Platonism."

sexual by the spiritual theme. But the "gospel" of Dante and Guinizelli, as Professor Fletcher has remarked, "is, obviously, a Catholic Christian conception, and quite distinct from the Platonic Love of the Renaissance."[35] It is not equivalent to the system described by Bembo in the *Courtier* and poeticized by Spenser in his *Fowre Hymnes*. The *Vita Nuova* sonnets, rather, give the first important literary treatment of courtly love as a spiritual union of lovers. For the later Renaissance, Christian, ascetic idealism was blended with a secular Platonism. Spenser for England and Bembo for Italy adopted this secular philosophy to explain and to accommodate an inherited sensual ideal of passion to the Renaissance conception of the well-rounded gentleman.

The furtive paganism of courtly love must have seemed fundamentally unpleasant to an Elizabethan poet such as Spenser, in whose mind the ethical tenets of the earlier church were still remembered.[36] But Dante's love experience, imitated and poeticized in the sonnets of Petrarch, had created a new and important conception of romantic delight,[37] one in which the physical assuagement of desire was left out. This conception could be assimilated and given expression by the Platonic philosophy of Ficino[38] and could thus thrust lovers' aspirations beyond the last boundary of possible physical corruption. In Ficino's writings, to be sure, neo-Platonism is an attempt to rationalize theology.[39] But Ficino's theorizing spread from the circle of the Medici poets in ever-widening arcs, until Platonism as an explanation of Christian doctrine was lost in much the same attitude of respect for a nonsexual kinship between a man and his mistress as that

[35] Fletcher, *Literature of the Italian Renaissance*, p. 52; see also pp. 44–53.
[36] Cf. Kate M. Warren's statement: "It is easy to understand, if we have at all realized the nature of Spenser, that the subject of Chastity, as he conceived it, was especially suited to his genius. It took him into the refined air of the world of spiritual ideas where he was always at home." (In Spenser, *The Works; a Variorum Edition*, Appendix I to the *Faerie Queene*, Bk. III, p. 313).
[37] See John, *The Elizabethan Sonnet Sequences*, pp. 138–139.
[38] Ficino himself noted Platonistic elements in Dante. See Robb, *Neoplatonism of the Italian Renaissance*, pp. 135 ff.
[39] *Ibid.*, pp. 58 ff.

Renaissance Adaptations

which Dante had lyricized. Hence, as spiritualized courtly love entered Elizabethan literature by way of the sonnet, and Platonic love by way of the conduct book, "Petrarchism" and "Platonism" became, for the most part, indistinguishable Elizabethan terms for the same sentiment.[40]

It was possible for Spenser, therefore, to deny the personal problems described by Wyatt or Sidney by presenting love, at its most exalted, not as a physical experience, but as an impalpable transport of the spirit. He portrayed it, in the manner of Dante and Bembo, as an emotion capable of purely spiritual satisfactions. The dichotomy between an ideal "reality" and the actual world seems about as permanent to the Calvinistic, Platonic Spenser as to the Catholic Chaucer. Wyatt struggled vainly to translate the delights of courtly romance into tangible fact. Sidney was baffled in his efforts to realize the courtier's perfect assuagement of his desire in an imperfect reality. Spenser avoided the difficulties of these poets either by disregarding the realities of an actual and passionate love affair or by looking beyond them.

Spenser does not deny sex a place in human affairs. In his *Fowre Hymnes*, which, as Professor Fletcher has aptly remarked, are actually "one complete doctrinal poem" [41] of Platonic love, physical passion is described as a primary but incomplete revelation of divine beauty, or "Sapience." [42] In his *Epithalamion*, likewise, carnal appetite, as such, is outlawed in favor of sex as a servant of a temperate, virtuous, self-controlled human being. The sensual impulses, that is, are acceptable only when in leash to the mind. Spenser illustrates what he considers an ideal attitude toward physical love in his portrait of his future wife, in his *Epithalamion*:

---

[40] *Ibid.*, p. 179, "Much of the so-called 'Platonism' of the sixteenth century is in reality 'Petrarchism.'"

[41] Fletcher, *The Religion of Beauty in Woman*, p. 118. See also "A Study in Renaissance Mysticism: Spenser's 'Fowre Hymnes,'" PMLA, Vol. XXVI (1911). Professor Fletcher remarks (p. 475) that in some ways these hymns are "the most perfect, as well as the fourth, gospel—after Dante, Cavalcante, Benivieni—of the medieval renaissance 'religion' of beauty and love."

[42] Spenser's *Fowre Hymnes*, ll. 183 *et sqq.*, in *The Poetical Works*, Vol. I, ed. by Ernest de Sélincourt.

> There dwels sweet love and constant chastity,
> Unspotted fayth and comely womanhood,
> Regard of honour and mild modesty,
> There vertue raynes as Queene in royal throne,
> And giveth lawes alone.
> The which the base affections doe obay,
> And yeeld theyr services unto her will,
> Ne thought of thing uncomely ever may
> Therto approch to tempt her mind to ill.[43]

By his choice of "Sapience" rather than Venus as the guide for lovers, Spenser links himself to the Reformation in a profound belief in the special human faculty of "reason." The church fathers' exhortations had yielded to humanistic criticism, and man emerged as a rational creature, capable of self-sufficiency on this earth, capable of discovering a "right" way of conduct and of following this way. It is out of this belief in rational choice [44] that Spenser spins his subtle allegory of conduct, *The Faerie Queene*. In the first book of this allegory its hero, Arthur, makes clear the intellectual method by which Spenser sought to bridle "will," or desire:

> But me had warnd old Timons wise behest,
> Those creeping flames by reason to subdew,
> Before their rage grew to so great unrest,
> As miserable lovers use to rew,
> Which still wex old in woe, whiles woe still wexeth new.[45]

In the second book of the *Faerie Queene* Spenser's philosophy of love is given elaborate expression. The reasonable man, in his ideal relationship to passion, is identified with "Temperance," who

> . . . with golden squire
> Betwixt them both can measure out a meane,
> Neither to melt in pleasures whott desire,

---

[43] *Op. cit.*, l. 191.
[44] See Craig, *The Enchanted Glass, the Elizabethan Mind in Literature*, for a discussion of "reason" and "will" in Elizabethan thought (pp. 25 ff.).
[45] *The Faerie Queene*, Bk. I, Canto IX, stanza ix, in *The Works of Edmund Spenser, a Variorum Edition*.

Renaissance Adaptations

> Nor frye in hartlesse griefe and dolefull teene.
> Thrise happie man, who fares them both atweene! [46]

Medina, in this book, the ideal feminine representative of moderate love sentiment, is controlled by reason. She sits between two couples, one (Elissa and Sansjoy) personifying irrational chastity, the other (Perissa and Sansloy) personifying provocative desire:

> With equall measure she did moderate
> The strong extremities of their outrage;
> That forward pair she ever would asswage,
> When they would strive dew reason to exceed;
> But that same froward twaine would accorage,
> And of her plenty adde unto their need.[47]

Spenser defends most clearly for his age his own conception of wisely tempered passion when he destroys the intemperate "Bowre of Blis" at the end of Book Two.[48] Guyon, aided by the Palmer, enters the garden "bridling his will." [49] The specific charge against the adamant Gryll, who refused to be freed from sensual delight, was that he did not wish to master his will, that he chose "to be a beast, and lacke intelligence." [50] At this point in his allegory Spenser seems to be bringing this same charge against the sensual delight idealized by courtly love.[51] Love, as Spenser conceives it, is not physical experience for its own sake. Physical passion is but a means of expressing a spiritual state of mind. This particular state of mind he had identified in his *Fowre*

---

[46] *Ibid.*, Bk. II, Canto I, stanza lviii.

[47] *Ibid.*, Bk. II, Canto II, stanza xxxviii.

[48] According to Legouis (in *Edmund Spenser*, pp. 245-247), this episode represents the triumph of the Reformation over the Renaissance, the brusque solution of a philosophic conflict in Spenser's own mind.

[49] *The Faerie Queene*, Bk. II, Canto XII, stanza liii, in Spenser, *The Works; a Variorum Edition*.

[50] *Ibid.*, Bk. II, Canto XII, stanza lxxxvii.

[51] See Lewis, *The Allegory of Love*, pp. 327 *et passim*, in which he contrasts the "Garden of Adonis" with the "Bowre of Blis." See also Fowler, *Spenser and the System of Courtly Love*, chs. i and v. The relationship between Bk. II, Canto XII, of the *Faerie Queene* and courtly love settings is discussed in the Appendix to Spenser, *The Works; a Variorum Edition*, under "Faerie Queene, Book Two," pp. 348-395, *passim*.

Hymnes with divine beauty, whom he personifies as "Sapience."

Spenser did not resolve the conflict expressed by Wyatt and Sidney, between sex experience and romantic idealism. Spenser found his choice of opposites to be between the "medieval renaissance 'religion' of love and beauty" [52] and the crudities of unbridled sex. Spenser's use of Platonic idealism should be distinguished, for this reason, from its use by Sidney. The latter casually embraces a spiritualized love theory as a mere passing refuge from a sensual ideal disintegrating under the touch of skepticism. Spenser uses it as a symbol of chastity (i.e., purity) more befitting the Renaissance than the hair shirt. By destroying the "Bowre of Blis" as unreasonable, Spenser denies the sensual romantic ideal that his age, generally, was trying to accommodate, to assimilate, in its notion of the well-rounded courtier,

> The glass of fashion and the mould of form,
> The observ'd of all observers.[53]

He poeticized for his age a philosophical study of love that was not generally practicable. Most sixteenth-century amorous poets were not prepared to accept Spenser's Platonic "reasonableness" as a substitute for the perplexities of a more realistic passion (any more than they were willing to accept Ovid's libertine notions or the medieval church's simple denial of sex). As Sidney stated it, in one of his sonnets to Stella,

> Reason, in faith thou art well serv'd that still
> Would'st brabling be, with sence and love in me:
> I rather wish thee climbe the Muses hill,
> Or reach the fruite of Natures chiefest tree;
> Or seeke heavens course, or heavens unusde to thee:
> Why should'st thou toyle, our thornie grounde to till?
> Leave sence and those that sences objectes be,
> Deale thou with powers, of thoughts leave thou to will.[54]

Spenser's philosophy of love, not immediately attractive to young and passionate courtiers, is isolated from the actual be-

---

[52] Fletcher, "A Study in Renaissance Mysticism," p. 475.
[53] *Hamlet*, Act III, scene i, l. 152.
[54] In Sidney, *The Complete Works*, ed. by Feuillerat, Vol. II, Sonnet 10.

havior of men and women at the Elizabethan court. His theory of conduct has remained to puzzle even the twentieth century—so that readers do not understand or are restive under the moral symbolism of the second and third books and prefer to read them for their "poetry," for their sweet verbal cadences. One wonders if his own age did not feel something of this same frustration before the "grave and moral" Spenser. Did it not sense the failure of his love-allegory to recognize what was at once the dividing line between the Middle Ages and the Renaissance and the cause of the basic conflict in all thought of the day: the acceptance of the validity of human experience as a criterion by which to judge preconceived, inherited ideals. Thus, one of the happiest Elizabethan references to the literary fashions of the medieval age, if it does refer to the *Faerie Queene,* refers as we do, not to its philosophy, but to its "poetry":

> Let others sing of Knights and Palladines,
> In aged accents, and untimely words:
> Paint shadowes in imaginary lines,
> Which well the reach of their high wits records;
> But I must sing of thee and those faire eyes.[55]

Despite Spenser's efforts to give a rational solution to the difficulties of love by presenting it as this Platonic transport, remote from usual or possible experience, Elizabethan amorous poetry continued to voice the protests of its suffering lovers against these difficulties. The Elizabethan sonnet continued to express a critical attitude toward love, an attitude that was not a sixteenth-century version of medieval imaginative escape, not a resignation before the rigors of human experience; it was a protest against their existence. The nature of the conflict is made clear if one reads first the *Vita nuova,* the most important of the early attempts to spiritualize courtly love, and then the *Astrophel and Stella* sonnets. In Dante's work love is presented as a spiritual ecstasy,

[55] Samuel Daniel, Sonnet XLVI, in *Poems and a Defence of Ryme,* ed. by Sprague, p. 33. See also Shakespeare's Sonnet CVI, of which Tucker Brooke says (*Shakespeare's Sonnets,* p. 308), "One would be happy to think that these lines were inspired, as Hales suggested, by looking into Spenser's *Faerie Queene.*"

which looks forward to Renaissance Platonism and to Spenser's philosophic ideal. Dante expresses no desire to touch his mistress, much less to possess her. To gaze on her is enough.

> The look she hath when she a little smiles
> Cannot be said, nor holden in the thought;
> 'Tis such a new and gracious miracle.[56]

In Sidney's sonnets one finds the poet in a perplexing dilemma. He is conscious that his desire cannot be satisfied by idealized drama or by ritual. He has become aware that love like his can never attain perfect satisfaction. He is nearer Catullus than Dante when he cries out against the Elizabethan representative of his ideal, "whose presence absence, absence presence is."[57] Dante, by his reinterpretation of courtly love, escaped the natural difficulties of rendering ideal a sexual passion. Spenser fled into philosophic seclusion. Sidney could take neither of these courses, conceiving his passion too literally for peace. He evidently began by accepting it as a sentiment which had, in some measure, served the Middle Ages as a poetic retreat from the vilifications of clerics and the anguish of actuality. But the object of his love always remained a human being, never quite the embodiment of a lady of the romances. This fact was the basis of his perplexity and despair.

The Marital Adaptation of Courtly Love

Troubadour amorous theory had prescribed a ritual of courtship which if literally followed would aid in preserving the lovers' belief in the idyllic nature of their relationship. Passion was to be secret and clandestine, not subject to the strain of daylight or the day's desires.[58] Its goal was distant. Ennobling passion was not the affair of a moment, but, as in Chaucer's "Knight's

---

[56] Dante, *The Vita Nuova with Rossetti's Version*, ed. by H. Oelsner, p. 91.
[57] *Astrophel and Stella*, Sonnet 60.
[58] Cf., for example, the change from sensual desire to work-a-day reality in the alternation of mood between Browning's "Meeting at Night" and his "Parting at Morning."

Tale," of a long and private torture. An amorous attachment, isolated in this fashion from the irritations and annoyances of too frequent meetings between courtier and lady, might well preserve the illusions of both parties. But such an attachment, by its very nature, could scarcely develop into a permanent and open relationship without losing some of its enchantment. Its allegorical setting, in the *Roman de la Rose*, was the Garden of Love, walled off from a harsh world and surrounded by hideous figures representing this world. The desires assuaged in this garden, seen—as in Chaucer's "Prologue to the Legend of Good Women"—just at daybreak in May, had the fragile perfection of a dream.

The final possession by the lover of his mistress, however, brought the amorous ritual to an end. The troubadour convention went no farther, suggested no realistic solution for the lovers' passion after their wooing had been brought to a climax. How long could human beings sustain such exalted desires? The courtly romances did not give a specific answer. *Fine amor* was both an imaginative, compensatory flight from the crudities of experienced love—as romantic literature often is—and also a flight from the limitations of moral theory. If a medieval poet insisted upon a tangible conclusion for his romance, he could marry his lovers, as Chaucer did in the "Knight's Tale," and leave their subsequent readjustment to the world beyond the Garden of Love unexplained. Or he could return to a theological attitude, as Chaucer did in the *Troilus*, and a final statement that all this sensual beauty was, indeed, the perishable stuff of dreams. He might caution his audience:

> O yonge, fresshe folkes, he or she,
> In which that love up groweth with youre age,
> Repeyreth hom from worldly vanyte,
> And of youre herte up casteth the visage
> To thilke God that after his ymage
> Yow made, and thynketh al nys but a faire
> This world, that passeth soone as floures faire.[59]

[59] *Troilus*, Bk. V, l. 1835.

When the Elizabethan dramatist made use of the sentiments and decorum of courtly love, however, he needed not only a definite and dramatically satisfying solution for his lovers' courtship, but also a conclusion which would justify their desires. Hence his denouement, characteristically, included a marital pairing off of the various couples of his play. Marriage was concrete and specific, and it was morally sound—attributes not found in the adulterous possession of a mistress. This marital solution had been suggested, earlier, by Chaucer's Franklin. It was given enhanced literary importance by the fifteenth-century *Kingis Quair*,[60] in which the poet is advised by Minerva to "ground and set" his desire "in Cristin wise." [61] For Shakespeare's century, idealized marriage as the goal for a courtier's passion is presented with great lyric beauty in Spenser's *Amoretti* sonnets and in his *Epithalamion*. It is given allegorical presentation in the third book of the *Faerie Queene*.

C. S. Lewis suggests that the legend of Britomartis's pursuit of Artegall, in the third book of the *Faerie Queene*, "tells the final stages of the history of courtly love," [62] "the last phase of that story—the final defeat of courtly love by the romantic conception of marriage." [63] But Spenser goes beyond the idealizing of married love suggested either by the "Franklin's Tale" or the *Kingis Quair*. Britomart is not sick with mere physical desire for Artegall.[64] Her love illustrates the "reasoned" passion which Spenser adapted from Platonism. Guyon's destruction of sensuality in general, in Book Two, is particularized in this third book —if we accept Professor Padelford's interpretation—as the destruction of sensuality for its own sake, in married love. Thus, in contrast to the more rugged Britomart is the character Amoret,

[60] Lewis remarks (*The Allegory of Love*, p. 237) that in the *Kingis Quair* "the poetry of marriage at last emerges from the traditional poetry of adultery. . . . It is the first modern book of love."
[61] *Kingis Quair*, stanza 142.   [62] *The Allegory of Love*, p. 338.
[63] *Ibid.*, p. 298.
[64] See *Faerie Queene*, Bk. III, Canto II, stanzas xxii ff., for a portrait of Britomart's physical symptoms of love.

who "could not refrain from surrendering herself to physical delight when once it had enjoyed the conventional sanction of marriage." She it is "who is chosen for discipline in chastity." [65] The defeat of Amoret's enchanter Busirane by Britomart is, to Spenser, the triumph of that

> Most sacred fire, that burnest mightily
> In living brests, ykindled first above,
> Emongst th'eternall spheres and lamping sky,
> And thence pourd into men, which men call Love;
> Not that same, which doth base affections move
> In brutish minds, and filthy lust inflame,
> But that sweet fit, that doth true beautie love.[66]

But the romance of marriage, whether a compromise between courtly love and theology, as in the *Kingis Quair*, or between courtly love and Platonism, as in Spenser's poetry, leaves untouched important difficulties. It is impossible to present marriage as if it had by domesticating lovers' passions solved the conflict between *fine amor* and actual experience. The romance of marriage, like the Platonism of Bembo or of Benivieni, is itself an ideal. Hence, what had served Spenser as a concrete illustration of the philosophic spiritualization of passion was often little more than a useful device for the Elizabethan dramatist. The final pairing of hitherto uncongenial couples in an Elizabethan play often seems merely abrupt and incredible as a solution to lovers' difficulties. For example, the duke in *Twelfth Night* turns from Olivia to Viola in the space of a few lines of unconvincing dialogue, and in like manner Demetrius, in *Midsummer Night's Dream*, turns from Hermia to Helena. In *Measure for Measure* even the austere Isabella graciously accepts the hand of the duke of Vienna, and in *As You Like It* Touchstone obliges by accepting Audrey in order to complete the list of "country copulatives." As Puck phrased it, satirically, for the sixteenth century:

[65] Padelford, in Spenser, *The Works; a Variorum Edition*, Appendix, "Faerie Queene, Book Three," p. 326.
[66] *Faerie Queene*, Bk. III, Canto III, stanza i.

> Jack shall have Jill;
> Nought shall go ill.[67]

The reason that in the drama marriage cannot present any real reconciliation of quarreling conceptions of love is that such a solution, if it really be one, is not an event or any series of events. It is a process of psychological adjustment of lovers' personalities which from its very nature would be almost impossible to dramatize. Yet something had to be done with the lovers, some final trick other than death or a sudden disavowal of love was needed to bring the story to an end. The conclusion to a medieval allegory of love such as the *Roman de la Rose*—the adulterous possession of one's mistress—was not only inherently incapable of satisfactory dramatization; it also ran counter to the entire Elizabethan code of morality, which was not separated from poetic (or dramatic) idyll as it had been in the Middle Ages.[68] The Renaissance writer then modified the climax of the courtly ritual of love, when he objectified it in drama, by legalizing the medieval pattern of amorous courtship. The dramatist who made use of the romance of marriage did not, with Spenser, spiritualize love in order to adapt it to the Elizabethan taste; he merely made love possible by making it respectable. Hence, as Touchstone's remark and Benedick's acceptance of Beatrice illustrate, a translation of passion into wedlock often suggested a kind of resigned acceptance by the lover of the contradictions of love. Thus, not only the inherited medieval romance, but marriage itself, as it had been idealized by poets, stood as a ready target for the teasing wit of the love-game comedy. The final legal union of lovers, as in *Romeo and Juliet*, guarantees the physical basis of love for Elizabethan literature, the conception that desire as described in medieval love poetry is worthy of emulation. But this legal union

---

[67] *Midsummer Night's Dream*, Act III, scene ii, l. 461.

[68] Cf. Craig's discussion (*The Enchanted Glass*, pp. 133–134) of Anne Frankford in a *Woman Killed with Kindness:* "She sorrows for the breach of her vow. The matrimonial sacrament in the Elizabethan ethical system was something fixed by God in His Church and supported by the law as a part of God's plan for governing the universe."

Renaissance Adaptations

also prepared such idealized love for dramatic treatment from a realistic and comic point of view.

Summary

It was from a complex, triangular antagonism of courtly love, ascetic idealism, and realistic skepticism that the Elizabethan amorist sought a tangible reality. Chaucer, as we have seen, represents the logic of the Middle Ages and expresses these mutually contradictory points of view, sometimes in the same poem. The Renaissance was no longer so sure or so tolerant of such inconsistency.[69] Theological objections to *fine amor* had been minimized by Platonic or by marital guarantees of sensuality. But the reinterpretations of courtly love itself, by Platonists or by exponents of the romance of marriage, served Elizabethan poets, for the most part, merely as expressions of escape from the unsatisfying nature of amorous experience.[70] There remained the quarrel over love as refined and sublimated by ritual and idealization and love as a realistic attitude toward physical passion. The latter point of view was derived partly from a tradition current in European literature at least from the time of Jean de Meung, partly from a fresh delight in the classics and in experience. The warm wind from Renaissance Italy was blowing across Europe to England to make the blood dance more quickly through the

[69] Cf. Renwick (*Edmund Spenser*, pp. 151–152): "The basic fact of the Renaissance, so difficult to isolate, has been held to be the escape of human reason from the bonds of authority. It would be true also to say that it was the escape of human temperament from the bonds of reason, from the habit of categorical division which is the mark of the legalistic mind of the Middle Ages. The medieval man kept things separate, and attended to one at a time. . . . This separation of human functions and interests could not last for ever, and when weakened there began the Renaissance, the discovery of man as a whole, indivisible, mind and body and soul together—the discovery of the central inclusive fact of life."

[70] Cf. Shakespeare Sonnet CXVI; Sidney, *Astrophel and Stella*, Sonnet LXXII. See also Harrison, *Platonism in English Poetry*, pp. 126 ff. Drayton, to be sure, prettified the notions of Platonism in his *Endimion and Phoebe*. For a discussion of this poem see Douglas Bush, *Mythology and the Renaissance Tradition*, pp. 156–163.

veins. In Elizabethan literature courtly love comes out of the sheltered garden into the world to be more sharply appraised than it had been in the Middle Ages. Allegory and romance are transformed into the debate of the conduct book and the autobiographical anguish of the sonnet. As C. L. Lewis has phrased it, "the wild Provençal vine has begun to bear such good fruit that it is now worth taming." [71]

The result of this invasion of a world eager to dramatize personal emotions by poetic fiction was to change what had been the exaggeration of idealized passion [72] into exaggeration of its contradictory nature. Conflict is always inevitable, as Catullus illustrates, between one's Lesbia that one wants to love and one's Lesbia that one has to love. But the Elizabethan conflict ran deeper than mere personal experience. In fact, the sixteenth century was never completely satisfied with its inherited psychology and description of love. Its conflict represented that between two ages, between two separate theories of existence. One period set aside for contemplation an idealized essence of experience. The other demanded that this idealized essence become real. For this reason Elizabethan literature continued to voice a recurrent protest that the "course of true love never did run smooth." [73]

[71] *The Allegory of Love*, p. 197.
[72] Cf. Renwick's statement: "Men discovered that their own actions and emotions were really the most interesting subject in the world, and felt they were not receiving the serious attention they deserved" (*Edmund Spenser*, p. 152).
[73] *Midsummer Night's Dream*, Act I, scene i, l. 134.

VII·
Renaissance Attempts to Actualize Theories of Courtly Love

Renaissance attempts to actualize troubadour sentiments of love were substantially aided by a general increase in respect for woman's emotional maturity and intellectual competence. A sixteenth-century Englishman was no longer expected, even by the church, to take the patient Griselda as a model of ideal femininity. It is true that during the Middle Ages women were not always and everywhere considered inferior to men, but their position, as described by the church fathers, at least, had been humble. But when love, under the influence of humanistic, ethical re-evaluations was accepted as part of the legitimate experience of a gentleman, the courtier's lady was not only given greater prominence, but love itself was also more accurately defined. Indeed, as Sidney's sonnets testify, the attempt to apply courtly modes of behavior to this newly appreciated woman was one of the forces which inspired a critical attitude toward romance.

For an actual change did take place in the position of the lady in the courtly society of Tudor England. With the beginnings of humanistic criticism in early sixteenth-century England, women had been allowed more and more education, and with it more liberty to develop personalities. When the last decades of this century had been reached, a sonnet sequence did not express a merely literary convention of servitude to a mistress. It portrayed an established social custom for one part of Elizabethan society.[1] Anne Boleyn was perhaps the first, certainly the most

[1] E. K. Chambers remarks (in *Sir Thomas Wyatt and Some Collected Studies*, pp. 98–99), "Catherine, worn early with the burden of ineffective child-bearing, soon dropped out. But Henry's lights of love were at hand to

prominent, woman of sixteenth-century England to embody all the freedom and the charm which the courtier sought in his beloved. To King Henry VIII his first wife, Katharine, must have seemed the embodiment of dreary old-fashioned ideals of wife and consort, while Anne Boleyn flashed upon him all the fascinations of the liberated mistress and companion.[2] Both women shared in the enlightenment of the sixteenth century, in the new education, but in contrasting fashion. Katharine's attitudes had been influenced by the medievally orthodox scholar, her tutor Juan Luis Vives; the only fiction permitted her was the story of the righteous Griselda.[3] Anne's philosophy, on the contrary, had been formed from a practical acquaintance with the romantic courtesy exhibited in the courts of Francis I and Marguerite d'Angoulême.

In his *Instruction of a Christen Woman* Vives presents a chaste and humble woman as his model of virtue; experienced passion forms no part of her life. In her social relations with young men, she is urged not to be a "talking stock" [4] or to participate in amorous badinage. Marriage, in his eyes, should be as clearly divorced from romance as it was to Juliet's father. Both regarded it purely as a family duty. Parents should choose husbands for their daughters, for "they that mary for love, shall leade their lyfe in sorowe." [5] Vives gives his own best summary of the severely restrictive attitude of the Middle Ages toward woman's intellectual life:

---

take her place. Pageant trod hard upon pageant, and Maying upon Maying. . . . In such an environment the encounter of bright eyes and warm bloods found its natural outcome in amorous versifying."

[2] See Einstein, *Tudor Ideals*, pp. 125–126: "The great changes which took place in the life and importance of women after the accession of Henry VIII, were due less to that prince's uxorious tastes than to the spirit of cultivation emulated from the Valois Court . . . everyone realized that the great reason for the divorce had been Katharine's personal unattractiveness compared with the French educated Anne Boleyn."

[3] See Watson, *Vives and the Renascence Education of Women*, p. 24.

[4] *Ibid.*, p. 98.

[5] Vives, *Instruction of a Christen Woman*, tr. by Richard Hyrd (1541). Bk. I, folio 60.

... in a woman, no manne wyll loke for eloquence, great wytte, or prudence, or crafte to lyve by, or ordrynge of the commen weale, or justice, or lyberalite: Finally no man wyl loke for any other thynge of a woman, but her honesty [chastity]: the whyche onely, if it be lacked, is lyke as in a man, if he lacke al that he shulde have. For in a woman the honestie is in stede of all.[6]

But it was precisely this "eloquence and great wytte," this ability to play the "talking stock," and a capacity for passion instead of "honesty" that characterized the woman praised by the Renaissance.[7] In court circles, where experienced love was becoming a necessary part of a gentleman's education, the mere condescension to women voiced by such an early humanist as Vives was old-fashioned and a little absurd. Anne Boleyn's marriage to Henry VIII became the first public triumph of the new woman of the sixteenth century.

Anne, the mother of Queen Elizabeth, represents a sixteenth-century attempt to live the poetic sensuality of medieval romances. She personified the Renaissance woman who had escaped from the control of clerical satirists and had assumed the "full right to flirt, to receive ballads, to keep trysts."[8] Judging from the surviving love letters and poems that he wrote,[9] Henry's courtship of Anne was conducted strictly according to the prescribed conventions of courtly love. Katharine absorbed herself in needlework and religious devotion,[10] while Anne flirted with the king and kept him in her service as pleading lover for more

[6] *Ibid.*, folio 17, verso.
[7] The contrast between the ideal woman of medieval tradition and that of the Renaissance is made with great plainness, if with some nostalgia, by the Earl of Northumberland, in his treatise written in the Tower after 1605, *The Management of Women*. He considered the men of his own day "with dalliances and attendances to be ridiculously obsequious." What had formerly been called a scold, one now called "a lady of good spirit." Quoted by Wilson, in *Society Women of Shakespeare's Time*, p. 175.
[8] Reich, *Woman through the Ages*, I, 235.
[9] See Henry VIII, *The Letters*, selected and ed. by St. Clare Byrne, ch. ii, p. 53, "from all other only to her I me betake."
[10] Wyat, *Extracts from the Life of the Virtuous, Christian, and Renowned Queen Anne Boleigne*, pp. 4 ff.

than a year.¹¹ And the adaptation of medieval romance to fact was never more complete than in these supplicating words from Henry's letter to Anne, written about 1527: "I promise you that not only shall the name be given you, but that also I will take you for my only mistress, rejecting from thought and affection all others save only yourself." ¹²

This contrast between Anne Boleyn and Katharine of Aragon, to be sure, did not set any mandatory precedent for sixteenth-century England. But the contrast between the Renaissance woman and the woman of the Middle Ages continued to become more and more striking as the century progressed.¹³ The contrast reached its climax, no doubt, in Elizabeth herself, who insisted upon being to her courtiers the embodiment of *fine amor*, and sent them from her, as unfaithful lovers, whenever they took a mistress or a wife.¹⁴ The shy Elizabeth Vernon, for example, who married Shakespeare's patron, Southampton, in 1598, seems to be almost an anomaly, a medieval survival in the late sixteenth century beside such a feminine representation of the age as Penelope Devereux, the supposed "Stella" of Sidney's sonnets. These two lived together at Essex's country house during his campaign in Ireland, in 1599. And when it was a mere question of going up to London, Elizabeth Vernon could not be tempted by Penelope until Southampton's consent had been obtained. She wrote to him: "For myselfe I protest unto you that your will is, either in this or in any thing elce, shale be most plesing to me. . . . If you wil have me goe with hir, she desires that you wil write a letter to my lorde Riche, that I may do so." ¹⁵ But Anne Boleyn,

---

¹¹ See Henry VIII, *The Letters:* Letter IV, p. 57 ". . . having been now above one whole year struck with the dart of love."

¹² *Ibid.*, Letter IV.

¹³ For a detailed discussion of this sixteenth-century woman see Violet Wilson, *Society Women of Shakespeare's Time;* see also Maulde la Clavière, *The Women of the Renaissance*, tr. by George Herbert Ely.

¹⁴ See the comment of Hubert Languet to Sidney (in Sidney, *Correspondence of Philip Sidney and Hubert Lanquet*, p. 185) "most of your noblemen appeared to me to seek for a reputation more by a kind of affected courtesy than by those virtues which are wholesome to the state."

¹⁵ Wilson, *Society Women in Shakespeare's Time*, p. 82.

Attempts to Actualize Theory

Queen Elizabeth, and Penelope Devereux were the coming to life of courtly love. Penelope Devereux, indeed, fulfilled the code even to the requirement of adultery. For whatever her relationship may have been with Sidney, she was the acknowledged mistress of Mountjoy, the great-grandson of Erasmus's patron, and she continued to remain legally married to Lord Rich. To her own age she might well have seemed the embodiment of the courtier's desire to experience the high ideals of twelfth-century Provence.

Conceptions of Courtly Love in Early Tudor Conduct Books

Because the Renaissance courtier attempted to experience love as it had been described in romantic poetry, he was almost inevitably unsuccessful. His reaction is found in the cries of despair which become conventional in the flood of sonnets in the last decades of the Elizabethan period. They bear acute witness to the difficulties [16] met in trying to attain the troubadour's picture of love in an actual love affair. One ought to find a steadily increasing critical and analytical consciousness of lovers' difficulties in the series of conduct books that succeeded each other in importance as the sixteenth century moved toward its Elizabethan zenith, but such is not the fact. Just as the Renaissance became sharply sensitive to poetry with the publication of *Tottel's Miscellany*, in 1557, so, too, this age found its attention focused on its own emotional confusion in an abrupt fashion when Sir Thomas Hoby published his translation of *Il cortegiano* in 1561.

In conduct books popular before Elizabeth's reign the suggested relationship of love to the life of a gentleman was fairly simple, because moral scruples remained to prevent a sudden acceptance of the principles of courtly love.[17] These books do not

---

[16] A particularly good example is John Donne's "Woman's Constancy," in *The Poems*, ed. by Grierson, p. 9.

[17] The first of these, in point of time, was La Tour-Landry's *Book of the Knight of la Tour-Landry, Compiled for the Instruction of His Daughters*, published by Caxton (1483). It amounts to a late medieval textbook in morals

so much question the practicability of passion, as its desirability. Discussion remains on the level of a critical concern over the place of woman and of desire in a well-regulated life. In Alexander Barclay's translation from Mancinus Dominicus, *The Mirrour of Good Manners* (1523), sex experience is denied much significance. It is considered less immoral than unreasonable. Hence,

> Those onely be good desires, cleane and sure
> Which nature requireth, obeying to reason.[18]

Again,

> Naught lightneth more mankinde to pass unreasonable
> Then gluttony and slouth, and lust without reason.[19]

In so far as it is from this world and not from revelation, the argument is that of the humanist, one notes, though the ideal is a moral one. When the appeal is to "reason," it is one that the sixteenth century could respect. Thus, amorous courtesy itself, and its little god "fayre flattering Cupid," [20] is put under control of the intellect, with the caution, "Let Venus fele bridle her pleasures to refrayne." [21]

In the writing of Sir Thomas Elyot, one of the most famous secular moralists of the sixteenth century, this "sensible" attitude toward love is presented in more costive fashion. In his *Boke of the Governour*, a good woman is described as "milde, timerouse, tractable, benigne, of sure remembrance, and shamfast." [22] Continence, with due respect to the new attitudes compressed into the single word, "pleasaunt," is "a vertue whiche kepeth the

---

and manners. The debate between the knight and his wife, in its final pages, concerning the effects of courtly love is almost wholly denunciatory.

[18] Mancinus Dominicus, *The Mirrour of Good Manners*, tr. by Barclay, p. 46. (Also tr. by G. Turbervile in 1568, as "A Plaine Path to perfect Vertue.")

[19] *Ibid.*, "Of lust Venerious to be refrayned," p. 56.

[20] *Ibid.*, p. 56. [21] *Ibid.*

[22] Elyot, *The Boke of the Governour*, ed. by Croft from the 1531 edition, I, 236. Elyot adds, "divers other qualities . . . mought be founde out, but these be moste apparaunt."

Attempts to Actualize Theory

pleasaunt appetite of man under the yoke of reason." [23] Elyot is blind to poetic excitations of sensuality, not as Chaucer's Parson might have been, but as a "reasonable" man of the Renaissance, when he cautions: "I wolde to God those names [Venus and Cupid] were nat at this day used in balades and ditties in the courtes of princes and noble men, where many good wittes be corrupted with semblable fantasies." [24]

After the elevation of Anne Boleyn to consort of Henry VIII, Elyot made an attempt, in his *Defence of Good Women*, to evaluate the sentiment of courtesy. He maintains that there are two common attitudes among men toward woman as objects of passion and that they are mutually exclusive. There is misogynic scorn, an "ungentyll custome of many men," [25] and there is excessive adulation: "Ye, whan theyr wanton appetite stereth them, they offer to serve them, and doo extoll them with prayses ferre above reason." [26] But Elyot, as a critical humanist, is much more interested in the latter excess than in the former. Thus, he finds that "lovers be dull and insensyble in feelynge of Sapience," [27] that they are "styll as blynde as [their] litel god Cupide." [28] The relationship between romantic sentiment and a gentleman's life is made clear. Poetry, Elyot says in irony, "is the onely study of you that be lovers; for that boke, which lacketh complayntes with wepynges and sighinges, is to you men that be amorouse wonderfull tediouse." [29]

The problem that Elyot sets himself in this book addressed to Anne Boleyn is to determine a temperate limit for the courtly sentiments of love in their relation to this new woman, this coequal of man. He suggests that a wise man should grant reason to woman as well as to man. To prevent any irrational perplexities that might arise from overpraise of woman as dispenser of love, he would have this creature's reason educated. He would have her follow the example of the Zenobia of his treatise and study moral philosophy that she might be a fit companion, not

---

[23] *Ibid.*, II, 305.
[24] *Ibid.*, II, 210–211.
[25] Elyot, *The Defence of Good Women* (1540), the preface.
[26] *Ibid.*
[27] *Ibid.*, sig. B$_3$ verso.
[28] *Ibid.*
[29] *Ibid.*, sig. B$_5$ verso.

for an excited lover, but for a sober man. Elyot and Barclay fail to express a consciousness of the special difficulties which faced the Renaissance courtier or poet who had accepted the illusions of romance, only to find them unstable in reality.

As the age progressed, more and more conduct books, most of them translations, began to circulate in England. Rationalization or condemnation of this romantic attitude became more and more important. One of the most popular, Guevara's *Libro aureo* (it had two important translations),[30] is almost wholly medieval, however, and contains the most eloquent denunciation of the emergent woman this side the Middle Ages. It illustrates the continued popularity of a misogynic attitude, even in courtly society, up to the mid-century mark. A more interesting book (because it is more nearly in the spirit of the high Renaissance), of the final quarter of this century is *The Nobility of Women*.[31] This treatise was partly translated from Lodovico Domenichi, in 1559. It was dedicated to the young Queen Elizabeth and remained in manuscript. Its translator, William Bercher (or Barker), owed a certain deference to women, since he had been sent to Cambridge before 1536 under the bounty of Elizabeth's mother. One is tempted to think that his translation was a counter blast to both Knox's and Calvin's caustic diatribes against the Renaissance woman of this same time. Thus, a conventional anti-feminism still lingers in this book of Bercher's, and the discussion hovers over the question, worn thin by 1559,[32] Are women inferior to men? Mr. Orlando, who pleads their equality before the Lady Philida, countesse of Elcie, argues not only that they are the equals of men but also that they would surpass their rivals if equally educated.[33] The opposition, represented by John Borghese, merely repeats the attitude familiar since St. Jerome, when he says:

[30] Published as *The Golden Boke of Marcus Aurelius*, 1535, tr. by Lord Berners; published as *The Diall of Princes*, 1557, tr. by Sir Thomas North.

[31] Bercher, *The Nobility of Women*, ed. by R. Warwick Bond, with introduction.

[32] Two years after the publication of *Tottel's Miscellany*, of the "new poetry."   [33] *The Nobility of Women*, p. 122.

ffor of them selves / and their bodis
they be so liberall / that the dystribution
of it [their charyte] to us men must nedes be
celebrated.³⁴

The Analysis of Love
in THE COURTIER

So long as it concerned itself with an impersonal discussion of the nature of woman and the limitations that wisdom should place upon a man's passion for her, the Tudor conduct book kept itself politely aloof from the emerging love-conflict. Its importance is that it makes articulate (though often grudgingly) for the court society preceding the Elizabethan period the swiftly disappearing condescension toward woman, which by the end of the century had vanished.³⁵ Possibly no single piece of Renaissance writing serves to isolate with great precision all the facets of the Elizabethan complexities of love. For the period of the high Renaissance, however, one book is most representative of the courtesy of the whole age.³⁶ This book, *Il cortegiano,* by Baldassare Castiglione, presents all sides of the humanistic attempt to accommodate romantic love sentiment to the newly apprehended woman and to include it as the legitimate emotional completion of the life of the Renaissance gentleman. *The Courtier* had been turned into Elizabethan idiom by Sir Thomas Hoby and had "long straid" ³⁷ in manuscript during the reign of Queen Mary. But from the time of its publication, in 1561, to the end of the century,³⁸ it was the accepted model for gentlemanly conduct,

---

³⁴ *Ibid.*, p. 107.

³⁵ In the sonnet sequences, the equality of the sexes is taken for granted. Such discussions weighing the virtues of men against those of women as those in *The Courtier* are purely academic.

³⁶ Cf. Walter Raleigh, in Hoby, *The Book of the Courtier,* Introduction, p. x, "Take it for all in all, the *Book of the Courtier* reflects as in a mirror the age that gave it birth."

³⁷ *Ibid.*, p. 5.

³⁸ Cf. Raleigh, *ibid.*, pp. viii ff. See also Tenison, *Elizabethan England,* I, 189–201. An interesting Elizabethan discussion of love later than the *Courtier* and much like it is the translation of Etienne Pasquier's *Le Monophyle,* tr.

despite the earlier Tudor old-school denunciation of the "Italianate Englishman" [39] by moralists such as Ascham and Norfolk. Because it described, purportedly, what the important courtiers assembled at Urbino actually thought about the problems of courtesy, *The Courtier* gave the final secular approval—which such early books as those of Elyot had withheld—to the Renaissance in its attempted adaptation of chivalric love to courtly life.[40]

The Courtier is quite the most leisurely and objective study of morals and manners that the Renaissance produced. Castiglione, far more skeptical than Elyot, remains aloof from the discussions that he reports. He has no obvious preference for the ideas of one character over those of another. He sets down all in friendly accuracy. The transcript begins, naturally, with a portrait of the court at Urbino, the courtiers and court ladies attendant, and the opening of their symposium. Lady Emilia Pia acts as deputy for the duchess of Urbino, and turns first to Lord Gaspar Pallavicino for his choice of a topic for discussion. Pallavicino, who is the most thoughtful—or at least the most realistic—of the courtiers, wishes to hear an analysis of the relationship between

---

by Geffray Fenton as *Monophylo; a Philosophicall Discourse and Division of Love* (1572). The three disputants are Monophylo, Glaphyro, and Phylopolo. The first "was so extreemely passioned with love, as all his thoughts and devotions tended directly to his Mystresse, upon whom he committed ydolatrie, as making hir the onely Idoll of his secrete contemplations" (sig. 1, verso). The second, "not so deeply distressed as he, preferring a civil and curteous behavior to the Ladies, seemed rather to holde an estate of a Courtyer, then to professe singuler love" (sig. 1, verso—sig. 2, recto). The third delighted "in a liberty of affection, without any peculiar choyse or regard" (sig. 2, recto).

[39] Ascham, of course, approved Castiglione's book (see *The Scholemaster*, in Ascham, *The English Works*, ed. by Wright, pp. 218, 235). For Norfolk's denunciation, see R. Warwick Bond's Introduction to Bercher's *The Nobility of Women*, p. 1.

[40] Sir Philip Sidney has often been suggested as the embodied pattern of Castiglione's book, since Sidney fulfilled all the requirements for the rounded gentleman, including that most fascinating to Castiglione's speakers, love. See Raleigh's statement (Introduction to *The Book of the Courtier*, p. xi). See also that of Tenison (in *Elizabethan England*, VI, 201) "Philip was to become the acknowledged incarnation of the blend of 'learning and chivalry' conspicuous in Castiglione."

Attempts to Actualize Theory

the perfection postulated by all lovers for their mistresses and the actual falling away from such perfection into fact: "to see who can fynde out most prayse woorthye and manlye vertues, and most tollerable vyces, that shoulde be least hurtefull bothe to hymn that loveth, and to the wyghte beloved." [41] But the rest of the company is not interested in his choice. Therefore, another suggestion is followed, and they settle down, first to define the attributes of a perfect courtier and then, on subsequent nights of their symposium, to determine the ways in which these attributes may be exploited.

An attempt to ascertain the nature of love and the relationship of courtier and court lady to it begins shortly before the close of the second evening's meeting and emerges from time to time during the remaining discussions. Such disagreements as occur, it should be noted, never slip back into the uneasy concern of Elyot, Guevara, and Bercher as to whether love should or should not be part of a gentleman's experience. The interlocutors of *The Courtier*, taking that for granted, present a highly sophisticated, critical examination of possible kinds of love.

The antifeminine point of view is voiced by Lord Gaspar. He remarks, early in the discussion of love, that a woman's amorous deeds and desires are out of all reason,[42] and he bases his evaluation of the courtier as lover on this assumption. But he uses the theories of medieval satirists somewhat jocularly, as a kind of balance to all attempts to idealize passion. He continually challenges the company to keep its descriptions of love well within the boundaries of possible experience. He rebels against the notion that the mistress of the courtier's fancy should be "reverenced and honoured of all gentilmen." [43] He comments that it "were good we might finde out some pretie rule howe to knowe" such a deserving lady, "bicause moste communlie the best in apparance are cleane contrarye in effect." [44]

The conception of love found in the medieval romances (and in Petrarch and his imitators) has many more advocates than has

---

[41] Hoby, *The Courtier*, p. 36.
[42] *Ibid.*, p. 144.
[43] *Ibid.*, p. 178.
[44] *Ibid.*, pp. 178–179.

the skeptical, realistic point of view maintained by Lord Gaspar. M. Bernarde, for example, suggests a suffering lover, a supplicating Lancelot, as the ideal:

> I beleave ech honest lover susteyneth such peynes, such watchinges, hasardeth himselfe in such daungers, droppeth so manie teares, useth so manie meanes and wayes to please the woman whom he loveth, not cheeflye to come bye her body, but to winne the fortresse of that minde, to breake in peeces those most harde Diamondes, to heate that colde yce, that lye manye times in the tender brests of these women. And this do I beleave is the true and sounde pleasure, and the ende wherto the entent of a noble courage is bent.[45]

Lord Julian, seconded by Lord Cesar Gonzaga, attempts to establish as the lady of the palace the provocative goddess of medieval poets. She brings out the nobility in the courtier. Hence, no court, Lord Cesar remarks,

> can have any sightlinesse, or brightnesse in it, or mirth, without women, nor anie Courtier can be gratious, pleasant, or hardye, nor at anye time undertake any galant enterprise of Chivalrye onlesse he be stirred wyth the conversacion and wyth the love and contentacion of women, even so in like case the Courtiers talke is most unperfect ever more, if the entercourse of women give them not a part of the grace wherwithall they make perfect and decke out their playing the Courtier.[46]

Her purpose is to create in fact the courtesy and the gentility described in romance. Thus, as Lord Julian continues the portrait of the lady of the Court her attributes follow naturally. She must always keep an air of the disembodied about her, of the impalpable. She should differ from the courtier (being more ideal than he), by never entering into the jocularities of wanton gossip or the outward shows of familiarity. She may "come just to certein limites, but not passe them." [47] That is, as in the courtly love ritual, this actual woman must keep herself aloof if she is to be worshiped. She should set herself apart, that "she be not only beloved, but reverenced of all men." [48]

[45] Ibid., p. 202.
[47] Ibid., p. 217.
[46] Ibid., pp. 214–215.
[48] Ibid., p. 219.

Attempts to Actualize Theory

Lord Gaspar, impatient with all attempts to portray love as an impalpable ideal, makes clear that M. Bernarde, in his search for a "perfect and true love," seeks an impossible absolute. According to Lord Gaspar Pallavicino, "alwayes he that possesseth the bodie of women, is also maister of the mind." [49] Likewise, disapproving all Lord Julian's contentions, the matter-of-fact Pallavicino voices the critical protest of the age, that this placing of woman on a pedestal is too fanciful altogether. It is too much out of harmony with experience, with what is practicable in love. He complains that Lord Julian has spoken of miracles, "and appointed to the gentilwoman of the Palaice certein fonde unpossible matters, and so many vertues that Socrates and Cato and all the Philosophers in the worlde are nothing to her." [50]

These interlocutors, arguing at cross-purposes, quickly reach an impasse. Cesar Gonzaga states that the nature of woman is actually idyllic because "noble yonge menne, discreete, wise, of prowes and welfavoured, spend many yeeres in lovinge, sparinge for nothinge that might entice, tokens, suites, teares: to be short, whatsoever may be imagined, and all but lost labour." [51] And further to prove that the painful ritual of medieval courtesy is a fact he confesses that he himself has played the prostrate lover more than once "nighe deathes doore" [52] and quite in vain. Gaspar Pallavicino, of course, turns such an argument for the withdrawn, intangible mistress of love against itself. This merely proves the complete unreality of such love, he notes; moreover, women scorn a prostrate lover and sue for themselves elsewhere.[53] But the Lord Cesar Gonzaga will not surrender romance so easily. He continues to cite the courtly virtues that follow the passion of love, calling in Petrarch's sonnets to Laura as tangible testimony.[54]

An effort is made to reconcile the conflict over the functions and the attributes of the lady of the palace by turning to an ex-

---

[49] *Ibid.*, p. 203.   [50] *Ibid.*, p. 222 (cf. also p. 219).
[51] *Ibid.*, p. 252 (see also pp. 248–265).
[52] *Ibid.*, p. 252.   [53] *Ibid.*
[54] *Ibid.*, p. 265.

amination of the symptoms and the nature of love itself.[55] Lord Julian describes it as it had been portrayed repeatedly by poets of the Middle Ages and of the Renaissance. True lovers have a "burninge hart . . . a colde tunge, with broken talke and sodeine silence." [56] But passion, if it is not to be disastrous, must end in marriage,[57] according to Lord Julian. Some of the courtiers oppose this legal circumscribing of desire. Pallavicino, however, objects not to the fashion in which the rites of love shall be enjoyed, but to the idealizing of simple passion. Once again he finds the woman involved in this theory too ethereal, too incorporeal.[58] But Julian rallies under attack to state that a virtuous courtier will desire only the spiritual appeasements of love, and divergent opinions begin to crystallize. Lord Julian makes it plain that there is inherent maladjustment in seeking to possess one's lady and seeking to revere her. The law of love, to him, is worship. Therefore, on final analysis it is the "soule of the lover" that "ought to be an obedient handmayden" [59] to his mistress.

Lord Gaspar, restive under this whole discussion of woman as part of an ostentatious ritual of desire rather than as a human being, draws his debate with Lord Julian and the others to a close. To Lord Julian love is emotional bondage to the court lady and cannot exist without the enslavement of the lover. This enslavement is still the product of the eye's glance which pierces the heart of the lover to inspire his prostration before a creature less woman than amorous symbol.[60] To Lord Gaspar the emotional impetus for this painful ritual is not passion, but feminine vanity. All women delight in being sued, though they may have no intention of satisfying the lover.[61] If one is to prove one's love by such torment, he concludes, it must be an odd emotion. For the lover, after his long and painful ordeal, can have left "no more sense to taste the delite or contentation offred him." [62] Gaspar is no religious misogynist, but a Renaissance critic. He finds no

[55] *Ibid.*, pp. 266 ff.
[56] *Ibid.*, p. 269.
[57] *Ibid.*, pp. 269 ff.
[58] *Ibid.*, p. 271.
[59] *Ibid.*, p. 277 (cf. p. 270 ff.).
[60] *Ibid.*, p. 278.
[61] *Ibid.*, p. 277.
[62] *Ibid.*, p. 287.

intrinsic evil in passion other than its supposed effects upon the courtier as lover. To him the Renaissance woman, as an object of love, is far less spiritual than the creature described by Julian —far more human than divine.

Pallavicino, the skeptic, and Lord Julian, the idealist, lack the capacity for the subtle rationalization that must resolve their contention and so make clear its bases. It is Cardinal Bembo, as befits a philosopher, that in the final night's symposium spins the fine thread of logic that can bridge the rift between the real and the ideal. It is true that this meeting starts off with an analysis of the relationship between the courtier and his prince. But the problem of adapting a romantic conception of love to the Renaissance world still troubles Lord Gaspar, and he interrupts the flow of talk to suggest that love be taken away from the experience of the courtier that he may live in peace.[63] Thereupon, Cardinal Bembo, who has heretofore done little to give direction to the conversation, replies that it is possible for the courtier (if not young) to love in a fashion that will be unperplexed and full of contentment. He then begins his analysis of Platonic love that serves to bring the whole book to a close and to define with new precision the Renaissance dilemma of love. His thesis is that love "is nothinge elles but a certein covetinge to enjoy beawtie." [64]

Lord Julian had attempted an idealistic description of sensuality, while Lord Gaspar had attempted a factual one. Cardinal Bembo would set up a dualism between the poetic embroidery of courtly love and its carnal fulfillment. Love sends its shaft through the eyes, as always, but when desire is pure, the arrow penetrates, not the heart, but the soul and creates a desire for mere spiritual possession.[65] The perplexities of love come when sensuality is confused with spirituality, when sense rather than the soul seeks appeasement.

Whan the soule then is taken wyth covetynge to enjoye thys beawtie as a good thynge, in case she suffre her selfe to be guyded with the judgement of sense, she falleth into most deepe errours, and judgeth

[63] *Ibid.*, pp. 340–341.   [64] *Ibid.*, p. 342.
[65] *Ibid.*, p. 343.

the bodie in whyche Beawtye is descerned, to be the principall cause thereof: whereupon to enjoye it, she reckeneth it necessarye to joigne as inwardlye as she can wyth that bodye, whyche is false.[66]

Sensual love, then, is an attempt to grasp the impalpable idea of beauty through carnal possession and results in the tormenting frustration of the lover. He is never satisfied by sexuality, because he is "deceyved through that likenesse" [67] to the intangible beauty he seeks. Thus he returns again and again to vain carnal pleasure: "they fall again into the raginge and most burninge thirst of the thinge, that they hope in vaine to possesse perfectlye." [68] Hence, the sensual lover, who has taken his romances too literally, recoils from fulfilled desire. Here, then, is the origin of the poetic ritual of the suffering lover that Lord Julian had prescribed and Lord Gaspar rejected.[69] It is a product of green youth, unable to distinguish sense from soul. It is beauty glimpsed, but corrupted by the touch of physical desire.

Cardinal Bembo presents Platonic love as a logical escape for those who seek such relief from the frustrations of a mutable physical ideal. Lord Julian had kept his lover in conflict, as Gaspar's comments on medieval sentiment had made clear, by trying to combine in him reverence and possessiveness. Bembo would keep him purely reverential; but M. Morrello denies even this rationalization. Before Bembo's frenzied description of the almost unknowable joys of Platonism is under way, M. Morrello challenges Platonic illusion merely by calling for a touch of sexuality in love: "The engendringe (quoth he) of beawtye in beawtye aright were the engendringe of a beawtyfull chylde in a beautifull woman." [70]

But nothing can stop Cardinal Bembo from describing the ascent, as by a ladder, from fleshly to divine ecstasy. It is curious evidence of the inexorable conflict of ideal and real that however far Bembo seeks to soar beyond the frustrating limitations of carnal experience, essentially he is tethered to these limitations.

[66] *Ibid.*, pp. 343–344.
[68] *Ibid.*
[70] *Ibid.*, p. 354.
[67] *Ibid.*, p. 344.
[69] *Ibid.*, pp. 344–345.

Thus, it is only older men, whose impulses have been subjugated either by will or by age, who can hope to love ecstatically. Furthermore, the rise from sensuality, through reason, to love as all-embracing idea, to the realm of perfect, unbodied desire, is described by a Bembo whose very figures of speech seem to belie his sentiment. They are suggested by the sexual love which he had sought to escape. The verb most used is "coupling." One may couple with beauty or with God: "all chast lovers covett a kisse, as a cooplinge of soules together." [71]

Whatever his failure to solve complexities of love for the young courtier, Bembo at least held his audience by his evocation of a passionate fulfillment beyond anything they would ever know. But it is precisely because Bembo refused to give up romantic ideals in favor of fact that he was forced to thrust his own picture of love beyond the disappointments of experience. Lady Emilia Pia is the one to dispel the hypnotic mood that Bembo has created. She plucks his garment, suggesting that he take heed lest "these thoughtes make not your soule also to forsake the bodye." [72] And thus Bembo's momentary vision of the Platonic ideal vanishes. One is back where one began. The desire for a perfect love and for a perfect woman is still unrealized. Bembo's Platonism is dream-like, without radical ties to experience. Lord Gaspar adds the final skeptical touch to dispel this fragile vision of an unperplexed passion beyond sense, when he says of Bembo's theory, "I beleave it be harde to gete up for men, but unpossible for women." [73]

Castiglione presents the most lucid analysis of the Renaissance effort to incorporate courtly love in reality, to accommodate a romantic sentiment to the life of a gentleman and a lady of the palace. Bembo represents the best that his age could do in adjusting poetic ideal to fact. But his resolution of conflict, from the point of view of a young sensualist certainly, is actually not one at all, but rationalized retreat. Experience is still unsatisfied. For all the various discussions of love during a four-evening sym-

[71] *Ibid.*, p. 356.   [72] *Ibid.*, p. 363.
[73] *Ibid.*

posium, for all the sifting of ideas to basic attitudes, love has not been bent to man's will, but remains to confound it.

It has often been suggested that the contention between Lady Emilia Pia and Lord Gaspar (which continually appears in *The Courtier* after the latter has made a vicious thrust at women) is the model for such quarreling lovers as Beatrice and Benedick in *Much Ado*.[74] Certainly one finds personified here something very like the witty debates that are found in Shakespeare's love-game comedies. Such debates are anticipated by Castiglione in the mocking disagreement between Emilia and Pallavicino. The court lady described by Lord Julian in the third book as the symbol of amorous perfection is brought to earth by Lord Gaspar. He says to Lady Emilia, laughingly, "Now . . . you can not complaine that the L. Julian hath not facioned this woman of the Palaice most excellent. And if perdee there be any suche to be found, I say that she deserveth well to be esteamed equall with the Courtier." [75] The Lady Emilia resents his literal mind and his jests at love. She replies, "I will at all times be bounde to finde her when you finde the Courtier." [76]

The similarity of these two attendants at the court of Urbino to two of Shakespeare's dramatic characters is, it would appear, not so much causal as parallel. That is to say, once the Renaissance assumed the social and emotional equality of the sexes, love generally became not a question of acceptance or denial (as it was to Elyot), but a quarrel between the ideal and the psychologically possible. This quarrel, which forms an important part of the conversation in *The Courtier*, by two of its speakers is presented in a fashion also found in certain comedies of Shakespeare. It is of interest that two literary reflections of the same Renaissance perplexity are much alike. But the quarrel was not limited to a minor pattern in a few pieces of Renaissance literature. It was a

---

[74] For example, Mary Augusta Scott, "The Book of the Courtyer," PMLA, XVI (1901), 475–502. R. Warwick Bond, Introduction to Bercher's *The Nobility of Women*, also suggests the debt of Elizabethan comedy to Renaissance attitudes toward love found in the conduct books. See also, Walter Raleigh, in his Introduction to Hoby, *The Book of the Courtier*, pp. lxxxiv–lxxxv.

[75] *The Book of the Courtier*, p. 271.   [76] *Ibid*.

Attempts to Actualize Theory

quarrel brought about by the sturdy, critical spirit of the age.

It is generally assumed that literature somehow reflects the life of its time.[77] Hamlet states it for the Elizabethan period. But this is not to assume that because Shakespeare's Beatrice is something like, let us say, Penelope Devereux or Emilia Pia therefore the one is the merely isolated product of the other. The aesthetic patterns of literature and the moral patterns of a section of a given society flow from the same inheritance of ideas. There may have been—indeed Castiglione indicates that there was—a sex duel in real life as well as in the love-game comedy. And in the special love conflict in Elizabethan thought, the one may have been very like, may even have suggested, the other. But historically the dramatic pattern is more significant than the actual embodiment. The latter can be described, at best, as only fragmentary, subject to the passing moods of the participants, to the disintegrating touch of time. But the dramatic reflection is complete in itself.[78] Borrowing from Hamlet's metaphor, it has the detached, intangible effect of the mirror image.

The attempt to accommodate a romantic attitude to the life of a gentleman and to the newly apprehended lady of the court, then, represents the intrusion of Renaissance reality into medieval courtly ideals whether illustrated in drama, in conduct book, or in fact. In point of time, it was not until the period of the high Elizabethan Renaissance (roughly, 1580–1600), that there was sufficient consciousness of the conflict caused by this attempt to give its dramatization importance. It is the growth of this consciousness, from the hesitant acceptance of "reasonable" passion in the writings of Elyot, to the complete clarification of the rea-

---

[77] See Wilson, *Society Women of Shakespeare's Time*, p. vii: "Shakespeare's heroines undoubtedly had their origin in the society women of the time."

[78] Castiglione poses his problems in terms of actual people, and therefore the problems remain aesthetically incomplete. The dramatist is less limited and translates his ideas into imagined embodiments and works them through to an imagined conclusion. (For the reality of Castiglione's portrait of Emilia Pia, cf. contemporary opinion, quoted by Maulde la Clavière, *The Women of the Renaissance*, p. 305: "Emilia Pia . . . writes almost as she speaks, with great liveliness and humour, and always with equal vivacity whether the subject be toilet specifics or philosophy."

sons for the difficulties of love in Hoby's translation, that is startling proof of the vitally humanistic impulse driving the age. In the sixteenth century, sentiment becomes a subject for logical analysis. Castiglione's treatise gives a coherent pattern to the courtier's contentious amorous attitudes, and the comedies of Lyly and Shakespeare dramatize his new consciousness of emotional difficulties.

·VIII·

AMOROUS CONFLICT IN ELIZABETHAN POETRY

SUCH a representative sixteenth-century treatise as *The Courtier* revealed the efforts of Italian aristocrats to adjust a medieval tradition of romance to the facts of their lives. The difficulties which arose because of a similar attempt by English courtiers were often reflected in their amorous verses. With the introduction of the sonneteering tradition into English literature, in the love poetry of Sir Thomas Wyatt, begins the involved, subjective analysis of love that was to make its perplexities a special part of Elizabethan thought.[1] The inspiration of this new poetry was almost entirely foreign. That is, it was an English adaptation of the tradition of courtly love which had been elaborated in the sonnets of Petrarch and his followers. This borrowed poetry assimilated not only the short, lyric sonnet-stanza and a whole catalogue of amorous metaphors[2] but also the autobiographical manner of its source.[3]

[1] Cf. Francis Meres's descriptive phrase, introducing his list of famous Elizabethan poets (in Meres, *Palladis Tamia, Wits Treasury,* London, 1598, ed. by Joseph Haslewood, *Ancient Critical Essays,* II, 154): "these are the most passionate among us to bewaile and bemoane the perplexities of love."

[2] A pedant such as Sperone Speroni compiled a dictionary of correct Petrarchan phrases. See Pearson, *Elizabethan Love Conventions,* p. 55.

[3] The immediate origins of Elizabethan conceptions of love are to be found largely in the Italian and French Petrarchists, though courtly ideas of love also came from Chaucer and his English followers. See Lee, Introduction to *Elizabethan Sonnets,* I, especially ix–xviii; Tillyard, Introduction to *The Poetry of Sir Thomas Wyatt,* pp. 23–25; Pearson, *Elizabethan Love Conventions,* especially ch. i; *Cambridge History of English Literature,* Vol. III, ch. vii, "The New English Poetry," and ch. xii, "The Elizabethan Sonnet."

It is true that from the time when Dante developed the poetic doctrines of Provence into a self-revealing description of personal experience, these doctrines became subject to the disintegrating influence of individual interpretation. However, such a potentially humanizing tendency did not lead to the skepticism concerning romance described by some of the speakers in *The Courtier*. By its emphasis on the spiritual side of passion, Petrarchan love tradition had remained relatively free from any complicating sense of reality.[4] Hence the sentiments of medieval romance in ascetic or Platonic guise lay as a common substratum under all the literary artifices of the poetry introduced by Wyatt. Sixteenth-century English love poetry adopts along with the Petrarchan conceits the whole troubadour doctrine of love which survived in the continental sonneteering tradition. The conception of love basic in all Elizabethan poetry, therefore, is precisely that current in the romances of the Middle Ages.[5] Love is everywhere described as an irresistible force. It is transmitted from the eyes of the mistress to those of the aspiring lover. It penetrates his heart, causing ecstatic love-sickness. Wherever one dips into the tremendous outpouring of the Renaissance English heart, he finds it is this courtly love doctrine,[6] either uncontaminated or in conflict with a skeptical outlook, that gives the pattern to expressions of passion.

Sir Thomas Wyatt makes use of this conception when he writes:

> Thorow myn Iye the strock frome hers did slyde
> Dyrectly downe unto my hert it ranne;
> In helpe wherof the blood therto did glyde,
> And left my face boeth pale and wann.

[4] Petrarch lends his name to the whole Renaissance lyric celebration of love that stems from Provence, whether the lyric is in strict sonnet form or not. His followers in Italy and in France did not always insist upon spiritualization of love.

[5] See Mott, *The System of Courtly Love*, ch. i. See also John, *The Elizabethan Sonnet Sequences*, pp. 55–56.

[6] This is true even in the satiric poetry of John Marston and John Donne. The former, to be sure, offers no substitute for Petrarchan courtesy; he merely denounces it.

> Then was I like a man for woo amasyd,
> Or like the byrde that flyeth into the fyer;
> For whyll that I on her beaulte gasyd,
> The more I burnt in my desyre.[7]

In Daniel's sonnets, as in those of Spenser, the origin of Platonic love, like that of sexual passion, is still that described in twelfth-century romance. Daniel thus speaks of his

> ... chaste desiers, the ever burning tapers,
> Inkindled by her eyes celestiall fiers.[8]

So, too, the eyes of Spenser's mistress are given as "hart thrilling,"[9] though Christianized to represent divine passion:

> ... to the Maker selfe they likest be
> whose light doth lighten all that here we see.[10]

Tottel's collection of lyrics bears witness that in the period before Elizabeth many writers were unconcerned with the validity of their romantic tradition. They were content merely to translate, to paraphrase, to manipulate romantic conceits into amorous verse.[11] The lyrics of Wyatt's most immediate disciple, Surrey, can stand for all. Here the expressions of passion are wholly conventional. Surrey shows little interest in the quarrel over traditional sentiment. The subject of his verse is the pleased despair [12] common to all sixteenth-century poetry. His poetic language is made up of standardized metaphor. He represents the Renais-

---

[7] *The Poems of Sir Thomas Wiat*, ed. by Foxwell, I, 288. See the commentary, II, 150–151, "The poem turns on the favourite Provençal conceit of the power of the eye, like a stroke of lightning, to pierce through to the heart of the lover ... Wiat collects conceits from Petrarch from stanza to stanza."

[8] Daniel, *Poems and a Defence of Ryme*, p. 35.

[9] *Spenser's Minor Poems*, ed. by Ernest de Sélincourt, Sonnet XII.

[10] *Ibid.*, Sonnet IX.

[11] See the remark of Sir John Harington, *Nugae antiquae*, II, 211: "The Queene stoode up and bade me reache forthe my arme to reste her theron. Oh, what swete burden to my next songe—Petrarcke shall eke out good matter for this business."

[12] The despairing lover pleading with an obdurate mistress in no sense illustrates the Renaissance conflict, but is part of the medieval testing of the amorous aspirant.

sance in its unquestioning acceptance of its romantic heritage.[13]

Many English writers of the new poetry were uninterested in critical analysis and were content with traditional habits of thought.[14] More than three decades after Surrey's lyrics had been published, both Daniel and Spenser kept alive a Platonized, romantic idealism, unchecked by any sense of its inadequacy as a transcript of normal experience. Indeed, Daniel's sonnet sequence, *Delia* (1592), does not even celebrate a personal love affair. It is merely a series of poetic compliments to Lady Mary, Countess of Pembroke, in which the theme of love is used as a fashionable literary device. In such a work, skeptical analysis of passion would be quite out of place. Whatever realistic suggestions of the momentary, physical nature of love appear in *Delia*, are purely decorative bits such as the following:

> But love whilst that thou maist be lov'd againe,
> Now whilst thy May hath fill'd thy lappe with flowers;
> Now whilst thy beautie beares without a staine;
> Now use thy Summer smiles ere winter lowres.[15]

We have already discovered a point of view similar to Daniel's in the *Faerie Queene*.[16] In Spenser's *Amoretti*, his personal celebration of love, there is also lack of insight into the nature of passion in real life. He accepts a Platonized garden of ideal love as a place of escape and solace, where

> . . . fayth doth fearlesse dwell in brasen towre,
> and spotlesse pleasure builds her sacred bowre.[17]

---

[13] Tillyard remarks, in *The Poetry of Sir Thomas Wyatt*, p. 35, that in Surrey "there is no more drama, no more sense of the here and now, than in most of the lyrics of Matthew Arnold."

[14] Lewis notes, in *The Allegory of Love*, p. 233: "Youthful vanity and dullness, determined to write, will almost certainly write in the dominant form of their epoch." This does not mean, however, that a real poet could content himself with mere poetic exercise, a customary charge against the Elizabethan sonneteer.

[15] Daniel, *Poems and a Defence of Ryme*, Sonnet XXXII, p. 26.

[16] See also the poetry of a host of minor Elizabethan sonneteers—e.g., Barnaby Barnes, Giles Fletcher, William Percy, William Smith, Bartholomew Griffin, Robert Tofte, Sir William Alexander, William Drummond.

[17] *Amoretti*, in *Spenser's Minor Poems*, Sonnet LXV.

Elizabethan Poetry

When he attempts to face passion realistically, as in the following lines, he is blind to any values in passion but lust.

> Let not one sparke of filthy lustfull fyre
> breake out, that may her sacred peace molest:
> ne one light glance of sensuall desyre
> Attempt to work her gentle mindes unrest.[18]

Poetry of Surrey, Daniel, and Spenser illustrates the fact that, during the entire Elizabethan period almost everyone who wrote of love began by accepting uncritically a romantic point of view. At the same time many lyricists sought, after the fashion of Lord Gaspar in *The Courtier*, to adapt to common experience these ideals that had been retained by the Petrarchan tradition. They were neither initially nor finally successful. All the forces that fed the humanistic thought of the day had failed to destroy belief in romantic sentiment. They merely turned the celebration of love in much of the new poetry into a kind of "amorous-odious sonnet." [19] Credulity was checked, not denied, by a consciousness of the difficulties one encounters in trying to keep romance alive in an actual love affair. Interest in conventional themes was shot through with distrust of their validity, not of their desirability.

Wyatt's Treatment of Lovers' Ideals

The first evidence in poetry of the sixteenth-century controversy over romance appears in the love lyrics of Sir Thomas Wyatt. They introduced the sentiments of Petrarch, complicated by a dominating sense of their unreality.[20] This individual quality

---

[18] *Ibid.*, Sonnet LXXXIV.

[19] The phrase is Gabriel Harvey's. (See Lee's discussion, *Elizabethan Sonnets*, I, cvi.) Lewis (*The Allegory of Love*, p. 145), remarks: "The history of courtly love from beginning to end may be described as an 'amorous-odious sonnet.'" But his reference is to the antifeminism which balanced medieval exaggerated ideals of love. There was always a kind of arrested conflict, in courtly love, as the palinode of Andreas Capellanus testifies. There is in Petrarch, and in Dante also, a residue of conflict between the imperfect nature of the lover and the perfection of love itself. One must distinguish such conflicts from that arising from the skeptical humanism of the Renaissance.

[20] This is not to imply that revolt from Petrarchan convention was an ex-

in his poetry is called by E. K. Chambers "the deeper accents of emotion,"[21] and has been described by Professor Tillyard as "not the personal but the dramatic element."[22] It was part of Petrarchan tradition to portray the mind as turned in upon itself, as exploring its own reactions to emotional experience. But with Wyatt this self-analysis is enlivened by the conviction that physical, not spiritual, possession should be the lover's goal. He tries, as did Lord Gaspar, to bring down to earth the highly imagined but impossibly poetic quality of the Petrarchan lyric. Wyatt's reaction is expressed succinctly in the following epigram. Here Wyatt voices a skepticism of ritualistic wooing much like that of the realistic lady in Chartier's fifteen-century poem, *La Belle Dame sans Merci:*

>Madame, withouten many wordes:
>Once I am sure, you will, or no.
>And if you will: then leave your boordes,
>And use your wit, and shew it so:
>For with a beck you shall me call.
>And if of one, that burns alway,
>Ye have pity or ruth at all:
>Answer hym fayer with yea, or nay.
>If it be yea: I shall be faine.
>Yf it be nay: frendes, as before.
>You shall another man obtayn:
>And I mine owne, and yours no more.[23]

Wyatt made his own age aware that there was a contention between love considered as a romantic ideal and the mutable fragments of an individual's passion. It is customary to say that

---

clusive Elizabethan phenomenon, but merely to show its presence as a part of the background of Elizabethan thought. For early satires on Petrarch in Italy see Pearson, *Elizabethan Love Conventions*, pp. 46–47.

[21] Quoted by Tillyard, in *The Poetry of Sir Thomas Wyatt*, p. 31.

[22] *Ibid.*, pp. 34 ff.

[23] In *Tottel's Miscellany*, ed. by Rollins, Vol. I, No. 53. Possibly from a douzaine of Mellin de Saint-Gelais (see Rollins's note, II, 171). The lady's answer to this poem, that the lover is not sufficiently aware of his subordinate, supplicating role in the ritual of adoration, is presented in Wiat, *The Poems*, ed. by Foxwell, I, 83.

Wyatt's affection for the nimble Anne Boleyn gave him the necessary insight for his revolt from traditional sentiment.[24] It may well be that Wyatt comments ironically, in such verses as the following, that he—a former suitor of the new queen—should have been one of the official party to accompany the royal couple to Calais in October, 1532:

> Some tyme I fled the fyre that me brent,
> By see by land, by water and by wynd;
> And now I folow the coles that be quent,
> From Dover to Calais against my mynde.
> Low how desire is boeth sprong and spent;
> And he may se that whilome was so blynd:
> And all his labor now he laugh to scorne
> Mashed in the breers that erst was all to-torne.[25]

The significance of this poem lies in its relation to the thought of the time, not in the fact that it may have arisen from the poet's own frustration. It represents the nascent Elizabethan sense of the destiny awaiting a romantic lover who ventures into the objective world. Regardless of the origin of the point of view, this poem makes clear Wyatt's critical perception of the painful results of lyric idealism.

The progress of the Elizabethan mind in attempting to divest itself of romantic artifice is reflected from the poetry of Wyatt to that of John Donne. In the history of this progress Wyatt is little more than a pioneer. He was the first to protest against the serious neglect of reality in the prescribed ritual of love. His poetry is the outpouring of his heart and may possibly be his despairing autobiography. His sense of the inadequacy of the Petrarchan descriptions of love reaches expression in the sharp contrasts of the poem "The lover waxeth wiser, and will not die for affection":

> Yet was I never of your love agreved,
> Nor never shall, while that my life doth last:
> But of hatyng my self, that date is past,

---
[24] See Chambers, *Sir Thomas Wyatt and Some Collected Studies*, pp. 130–145.
[25] In Wiat, *The Poems*, ed. by Foxwell, I, 49; see commentary, II, 64.

> And teares continual sore have me weried.
> I will not yet in my grave be buried,
> Nor on my tombe your name have fixed fast,
> As cruel cause, that did my sprite sone hast.
> From thunhappy boones by great sighes stirred.
> Then if an hart of amorous fayth and will
> Content your minde withouten doyng grief:
> Please it you so to this to do relief.
> If otherwise you seke for to fulfill
> Your wrath: you erre, and shal not as you wene,
> And you your self the cause thereof have bene.[26]

Conflict in Astrophel and Stella

In Sir Philip Sidney's *Astrophel and Stella* an important Elizabethan first made excellent poetry from the conflict which had been baldly expressed by Wyatt. The latter had been content to point out that traditional romance painted a thoroughly inadequate picture of amatory experience. Sidney carries the analysis of love further in the direction of realism. He suggests, on the one hand, that the surviving ritual of romance does not allow for a psychological adjustment between an actual lover and his mistress. On the other hand, he notes that the transient, sexual nature of love [27] makes the faithfully despairing, unrequited lover of poets an absurd figure. In the second sonnet of *Astrophel and Stella*, for example, Sidney denies the time-honored convention that love must be awakened at first sight:

> I sawe and lik'd, I lik'd but loved not,
> I lov'd, but did not straight what Love decreede.

His rejection of romantic convention is expressed again in the fifth sonnet. The poet doubts the truth of the psychology of love which had survived in Petrarchan conceit.

---

[26] *Tottel's Miscellany*, ed. by Rollins, Vol. I, No. 38. This sonnet is an adaptation from Petrarch. Yet, as Miss Foxwell points out (Wiat, *The Poems*, II, 31), Wyatt completely reverses all that Petrarch says.

[27] The troubadours of Provence and the writers of courtly romances poeticized a love that was, in contradistinction, sexual in a highly idyllic fashion, and was never transient.

> It is most true, what wee call *Cupids* dart
> An Image is, which for our selves we carve:
> And fooles adore, in Temple of our hart.

Sidney's skepticism of poetic symbols turns Cupid and all his crew out of the Garden of Love, for a moment, to fend for themselves in the rude world of experience.

Sidney, however, reproduces the conflicting humanistic and idealistic impulses of his age in a quarrel more fundamental than one with poetic conceit. In the midst of his concern with purely lyric love he launches a critical, objective search for a more tangible reality. This conflict is expressed in such lines as those concluding sonnet fifty-two.

> Well Love, since this Demurre our sute doth staie,
> Let Vertue have that *Stellas* selfe, yet thus,
> That Vertue but that body graunt to us.

The same conflict is a constantly recurring theme in his sequence. It is expressed in the seventy-first sonnet.

> See while thy beautie drives my hart to love,
> As fast thy vertue bends that love to good:
> But ah, Desire still cries, give me some food.

The thought appears again in the seventy-second sonnet.

> But thou Desire, because thou wouldst have all:
> Now banisht art, but yet within my call.

Because this quarrel between physical and spiritual passion resulted from his acceptance of Petrarchan ideals, no satisfactory synthesis of the two was possible for Sidney. This quarrel suggests his wish to maintain the illusory lyricism of love and at the same time to make this lyricism come to life. That is, Sidney, like Lord Octavian in *The Courtier*, has attempted to force his lady to play the role of the mistress in the ritual of courtship. This was the Renaissance way of exalting love. At the same time, like Lord Gaspar, Sidney derides the traditional amorous system, because he finds that he needs something more substantial. Sidney's extremely literal reaction to romantic convention led to despair. Hence Sidney, seeking an escape from conflict as Cardinal Bembo had done, and Lucretius before him, is finally driven to conclude that the pursuit of love is a form of madness. He escapes from a tangle of inconsistent attitudes by denying the very palpable facts with which he had challenged romance. Love and sexuality become identified, only to be dismissed together.

> Thou blind mans marke, thou fooles selfe chosen snare,
> Fond fancies scum, and dregs of scattred thought,
> Band of all evils, cradle of causelesse care,
> Thou web of will, whose end is never wrought.
> Desire, desire I have too dearely bought,
> With prise of mangled mind thy worthlesse ware,
> Too long, too long asleepe thou hast me brought,
> Who should my mind to higher things prepare.[28]

While Lucretius, influenced by Roman modes of thought, concluded that all "love" (that is, any imagined perfection beyond sexuality) is madness, Bembo and Sidney, with a twelfth-century heritage, came to the opposite conclusion. They voice, on the one hand, a Platonist's, on the other, an ascetic's retreat from contending points of view. For Sidney, however, the surrender of romance was a somewhat despairing one. In his final retraction Sidney grudgingly returns to the philosophy of the medieval church.

> Leave me ô Love, which reachest but to dust,
> And thou my mind aspire to higher things:
> Grow rich in that which never taketh rust:
> What ever fades, but fading pleasure brings.[29]

Realistic Greville

What had been suggested conflict in Wyatt becomes explicit in Sidney. But Sidney does find a way out, if somewhat belatedly,

---

[28] Sidney, *Certaine Sonets Written by Sir Philip Sidney: Never before Printed* (1598), in his *The Complete Works*, ed. by Feuillerat, II, 322. For the relationship of this and the following sonnet to *Astrophel and Stella*, see Wilson, *Sir Philip Sidney*, p. 202. It has been suggested that Bruno's attack on the courtier's worship of woman, in *De gli eroici furori* (1585) influenced this particular lyric. Bruno's work was dedicated to Sidney. See Yates, *A Study in Love's Labour's Lost*, pp. 104–105; see also Boulting, *Giordano Bruno, His Life, Thought, and Martyrdom*, pp. 96–97.

[29] Sidney, *The Complete Works*, II, 322.

Elizabethan Poetry 133

by accepting an older religious pattern. Not so Sidney's friend Fulke Greville, the author of the realistic *Caelica* [30] sonnets, a cynical humanist, more intellectually than emotionally conscious of the fundamental dilemmas of his time. Greville's less famous poetry is interesting, not as giving direction to the Elizabethan conflict of amorous attitudes, but as taking direction from it. The burden of his general censure of the Elizabethan Renaissance, which he applies, specifically, in his profoundly anti-romantic *Caelica*, is that there is no practicable relationship between intellectual concepts (the imagined ideals which the mind begets) and the life of man. He sees the objective world of experienced reality, with which man must come to terms, forever in conflict with the ideal "knowledge" that haunts his brain.[31] Reality, to Fulke Greville, is the concrete, the definite, the palpable. Man's knowledge, therefore, is "neither to be enjoy'd, nor yet discarded." [32] It is, perhaps, a necessary illusion, which, however, is seen as precisely that by the intuitive nature of man.

> Yet when each of us in his owne heart lookes,
> He findes the God there farre unlike his bookes.[33]

Greville joins with other poets of his time in paying tribute to love. But he brings the whole system of Provençal sentiment preserved in Petrarchan convention into conflict with a desire to give body to lovers' ideals. For Greville the objectivity of the realist always triumphs over the insecure knowledge of the romanticist. Passion, as described by the systematized courtesy of

[30] For the date of *Caelica* see Croll, *The Works of Fulke Greville*, pp. 7–17. The first 40 sonnets he places before 1586; 40–84, between 1586–1600; 85–110, after 1600.

[31] See Una Ellis-Fermor's comment (Introduction to Brooke, Fulke Greville Caelica, p. viii), "For him, man's knowledge is a subjective delusion, resting upon the evidence of imagination, reason and the senses, not necessarily connected at any point with the reality beyond him; his thinking life is a dream which, for the thinker who perceives that he is dreaming, becomes a nightmare."

[32] Brooke, Fulke Greville, *A Treatie of Humane Learning*, in *The Works in Verse and Prose Complete*, ed. by Grosart, Vol. II, stanza 120. See also stanzas 26–29, 34, 123.

[33] "Mustapha," in *The Works in Verse and Prose Complete*, III, 417 (final couplet from "Chorus Sacerdotum").

the Middle Ages must therefore be recognized as an abstraction, not as a fact. Hence, Greville's admonition to a lover,

> For those sweet glories, which you doe aspire,
> Must, as Idea's, only be embraced.[34]

This point of view, though stated with different symbols, runs through his whole sonnet sequence. His suggested escape is not Platonic doctrine, not spirituality. It is to abandon amorous dreaming for the sharp actualities of experience.

> Angells enioy the heavens' inward Quires:
> Starre-gazers only multiply desires.[35]

There is no palinode, no retreat, in Greville. Analysis is more important to him than emotional tranquility. Love is complex only when it confuses a romantic absolute with mutable reality. This is shown in his address to Cupid.

> I tooke your oath of dalliance and desire,
> Myra did so inspire me with her graces,
> But like a Wag that sets the straw on fire,
> You running to doe harme in other places,
> Sware what is felt with hand, or seene with eye,
> As mortall, must feele sicknesse, age and dye.[36]

Phrased in slightly different fashion, the same thought appears in the lines

> Thus our Delights, like faire shapes in a glasse,
> Though pleasing to our senses, cannot last.[37]

Intellectually (though certainly not emotionally) Greville's conception of love often approaches the disenchanted attitude of the Ovid of *Ars amatoria*. But the parallelism between the two is no more exact than that between Bembo and Lucretius; the Middle Ages lies between them. Whereas Ovid expressed amusement at the fantastic, preposterous illusions of the Roman lover,

---

[34] Brook, *Caelica*, Sonnet X, in *Certaine Learned and Elegant Workes*.
[35] *Ibid.*, Sonnet XVII (with a possible reference to Sidney's *Stella*).
[36] *Ibid.*, Sonnet XXVII.
[37] *Ibid.*, Sonnet XLI.

Elizabethan Poetry

Greville, in conflict with an accepted romanticism, expressed only resignation.

> Let no Love-desiring heart,
> In the Starres goe seeke his fate,
> Love is onely Natures art,
> Wonder hinders love and hate.
> None can well behold with eyes,
> But what underneath him lies.[38]

Minor Amorous Poets

The conventions and sentiments of courtly love continued to be celebrated in the amorous verse of nearly all Elizabethan poets down to about 1600, when Elizabethan literary taste moves toward seventeenth-century skepticism.[39] As one approaches the end of the century, however, he finds that this Renaissance quarrel with romantic convention has penetrated sonnet sequences which are mere collections of literary artifice. Thus, in Robert Tofte's sonnets,[40] published in 1597, which follow for the most part the well-worn complimentary pattern, love is a customary swooning to death.

> Content am I to loose this life of mine,
> Whilst I doo kisse that lovely lip of thine.[41]

But spread thinly through one sonnet in Tofte's series and almost lost in the manipulation of stock figures of speech, there emerges the perplexity voiced by Wyatt, Sidney, and Greville.

> The Beautie that in Paradice doth grow,
> Lively appeares in my sweet Goddesse face,
> From whence (as from a christall River) flow
> Favour devine, and comelines of grace.
> But in her daintie (yet too cruell) Brest
> More crueltie and hardnes doth abound,

---

[38] *Ibid.*, Sonnet LV.

[39] This fact is witnessed in drama, as well as in poetry, in the comedies of Ben Jonson, John Marston, and Shakespeare.

[40] Tofte, *Laura, the Toyes of a Traveller; or, The Feast of Fancie*, dedicated to Lady Lucy, sister to Henry, Earl of Northumberland.

[41] *Ibid.*, Sonnet X, Part I.

> Than doth in painfull Purgatorie rest:
> So that (at once) she's faire and cruell found
> When in her face and breast, (ah grief to tell)
> Bright Heaven she showes, and craftie hides dark hell.[42]

One cannot mark the precise moment when poets who expressed a skeptical, realistic attitude (which had invaded and complicated even the works of such a minor poet as Tofte) turned from questioning the Petrarchan tradition to mock it. Shortly before 1600, however, interest in the monotonous artifice of both the matter and the manner of Elizabethan sonneteering love began to decline. With the passing of an age values had changed. The pained astonishment voiced by both Wyatt and Sidney that their heritage of romance could not be assimilated into experience turns to a cry of annoyance. The traditional ideals, themselves never wholly denied even by Greville, begin to be reviled. They become targets, not for complaint, but for satiric jest. It has been suggested that such a triumph for skepticism appears first in the sonnet sequence of Richard Linche, *Diella*.[43] The voluptuous titillating figures of speech with which Linche occasionally embellishes this sequence are, indeed, a flippant rather than a seriously considered questioning of romance. Linche himself, in his one memorable use of stereotyped conceit, admits as much. He has a wandering and a too curious eye.

> Mine eyes were greedy whirlepooles sucking in
> that heavenly faire which me of rest bereaves.[44]

But even his most erotic sonnets, in which Miss Pearson finds "the coarse, the obscene," [45] are objective, and express no great surge of revolt. His romantic flights are somewhat restrained by his awareness that love is part gossamer, part sex.

[42] *Ibid.*, Sonnet XII, Part I.
[43] Pearson, *Elizabethan Love Conventions*, pp. 136 ff., groups together with Lynche, the author of *Zepheria*, Barnfield, Constable, and Lodge.
[44] Lynche, *Poems by Richard Linche, Gentleman* (1596), ed. by Grosart, Sonnet VIII.
[45] Pearson, *Elizabethan Love Conventions*, p. 137.

Satire in Drayton and Marston

An actual change in attitude toward romantic love sentiment appears almost simultaneously in the poetry of Michael Drayton, John Marston, and John Donne.[46] One becomes aware of this change when one finds these writers treating the traditional celebration of love as though it were a kind of polite fiction.[47] Drayton expresses this novel point of view infrequently. He never dismisses tradition in the downright fashion of either Marston or Donne. Indeed, in Drayton's initial sequence, published in 1594,[48] his sonnets are largely conventional renderings of Petrarchan sentiment, with only a slight sense of its Renaissance incongruity in evidence. The neophyte, the amorous aspirant, prostrates himself in adoration, begging his lady to

> Receave the incense which I offer heere,
> By my strong fayth ascending to thy fame.[49]

But even in such a mood, Drayton occasionally lets his eyes wander from the adored lady, to become fully aware of the contradictions of passion.

> But still, distracted in loves lunacy,
> And Bedlam like thus raving in my griefe,
> Now rayle upon her hayre, now on her eye,
> Now call her Godesse, then I call her thiefe;
> Now I deny her, then I doe confesse her,
> Now I doe curse her, then againe I blesse her.[50]

With the publication of his sonnets to *Idea*, in 1599, however,

---

[46] The "gulling" sonnets of Sir John Davies ought, possibly, to be mentioned. But they are a mere *tour de force*, symptomatic rather than significant. See Lee, *Elizabethan Sonnets*, I, cvi–cvii.

[47] Except for Shakespeare's *Sonnets*, reserved for a later and special treatment, the poems of these men were the first to express this liberating point of view.

[48] Drayton, *Ideas Mirrour, Amours in Quatorzains*, 1594.

[49] Drayton, *Ideas Mirrour*, in *Minor Poems of Michael Drayton*, ed. by Brett, Sonnet I, p. 2. Drayton's additions to his sequence are not given chronologically in the more recent text, *The Works of Michael Drayton*, ed. by Hebel.

[50] *Ibid.*, p. 23, Sonnet XLIII.

Drayton begins to prey upon Petrarchan sentiment as do Marston and Donne in their satires. In his second sonnet of this year, Drayton shows a change in attitude from that of 1594.

> No far-fetch'd sigh shall ever wound my brest,
> Love from mine eye, a teare shall never wring,
> Nor in ah-mees my whyning Sonets drest,
> (A Libertine) fantasticklie I sing;
> My verse is the true image of my mind,
> Ever in motion, still desiring change,
> To choyce of all varietie inclin'd,
> And in all humors sportively I range;
> My active Muse is of the worlds right straine,
> That cannot long one fashion entertaine.[51]

This revolt is not like that found in Sidney or Greville. It is a change in concept. The closing couplet gives the clew. Drayton views the old ritual of adoration more in the spirit of the seventeenth-century Suckling: that is, as a mere fashion, a whim, a mannerism of the social world. In this 1599 series Drayton further elaborates his divergence from the conflict of attitudes expressed in the earlier Elizabethan sonnet. Let those who will, return to earlier times and read "some Sidney, Constable, some Daniell," Drayton admonishes. His "wanton verse nere keepes one certaine stay":

> Like me that lust, my honest merry rimes,
> Nor care for Criticke, nor regard the times.[52]

Two or three of the poems added to the final edition of his sequence, in 1619, carry the Elizabethan conflict quite beyond the romantic age from which it draws significance. In at least one sonnet Drayton makes realism too oppressive. He exaggerates his denial of what conventionally was supposed to be immutable love, until it becomes vicious satire and not at all in the spirit of the age that was disappearing. The sonnet in question depicts his bitter regret that he cannot take revenge for his lady's disdain by seeing her in her haggard age:

[51] *Ibid.*, p. 28, Sonnet II.   [52] *Ibid.*, p. 29, Sonnet III.

There's nothing grieves me, but that Age should haste,
That in my dayes I may not see thee old,
That where those two cleare sparkling Eyes are plac'd
Onely two Loope-holes, then I might behold.
That lovely, arched, yvorie, pollish'd Brow,
Defac'd with Wrinkles, that I might but see;
Thy daintie Hayre, so curl'd, and crisped now,
Like grizzled Mosse upon some aged Tree;
Thy Cheeke, now flush with Roses, sunke and leane,
Thy Lips, with age, as any Wafer thinne,
Thy Pearly teeth out of thy head so cleane,
That when thou feed'st, the Nose shall touch thy Chinne:
These Lines that now thou scorn'st, which should delight thee,
Then would I make thee read, but to despight thee.[53]

The concern of the strictly Elizabethan contention, from its beginning in Wyatt, had been with the unreality of both the Petrarchan asceticism and the prescribed ritual of conquest. Possibly with the eroticism of Linche, certainly with the satiric use of conceited artifice in Drayton, both burdens of Elizabethan romantic idealism begin to be dropped. In Marston's satires this process is further advanced. Influenced, perhaps, both by Ovid and by the changing taste of the closing century, which was beginning to view romance as old fashioned, Marston mocks the courtier who tries to shape his passion in the mold of courtesy.

> He that can purpose it [54] in dainty rhymes,
> Can set his face, and with his eye can speak,
> Can dally with his mistress' dangling feak,
> And wish that he were it, to kiss her eye
> And flare about her beauty's deity:—

[53] *Ibid.*, p. 52, Sonnet VIII. The theme of passing youth need not descend to such realism. See the idyllic quality of this same theme in the more famous sonnets of Ronsard, "Quand vous serez vielle," and "Mignonne, allons voir si la rose." The details in Drayton's poems are very like those found in verses from Villon's *Grand Testament*. But in Villon it is an old prostitute who examines her own infirmities as she laments her former charms. Drayton's point of view is slightly different. See Villon, *The Complete Works of François Villon*, tr. by Nicolson, pp. 38-40.

[54] That is, his lust.

> Tut! he is famous for his revelling,
> For fine set speeches, and for sonnetting;
> He scorns the viol and the scraping stick,
> And yet's but broker of another's wit.
> Certes, if all things were well known and view'd
> He doth but champ that which another chew'd.
> Come, come, Castilion, skin thy posset curd,
> Show thy queer substance, worthless, most absurd.
> Take ceremonious compliment from thee!
> Alas! I see Castilio's beggary.[55]

Marston here clearly regards the conventions of courtly love as disingenuous disguises for mere sexuality and ruthlessly strikes them down. Even more vehement is Marston's castigation of the Elizabethan gentleman who performs the old prescribed ritual of suffering, despairing courtship. The amorist who used it as cloak for his lust was a hypocrite. The lover who believed in its truth and beauty was a fool and a natural object of derision.

> For when my ears received a fearful sound
> That he was sick, I went, and there I found
> Him laid of love, and newly brought to bed
> Of monstrous folly and a frantic head.
> His chamber hang'd about with elegies,
> With sad complaints of his love's miseries;
> His windows strew'd with sonnets, and the glass
> Drawn full of love-knots. I approach'd the ass
> And straight he weeps, and sighs some sonnet out
> To his fair love! And then he goes about
> For to perfume her rare perfection
> With some sweet-smelling pink epitheton;
> Then with a melting look he writhes his head,
> And straight in passion riseth in his bed;
> And having kiss'd his hand, stroke up his hair,
> Made a French conge, cries, "O cruel fair!"
> To the antic bedpost.[56]

---

[55] Marston, *The Metamorphosis of Pygmalions Image and Certain Satyres* (1598), in Marston, *The Works*, ed. by A. H. Bullen, III, 264–265, "Satire I."
[56] *Ibid.*, III, 278, "Satire III."

Elizabethan Poetry

This poem signalizes the complete disintegration of a purely romantic attitude, but it fails to clear the way for the emergence of a new point of view. Save for references to sonnets, Marston's excoriation might be directed at Chaucer's Troilus, so closely does it ridicule the traditions of medieval romance. Such triumph as cynical realism enjoyed in Drayton or in Marston, then,[57] goes too far. It is, like Bembo's Platonism, an exaggeration of one of the bases of the conflicting attitudes toward love current in the Renaissance. Thus it serves its writer as a momentary retreat from inconsistencies, but does not suggest a way to harmonize them.

Donne's Solution to Lovers' Difficulties

Only with John Donne, the last of the great poets whose conceptions of love were formed out of the complex fusion of medieval tradition and Renaissance humanism, do the perplexities of love give way to enlightenment. John Donne, like Fulke Greville, represents the Renaissance mind at its subtlest—turning in upon itself, examining subjectively traditional emotions and attitudes. He is quite aware that the Elizabethan difficulties of love are reducible to the conflict between sex experience and the idealized experience formalized by the medieval imagination.

> . . . lovers dreame a rich and long delight,
> But get a winter-seeming summers night.[58]

But he tries to get beyond this incongruity to something more quintessential. Hence he expresses the wish to return to a time before these amorous conventions of romance were established.

> I long to talke with some old lovers ghost,
> Who dyed before the god of Love was borne:
> I cannot thinke that hee, who then lov'd most,
> Sunke so low, as to love one which did scorne.
> But since this god produc'd a destinie,

[57] As has already been indicated in Chapter II.
[58] Donne, *The Poems*, ed. by Grierson, "Loves Alchymie," I, 39.

> And that vice-nature, custome, lets it be;
> I must love her, that loves not mee.[59]

In his desire to escape a customary fidelity to his lady, whether she would or no, Donne praises the quite opposite attitude of complete inconstancy. This is the theme of such poems as "Womans Constancy" and "The Indifferent."

> Rob mee, but binde me not, and let me goe.
> Must I, who came to travaile throw you,
> Grow your fixt subject, because you are true?[60]

A philosophical wit keeps this libertine poetry of John Donne from descending to the exaggerated mockery of John Marston's portraits of traditional lovers, on the one hand, or the ribaldry of Ovid, on the other. Donne's love poetry is essentially a search for a new emotional or moral pattern to be formed from the complicated snarl of Renaissance thought. He teases romantic idealism outrageously. Yet in a few of his lyrics he seems gradually to grow to an understanding that the romance and the realities of passion can exist side by side. This understanding lends meaning to the paradoxical ideas expressed in his poem "Lovers Infiniteness."[61] The following verses from "A Valediction: Forbidding Mourning" illustrate Donne's attempt to express the coexistence of the flesh and the spirit.

> Dull sublunary lovers love
> (Whose soul is sense) cannot admit
> Absence, because it doth remove
> Those things which elemented it.
>
> But we by a love so much refin'd,
> That our selves know not what it is,
> Inter-assured of the mind,
> Care lesse eyes, lips, and hands to misse.[62]

Donne's verses show that he realizes that an individual must make subtle psychological adjustments between illusion and fact before he can resolve the conflict inherent in love as the Renais-

---

[59] *Ibid.*, "Loves Deitie," I, 54.
[60] *Ibid.*, "The Indifferent," I, 12.
[61] *Ibid.*, I, 18.
[62] *Ibid.*, I, 50.

sance conceived and repeatedly described the passion. Out of the tremendous outpouring of amorous complaint of the whole age, only in Donne's poetry, as in the love-game comedy, does there emerge what is, according to Professor Grierson, "the suggestion of a new philosophy of love, which, if less transcendental than that of Dante, rests on a juster, because a less dualistic and ascetic, conception of the nature of the love of man and woman." [63] The whole body of poetry in which the Elizabethan humanistic impulse clashed with traditional, exaggeratedly idyllic love comes to rest in verses of Donne's such as these from "The Ecstasy."

> As our blood labours to beget
> Spirits, as like soules as it can,
> Because such fingers need to knit
> That subtile knot which makes us man:
>
> So must pure lovers soules descend
> T'affections, and to faculties,
> Which sense may reach and apprehend,
> Else a great prince in prison lies.[64]

Donne's perception, however, was too ingenious. His suggestion that the imaginative, amorous flights of the spirit are merely complementary to transient, physical desires, that an adjustment can be made whereby both take on significance, placed too great a strain on the credulity of his own time.[65] He established no philosophy of love easily understood and assimilated as was that of Ovid. A paradoxical conception of love is best presented for intuitive acceptance, as it was in comedy, not in cunning, analytic exposition. Elizabethan comedy gave its answer to the Renaissance conflict in a paradoxical fashion, as did Donne in his poetry, but with a difference. Both draw sustenance, take on meaning, when viewed as partial expressions of the complex Elizabethan preoccupation with a medieval romantic inheritance. But the acceptance in comedy of the ideal as the complementary half of

---

[63] *Ibid.*, II, xxxv.   [64] *Ibid.*, I, 53.
[65] See Ben Jonson's famous remark that Donne, "for not being understood, would perish" (*Ben Jonson's Conversations with William Drummond of Hawthornden*, ed. by Patterson, p. 18).

the real is purely emotional. Such acceptance is possible only after a momentary, unmarked surrender by the audience of its difficulties. It is the abandonment of conflict through comic and irrational response.

Conflicting Ideas in Elizabethan Poetry and Comedy

What such a book as *The Courtier* and four decades of Elizabethan amorous complaint did for comedy was to make current and important an emotional difficulty that could serve the purposes of drama. The Elizabethan poet's critical approach to traditional romance created a tension between opposing conceptions of love. Natural difficulties of lovers were exaggerated. From the introduction of Petrarchan courtly love in Wyatt's verse to its castigation in that of Drayton and Marston, the conflict became increasingly apparent. Writers expressed various degrees of despair over their inability to reconcile romantic love with the limitations of their ladies, or more broadly with the effects of time upon their beauty, or with the mutability of desire. The reasons for this despair were acknowledged with varying degrees of awareness. The only constant element in this poetry was the display of incompatible attitudes. There were such forms of palinode and retreat as that offered by Platonism (as in Spenser and, to some degree, in Sidney), by resignation (as in Greville), and by ridicule (as in Drayton and Marston). But they were all makeshifts. What the poets actually accomplished was to create a need for a practicable, emotional release, an escape from perplexity that should lead, not to despair, but to delight. And it was this psychological need, this emotional turmoil, that was satisfied dramatically by the love-game comedy.

There is evidence more specific than identity of conflicting attitudes in two literary mediums that links the love-game comedy to the amorous problems of the Elizabethan lyric. Much of the poetry in the Petrarchan tradition is itself dramatic. When controversial conceptions of love are made articulate in poetry, it is often in the form of a contention between the poet and his lady.

Elizabethan Poetry

A conflict of attitudes is easily and naturally personified, and at such a moment in Elizabethan poetry, as in *The Courtier*, fragments of a sex duel appear. Such dramatization is apparent, for example, in Wyatt's lyric already referred to.

> Madame, withouten many wordes,
> Once I am sure, you will, or no.[66]

Here, like Shakespeare's Berowne, Wyatt momentarily makes a realistic approach to traditional courtship. In the sonnet below Sidney dramatizes a similar situation. Like Wyatt, he takes the humanistic, critical point of view in controversy with Stella, who maintains the Petrarchan, spiritualized sentiment.

> Late tyr'd with woe, even ready for to pine
> With rage of love, I call my Love unkinde.
> She in whose eyes, loves fyres unfelt doe shine,
> Sweetlie saide; I true love in her shoulde finde.
> I joy, but straight thus watred was my wine:
> That love she did, but with a love not blinde.
> Which would not let me, whome she lov'd decline,
> From Nobler course, fit for my birth and minde.
> And therefore by her loves Authoritie;
> Wilde me these Tempests of vaine love to flee:
> And Anchor fast my selfe on vertues shore.
> Alas if this the onelie mettall be,
> Of love newe coyn'd to helpe my beggery:
> Deere, love me not, that you may love me more.[67]

It is when the poet's "Stella" bears the attack, only to return it, as does the lady in *The Courtier*, that one is on the way to the fully developed sex duel of drama. Sidney even hints that his mistress expressed some of the witty scorn of Benedick's Beatrice.

> . . . her heart is such a Cytadell.
> So fortified with wit, stor'd with disdaine:
> That to winne it, is all the skill and paine.[68]

---

[66] Wyatt, *Tottel's Miscellany*, No. 53. See also, No. 54, "To his love whom he had kissed against her will"; No. 56, "To his love from whom he hadd her gloves."
[67] Sidney, *Astrophel and Stella*, Sonnet LXII.
[68] *Ibid.*, Sonnet XII.

The well known poetic debate between Marlowe's passionate shepherd and Raleigh's realistic nymph, although part of a pastoral rather than a Petrarchan fashion, personifies and therefore dramatizes this essential conflict between idyllic courtesy and experienced love. As in Sidney, so here, suggestions of the satirically critical and at the same time witty possibilities of the sex duel in drama appear in the nymph's reply:

> But could youth last, and love still breede,
> Had joyes no date, nor age no neede,
> Then these delights my minde might move,
> To live with thee, and be thy love.[69]

John Donne's metamorphosis of Marlowe's poem into "The Baite" likewise presents contention in dramatized form. But it is personified libertinism and far too satiric to parallel the sex duels found in Shakespeare's light comedies. This is what one might expect in the period when Elizabethan literary taste was undergoing rapid, realistic transformation. Since Donne and Shakespeare reconcile lovers' difficulties, one might expect the poetry of the one to resemble the comedies of the other. Donne's attitude toward the paradoxical nature of love remained a closely reasoned one, quite outside the realm of drama.

All Renaissance discussion of the problems of love, whether in conduct book or in poetry, made current a psychological dilemma that could be used by the dramatist. Although no strictly chronological analysis of the progression of this Elizabethan conflict is valid, during the decade 1580–1590 the issues had been made clear enough. Thus, when the dramatization of these contending attitudes first appeared in the plays of John Lyly, it had as a background the discussions of *The Courtier* and the poetry of Wyatt and Sidney. The final five years of the sixteenth century mark the emergence of the completed pattern of the love-game in Shakespeare, which parallels in time the poetry of Donne. But besides making articulate the love conflict of the Renaissance, this Elizabethan poetry occasionally goes farther and dramatizes the

---

[69] *England's Helicon*, ed. by Rollins, I, 186, No. 138. Rollins challenges Raleigh's authorship, II, 189–190.

conflict. The sonnet, as a sequence of incidents in the poet's court ship, as a poetic dialogue to one's lady, always suggested drama in miniature. When dramatically apprehended individuals occasionally emerge from such poetry, the lover's problems may be for a moment incarnate. But in such poetry there is always lacking the final element essential to the comedies of Lyly and Shakespeare: the comic illusion of a resolution of forces.

Professor Tillyard has remarked that "it was Donne who carried on the movement that Wyatt had begun, and let the Elizabethan drama he loved into the Elizabethan lyric he despised." [70] The reverse of this statement is also true. To permit the conflict of attitudes that has been described in the Elizabethan lyric to enter the drama, was to transform the sex duel into the love-game comedy.

[70] Tillyard, *The Poetry of Sir Thomas Wyatt*, p. 36.

· IX ·

Lyly's Quarreling Lovers

ROMANCE had been rejected by Drayton and Marston; it had been idealized beyond contamination from real life by Spenser and Cardinal Bembo; it had been described by John Donne as the spiritual half of love, which in normal experience exists on both spiritual and physical levels. John Lyly was the first Elizabethan writer to perceive that the opposed attitudes in this quarrel over romance could be used for another purpose. They could be embodied in a series of characters whose conflicts could be used as the basis of a sustained narrative and at the same time illustrate one of the significant problems of the day. Lyly explores the possibilities of his discovery [1] in the two parts of his novel *Euphues, the Anatomy of Wit* (1578) and *Euphues and His England* (1580). He turns his back on the bucolic enchantments which sustain Sidney's *Arcadia*,[2] for example. There is no escaping the realities of the actual world in *Euphues;* [3] its

---

[1] Bond, in Lyly, *The Complete Works* (I, 159), notes the advance in *Euphues* over the mere recapitulation of medieval idyllic sentiment in other Elizabethan romance, when he states that *Euphues* is "the first holding-up to English men and women of the mirror of their own life and loves." Because this novel displays the "inner or mental side, the subjective history, of the tender passion . . . we pass at once from mediaevalism and classic survival, and enter the modern world" (*ibid.*, I, 161).

[2] The usual Elizabethan prose romance, like Sidney's *Arcadia*, ca. 1580, combines the medieval idealized conception of love and the ritual and psychology of courtly romance with the pastoral tradition inaugurated by Boccaccio in his *Ameto*. It also incorporates some of the spirit as well as the narrative material of the late Greek romances. See *Cambridge History of English Literature*, III, 351–355, "Elizabethan Prose Fiction." See also Wolff, *Greek Romances in Elizabethan Prose Fiction*. For the followers of Sidney, cf. Greene's *Pandosto* (1588), *Menaphon* (1589), and Lodge's *Rosalynd* (1590).

[3] For contrast see *The Countesse of Pembrokes Arcadia*, original version,

main concern is to exhibit the perplexities of love as they appeared to the ladies and gentlemen of the sixteenth century.

The plot of *Euphues* concerns three lovers, each of whom fails in his attempt to experience traditional romantic passion. The most realistic of the three, the one least subservient to the despairing ritual of adoration which convention decreed, is Euphues. This is not to say that he escapes romance. Love enters his heart through the eye and at his first sight of his lady. He is seated opposite her at dinner, and he "fed of one dish which ever stoode before him, the beautie of Lucilla. Heere Euphues at first sight was so kyndled with desyre, that almost he was lyke to burn to coales." [4] He also endures the customary love-sickness for his mistress, crying out in his pain, "can men by no hearb, by no art, by no way procure a remedye for the impatient disease of love?" [5]

But the goal of Euphues's desire is far less exalted than that stipulated by courtly or Petrarchan ideals. He is indifferent to the ennobling power of love and to lovers' spiritual ecstasies. His wooing seeks only sexual union. He presents his suit to Lucilla, after the fashion of Drayton and Donne, by urging the very perishable nature of love. Of obdurate mistresses he says:

When the blacke crowes foote shall appeare in theyr eye, or the blacke Oxe treade on their foote, when their beautie shall be lyke the blasted Rose, theyr wealth wasted, their bodies worne, theyr faces wrinckled, their fyngers crooked, who will lyke of them in their age, who loved none in their youth? [6]

Furthermore, Euphues woos the lady already supposedly won

---

in Sidney, *The Complete Works*, ed. by Albert Feuillerat, IV, 9, where the Arcadian lover, Pyrocles, says that he "sawe no grass upon which hee thoughte Philoclea mighte happ to treade, but that hee envyed the happynes of yt."

[4] *Euphues, the Anatomy of Wit*, in Lyly, *The Complete Works*, ed. by Bond, I, 201. This much Euphues shares with Pyrocles of Sidney's *Arcadia*, who, merely seeing the picture of his lady, exclaims: "that beauty did pearse so through my eyes to my hart . . . that . . . the questyon ys . . . whether Loving I shall live or dye." Sidney, *The Complete Works*, IV, 14–15.

[5] *Euphues, the Anatomy of Wit*, in Lyly, *The Complete Works*, ed. by Bond, I, 208.

[6] *Ibid.*, I, 203.

by his friend Philautus,[7] and he justifies his treachery by mocking the idea that love is the one supreme, inviolable emotional experience; "he that cannot dissemble in love, is not worthy to live. I am of this minde, that both might and mallice, deceite and treacherie, all perjurie, anye impietie may lawfully be committed in love, which is lawlesse."[8]

When Euphues finds that Lucilla has forsaken him, even as she did Philautus, he repudiates romance, much as Sidney had done, by crying out against his own practices.

> What greater infamye, then to conferre the sharpe wit to the making of lewde Sonnets, to the idolatrous worshipping of . . . Ladies, to the vaine delights of fancie, to all kinde of vice as it were against kinde & course of nature?[9]

Henceforth he becomes a critic of the very ideals of love to which, despite his sense of reality, he had paid allegiance.[10] On the one hand, he generalizes skeptically from his own experience, finding that the ideals common to his age are remote from actual life. He attacks the principle of love at first sight by pointing out that "Love which should continue for ever, should not be begon in an houre, but slowly be taken in hande."[11] On the other hand, he cannot rid himself of the lingering conviction that all human love is wrong because it is basically carnal. We need not then be surprised that Euphues's advice to Philautus turns into a rehearsal of a kind of dismal, worldly wisdom, a Puritan's cry to avoid the snares of courtly romance: "if thou canst not live chastly, chuse such an one, as maye be more commended for humilitie than beautie . . . Fond lust, causeth drye bones: and lewd pastimes, naked pursses."[12]

---

[7] The ubiquitous Renaissance quarrel over the relative value of friendship and love was one way of showing the unreality of traditional romance.

[8] *Ibid.*, I, 236.   [9] *Ibid.*, I, 252.

[10] Bond observes in Lyly, *The Complete Works*, I, 161–162, that "Euphues is the story of a young man's passion and disillusion . . . taking a somewhat melancholy pleasure in observing the workings of a passion in which he has no further share."

[11] *Euphues and His England*, Lyly, *The Complete Works*, II, 156.

[12] *Ibid.*, II, 16–17. This same note is struck when Euphues complains that

The second lover in Lyly's novel, Philautus, is less concerned than Euphues had been with the physical side of love. He seeks quite candidly the experience that had been described in twelfth-century romance. But Philautus is too ingenuous in his attempt, as his remarks to Euphues indicate:

> . . . let us goe devoutly to the shrine of our Saincts there to offer our devotion, for my books teach me, that such a wound must be healed wher it was first hurt, and for this disease we will use a common remedie . . . The eye that blinded thee, shall make thee see . . .[13]

The first woman to receive his attentions, Lucilla, leaves him for Euphues. Her infidelity, however, far from making him skeptical, acts as a spur to send him on still further quests for an earthly ambassadress from the medieval Garden of Love. And he enters England, so Lyly tells us, "carying the Image of Love, engraven in the bottome of his hart, & the picture of courtesie, imprinted in his face." [14] A man under the dominance of such an ideal is immediately re-entangled in the same despair over the witty Camilla [15] that he had already suffered for Lucilla. Following his lack of success with Camilla, he proceeds to woo and to wed Frauncis.

He represents the Renaissance in its absurdly determined effort to actualize an inherited theory of love. He is a follower of troubadour ideals, however, rather than Petrarchan, and shows the futility of most attempts to spiritualize passion. In reply to Euphues's philosophy, after the latter's reformation, that "the effect of love is faith, not luste, delightfull conference, not detestable concupiscence," [16] Philautus denies ascetic ideals a place in courtship.

---

passion has become the property of the lower classes. Everyone is now in love, craftsman, clown, and beggar. "And what can be the cause of these loving wormes, but onely idlenesse?" (*ibid.*, II, 181–182). Philautus accuses Euphues of alternating between St. Paul and Ovid in his attitude toward love (*ibid.*, II, 93).

[13] *Euphues, the Anatomy of Wit*, in Lyly, *The Complete Works*, ed. by Bond, I, 214–215.
[14] *Euphues and His England*, II, 84.
[15] *Ibid.*, II, 85–86.   [16] *Ibid.*, II, 158.

... it would doe me no more good, to see my Lady and not embrace hir, in the heate of my desire, then to see fire, and not warme me in the extremitie of my colde. No, no, Euphues, thou makest Love nothing but a continuall wooing, if thou barre it of the effect, and then is it infinite, or if thou allow it, and yet forbid it, a perpetuall warfare, and then is it intollerable.[17]

The third of these lovers to personify an aspect of the amorous conflict of the Renaissance, Fidus, is the least realistic and the most courtly. In his wooing of Iffida as if she were a lady out of medieval romance he shows that his bondage to idyllic love is almost complete. Of the three, only for Fidus the "measure of love is to have no meane, the end to be everlasting." [18] His final loss of his lady and his discovery that love is subject to the changes of time are not enough to make him disavow it, like Euphues, or to pursue it farther, like Philautus. He retreats from the world of experience and becomes a hermit in order to preserve his illusions. Fidus is not unaware of reality. Like Philautus he wishes the fruition of his idealized conception of love. Fidus is singular only in that he can be content with no less than such ideal fruition. Hence, though he has become one of love's anchorites, he realizes that he cannot escape the penalties of clinging to illusion. For all his fidelity, he concludes that love has "so many inconveniences hanging upon it, as to recken them all were infinite, and to taste but one of them, intollerable." [19]

By means of these three characters in *Euphues* Lyly suggests some of the difficulties which beset young men seeking the ideals of romance in the real world. Furthermore, here and there in his narrative Lyly anticipates the pattern of the love-game comedy by presenting the quarrel over the nature of love as a witty duel between the lovers and their ladies. Euphues and Lucilla, for

---

[17] *Ibid.*, II, 158–159. Violet Jeffery, in her book, *John Lyly and the Italian Renaissance*, p. 34, finds the Italian poets of the "dolce stil nuovo" to be the origin of Lyly's traditional amorous idealism, with this difference: "The Italian could treat of love from the purely intellectual point of view, quite apart from moral considerations, and could maintain sincerely in theory an attitude belied by practical life. Lyly, the Englishman, failed to separate theory and practice. His common sense as used in practical life, must of necessity step in. For him, theory and practice must be in complete harmony."
[18] *Ibid.*, II, 52.
[19] *Ibid.*, II, 80.

example, come to accept each other (and romance of a sort) only after a sharp verbal skirmish concerning current and inconsistent attitudes toward love.[20] Fidus, in his duels of wit with Iffida, defends the ritual of courtesy, while she advocates a realistic contempt of it. He is appalled by her refusal to accept either the idealized sentiment of love or the adoration of a would-be suitor [21] and pours scorn upon her skepticism:

> Is this the guerdon for good wil, is this the courtesie of Ladies, the lyfe of Courtiers, the foode of lovers? Ah Iffida, little dost thou know the force of affection, & therefore thou rewardest it lightly, neither shewing curtesie lyke a Lover, nor giving thankes lyke a Ladye.[22]

But Iffida is moved only to derision. She mocks Fidus by suggesting: "And to the ende I might stoope to your lure, I pray begin to hate me, that I may love you." [23]

Philautus quarrels with Camilla in a different fashion. Although suffering all the required despair of the aspiring lover, he lets his own common sense triumph. He approaches his lady, not protesting humility and adoration, but, like Berowne and Benedick, almost denouncing that for which he sues. Ladies pretend, he says, "a great skyrmishe at the first, yet are boorded willinglye at the last. I meane therefore to tell you this which is all, that I love you." [24] But he concludes this speech, belying himself, "wringing hir by the hand," and Camilla turns upon him for his lack of romantic pretense, crying, "You fall from one thing to an other, using no decorum, except this, that you study to have your discourse as farre voyde of sence, as your face is of favor." [25]

In these lovers' skirmishes is found a sophisticated banter be-

---

[20] See *Euphues, the Anatomy of Wit*, in Lyly, *The Complete Works*, ed. by Bond, I, 220: "in the ende, arguing wittilly upon certeine questions, they fell to suche agreement as poore Philautus woulde not have agreed unto if hee had bene present, yet alwayes keepinge the body undefiled."
[21] See Iffida's speech (*Euphues and His England*, II, 64): "if your request be reasonable a word wil serve, if not, a thousand wil not suffice . . . use not tedious discourses or colours of retorick, which though they be thought courtly, yet are they not esteemed necessary."
[22] *Ibid.*, II, 66.　　[23] *Ibid.*, II, 67.　　[24] *Ibid.*, II, 105.
[25] *Ibid.*, II, 106. Philautus's final, successful wooing of Frauncis is carried on by a sex duel (see *ibid.*, II, 174–180).

tween courtier and lady like that in Castiglione's treatise. It was this sort of dialogue, expressing inconsistencies in love, that was elaborated to carry the burden of lovers' quarrels in Shakespeare's comedies. Lyly, both as a stylist and as a Renaissance psychologist, was quite aware that this method of presenting men and women in love was new to his age. He comments that the amorous language of Henry VIII's time is now considered "barbarous": "in tymes past they used to wooe in playne tearmes, now in piked sentences.... And to that passe it is come, that they make an arte of that, which was woont to be thought naturall." [26] Even the despairing Fidus confesses that the one attribute in a woman that most sets his "fancies on edge" is her wit. When he is driven by Iffida's raillery to make a theoretical choice among three possibilities—a witty wanton, a fair fool, and an ugly saint —he chooses the one with wit, because "by hir wit she will ever conceale whom she loves, & to weare a horne and not knowe it, will do me no more harme then to eate a flye, and not see it." [27]

Pairs of contending lovers, as they emerge occasionally from *The Courtier* or from Elizabethan poetry, have been shown neither to solve their own conflict nor suggest a generally acceptable solution. In *Euphues*, however, wholly imaginary characters are involved in an imaginary narrative. They are free from the restrictions imposed by reality. Therefore Lyly is free, as neither Castiglione nor Sidney was, to harmonize these discordant concepts of love by the final union of the lovers who represent the conflict. He is free to present his characters as con-

[26] *Ibid.*, II, 57. For the relationship of wit, of rhetorical dialogue to discussion of amorous problems, see Crane, *Wit and Rhetoric in the Renaissance, the Formal Basis of Elizabethan Prose Style*, ch. xii, pp. 179-180, 195-202. Lyly gives explicit illustration of this new, controversial language of love when he cites the story of the "Magnifico" of Sienna (*Euphues and His England*, in Lyly, *The Complete Works*, ed. by Bond, II, 60).

[27] *Ibid.*, II, 63. For a discussion of parallels to this "question of love" debate, in the Italian Renaissance, see Jeffery, *John Lyly and the Italian Renaissance*, pp. 11-28. For a discussion of this same problem, in medieval parallel, cf. La Tour-Landry, *The Book of the Knight of La Tour-Landry*, pp. 15 ff.; see also Chaucer's "Wife of Bath's Tale," ll. 1219-1227.

cluding their sex duels by accepting each other and therewith the natural paradoxes of idyllic love in a skeptical world. But Lyly, at least in *Euphues*, only partially realized the dramatic and comic potentialities of this acceptance. The contentions in the two parts of *Euphues* give dramatic force to the amorous problem they present. But the lovers' quarrels, with the exception of that between Philautus and Frauncis, serve rather to separate the contestants and the attitudes they embody than to bring them together in any kind of harmony (as is done in *Much Ado*). Fidus accurately summarizes all their sex duels when he describes his own battle of wits with Iffida: "Many nips were returned that time betweene us, and some so bitter, that I thought them to proceede rather of mallice, to worke dispite, then of mirth to showe disporte." [28]

In *Euphues*, even when diverse opinions are reconciled by the marriage of the two contestants, comedy is not evoked. The ultimate surrender of Camilla to Surius is merely noted by Lyly in passing. It is highly anticlimactic, breaks no tension, comes almost as an afterthought. "By the preamble, you may gesse to what purpose the drift tended," he says. He draws a moral out of that which to be most effective dramatically should be immediately understood by the audience. There should be no such pointed comment as "This I note, that they that are most wise, most vertuous, most beautiful, are not free from the impressions of Fancy: For who would have thought that Camilla, who seemed to disdaine love, should so soone be entangled." [29] The final solution to the difficulties which have beset Philautus in his effort to find an acceptable mistress is presented in a similar manner. Lyly breaks the news of Philautus's successful pursuit of Frauncis in an exchange of letters (between Philautus and Euphues) which are mainly concerned with the lady's dowry and with the requisites of a successful married life.[30]

In *Euphues* Lyly presents the fact, of which his age was well aware, that men and women in love do not follow any rigidly

---

[28] *Euphues and His England*, II, 70.   [29] *Ibid.*, II, 184.
[30] *Ibid.*, II, 218–227.

prescribed code of behavior. The witty, consciously rhetorical dialogues between lovers show Lyly putting legs to a quarrel over romance and making it walk. His lovers' predicaments are not merely the hazards set up by the improbable events found, for example, in Sidney's Arcadian romance. The characters in *Euphues* dramatize the gulf between the effects of an actual love affair and the supposed effects prescribed by genteel tradition. But Lyly's lovers fail to create the illusion that they have solved the problems which beset them. They illustrate no dramatic and concerted reconciliation, as do the contestants in Shakespeare's *Much Ado*. For this reason, in Lyly's novel the pattern of the love-game comedy remains incomplete.

Contending Attitudes in Lyly's Comedies

In most of Lyly's comedies [31] (as in *Euphues*) he creates a series of lovers whose difficulties are the result of the sixteenth-century rebellion of common sense against the attenuated sentiments of romantic tradition. Lyly's presentation of this conflict in his dramas, however, is complicated by the fact that his characters are usually thought to reflect the ever changing infatuations of the queen and her courtiers.[32] Indeed, the allegorical significance of these characters may well have been Lyly's chief personal interest in them, since he hoped to make them appeal eloquently for his own preferment. For example, in Lyly's first

---

[31] The exceptions are *Midas*, a study of avarice, probably an allegory of Philip of Spain; *Mother Bombie*, an Elizabethan attempt at a Roman farce; and *Gallathea*, a pastoral comedy in which the traditions of romance are, for for the most part, accepted as valid. Love is no problem, but all fine gossamer, as stated in the epilogue (Lyly, *The Complete Works*, II, 472, ll. 8 *et sqq.*): "Cupid was begotten in a miste, nursed in Clowdes, and sucking onelie upon conceits. Confesse him a Conquerer . . ."

[32] I follow Bond's analysis of the allegorical meanings in Lyly's plays (*ibid.*, II, 256–260; III, 81–103). G. Wilson Knight, while not minimizing the "masked contemporary meanings" in Lyly's plays, agrees in general with the theme presented here. He comments, "Love, as in *Euphues*, is his whole theme. He is as aware as Spenser of its complexities: he is more aware than Spenser of its inward contradictions" ("Lyly," in *Review of English Studies*, Vol. XV, April, 1939). See also Thorndike, *English Comedy*, pp. 80–83.

comedy,[33] *Alexander and Campaspe,* Alexander was no doubt meant to be in part a flattering portrait of Elizabeth complacently conquering her desire for an unworthy lover. But he also exists to voice an impersonal protest against those who allow themselves to be overwhelmed by romantic passion. Lyly's prudence, as well as his artistry, dictated that the allegorical meanings of these plays be kept imprecise and the import of their love conflicts general. Although the allusions to specific men and women of his time are too amorphous to make his comedies accurate social history, his presentation of attitudes of actual Elizabethans is important because it emphasizes the very real nature of the sixteenth-century quarrel over romance.

In *Campaspe* Lyly presents love as a quarrel of impulses within the mind of the protagonist, Alexander, who suffers for his Theban captive the languishing despairs of the courtly lover. His problem is whether he shall possess her against her will and be recreant to all the ideals of romantic love or conquer his passion and so deny love itself.[34] Hephestion, who acts as Alexander's moral counselor, insists that romance is mutable and merely a delusion arising from sexual desires. He cautions Alexander that "time must weare out that love hath wrought, and reason weane what appetite noursed." [35] He defines love as "a word by superstition thought a god, by use turned to an humour, by selfwil made a flattering madnesse." [36] Lays, the courtesan, acts as Alexander's realistic counselor. She suggests ironically that the achievement of worldly ambition is for Alexander more important than his realization of a romantic idyl: "You may talk of warre, speak bigge, conquer worldes with great wordes: but stay at home, where in steede of Alarums you shall have daunces,

---

[33] See Lyly, *The Complete Works*, II, 309.

[34] *Alexander and Campaspe*, Act II, scene ii. Not the predicament, but the romantic sentiment with which Alexander wishes to come to terms, is of the Renaissance.

[35] *Ibid.*, Act III, scene iv, l. 120.

[36] *Ibid.*, Act V, scene iv, l. 35: This regarding of traditional romance as a mere cloak for sexual passion is stated more bluntly by Diogenes:
> Your filthy luste you colour under
> courtly colour of love. (Act IV, scene i, l. 36.)

for hot battelles with fierce menne, gentle Skirmishes with fayre womenne." [37]

Alexander finally extricates himself from his entanglement in about the same manner as did Euphues, by accepting asceticism as "reasonable." [38] He is thus enabled to contradict in jocular fashion conventional descriptions of love. Henceforth, he concludes, he will use "fancy as a foole to make his sport, or a minstrell to make him mery. It is not the amorous glaunce of an eie can settle an idle thought in the heart; no, no, it is childrens game, a life for . . . scholers (who) picking fancies out of books, have little els to mervaile at." [39] Alexander does not come to terms with romance, but eludes it, as his final comment illustrates: "It were a shame Alexander should desire to commaund the world, if he could not commaund himselfe . . . good Hephestion, when al the world is woone, and every country is thine and mine, either find me out an other to subdue, or of my word I wil fall in love." [40]

In *Sapho and Phao*, Lyly's second play, Phao, the humble lover of Sapho,[41] was probably meant to suggest the Duc d'Alençon, in whom Elizabeth pretended a teasing sort of interest. Phao also represents the naïve lover, unaware of the actual nature of the world in which he is seeking romance. His love for Sapho follows courtly tradition. He is stricken nearly speechless at his first sight of her, finally declaring: "Madame, I crave pardon, I am spurblinde [i.e., purblind] I could scarse see." [42] He exhibits all the physical anguish that was part of the pattern,[43] only to

---

[37] *Ibid.*, Act V, scene iii, l. 15. The problem here is not unlike that faced by Aeneas when he turned from Dido.

[38] *Ibid.*, Act II, scene ii, l. 77: "my case were light . . . if reason were a remedy," he says to Hephestion, as part of the dramatic irony. To the Renaissance, "reason" no longer meant the logic of the theologian. It meant what we would call "reasonableness" or "rationality."

[39] *Ibid.*, Act V, scene iv, l. 133. [40] *Ibid.*, Act V, scene iv, l. 150.

[41] Sapho probably represents Elizabeth. Like the Queen, Sapho uses love as a means to other ends (*Sapho and Phao*, Act I, scene i, l. 39). She is momentarily overcome by the trickery of Venus and Cupid, but easily escapes passion, as had Alexander, with "reason not yeelding to appetite" (*ibid.*, Act V, scene ii, l. 36).

[42] *Ibid.*, Act II, scene ii, l. 20. [43] *Ibid.*, Act II, scene iv.

be refused by Sapho at the end of his wooing. Then he turns from her court back to his ferrying, to endeavor, as he says, "with mine oare to gette a fare, not with my penne to write a fancie." [44] Yet like Fidus, Phao can neither reject romance nor accept a less ideal reality. He finally admits that "loves are but smokes, which vanish in the seeing, and yet hurte whilest they are seene." [45] But he remains faithful to his ideal: "This shal be my resolution, where ever I wander to be as I were ever kneeling before Sapho, my loyalty unspotted, though unrewarded." [46]

Mileta of this play, the lady-in-waiting to Sapho, represents (in contrast to Phao) the unadulterated skepticism of the Renaissance. To her feminine companions she cries out her protests against the courtly tradition which Phao dramatizes: "I laugh at that you all call love, and judge it onely a worde called love. Me thinks lyking, a curtesie, a smile, a beck, and such like, are the very Quintessence of love." [47] She finds the sighs and sonnets of a lover quite as ridiculous as, a decade later, did such satirists as Marston and Donne. She assumes the regular anti-Petrarchan attitude when she describes these conventional courtiers as "wearing our hands out with courtly kissings, when their wits faile in courtly discourses. Now rufling their haires, now setting their ruffes, then gazing with their eies, then sighing with a privie wring by the hand, thinking us like to be wowed by signes and ceremonies." [48]

In Lyly's third play, *Endimion*, as Bond suggests, "the allegory *is* the plot." [49] Indeed, the Elizabethan audience could scarcely have failed to look for hidden significances in *Endimion*, since it was warned not to do so by the author in his prologue.[50]

[44] *Ibid.*, Act V, scene iii, l. 10.
[45] *Ibid.*, Act V, scene iii, l. 11. This is not Chaucer's medieval, moral skepticism, but a Renaissance realistic appraisal. This conflict is not new to the sixteenth century. The important fact is that it exists in Phao's mind.
[46] *Ibid.*, Act V, scene iii, l. 17.   [47] *Ibid.*, Act I, scene iv, l. 15.
[48] *Ibid.*, Act I, scene iv, l. 36.
[49] Bond, in *The Complete Works of John Lyly*, II, 259.
[50] "It was forbidden in olde time to dispute of Chymera, because it was a fiction: we hope in our times none will apply pastimes, because they are fancies." *Ibid.*, III, 20.

Again the characters reflect both court intrigues and the more general conflict of Renaissance attitudes toward love. Endimion, whose name gives title to the play, is probably meant to be Leicester, languishingly but ascetically devoted to Cynthia, or Elizabeth, "the Ladie that hee delightes in, and dotes on every day, and dies for ten thousand times a day." [51] He is also the perfect Petrarchan lover; all his amorous thoughts "are stitched to the starres." [52] Eumenides, his friend and rescuer, seems to be something like Sir Philip Sidney. The sharp-tongued Semele, whom he woos, may very well have suggested Penelope Devereux, or "Stella." But these contrasting pairs of lovers also dramatize the general difference between a Platonic respect for one's mistress and a courtly solicitation of her favors.

Endimion, in his absolute devotion to Cynthia, is the romantic lover incarnate. To him love is the only significant human experience. He cries:

> There is no Mountain so steepe that I will not climbe, no monster so cruell that I will not tame, no action so desperate that I will not attempt . . . Beholde my sad teares, my deepe sighes, my hollowe eyes, my broken sleepes, my heavie countenaunce. . . . Have I not spent my golden yeeres in hopes, waxing old with wishing, yet wishing nothing but thy love.[53]

Like Fidus, like Phao, Endimion becomes one of love's anchorites, "divorsing himselfe from the amiablenes of all Ladies, the braverie of all Courts, the companie of al men . . . accounting in the worlde (but Cynthia) nothing excellent." [54] And like Phao, Endimion is untouched by skepticism, although his only reward for his fidelity to Cynthia has been a single kiss.[55]

The attitude of Eumenides, on the other hand, is that of a matter-of-fact lover who is content to have his fortunes "creepe on the earth." [56] He lightly mocks the Petrarchan amorist when he warns Endimion that sleep will do him more good than his

---

[51] *Endimion*, Act I, scene iv, l. 37. [52] *Ibid.*, Act I, scene i, l. 5.
[53] *Ibid.*, Act II, scene i, l. 6. [54] *Ibid.*, Act II, scene i, l. 39.
[55] *Ibid.*, Act V, scene i, l. 18 and Act V, scene iii, ll. 162 *et sqq.*
[56] *Ibid.*, Act I, scene i, l. 73.

ecstatic reverie.⁵⁷ Eumenides, like Philautus, seeks a substantial reward for his wooing. To him the goal of courtesy is the yielding by a virtuous lady to her lover.⁵⁸ Indeed, he is so much a virtuoso in sensuality that his imagined delight at Semele's final surrender almost overcomes him. He cries out, "I pray thee, fortune, when I shall first meete with fayre Semele, dash my delight with some light disgrace, least imbracing sweetnesse beyond measure, I take surfit without recure . . ."⁵⁹ His only difficulty is that the object of his devotion, like Sidney's "Stella," refuses to conform to his realistic conception of love.

In portraying the character Sir Tophas in this play, Lyly goes beyond a commonsense realism and actually derides romantic ideals. Sir Tophas is a braggart, a pedant, a social climber, and a foolish amorist. His courtship of the old hag Dipsas is a gross parody of the proper ritual of adoration. It may have been meant merely to ridicule some unlucky Elizabethan would-be courtier.⁶⁰ But the conduct of Sir Tophas is also a violent caricature of the lover's pageant of woes. Like the neophyte in a twelfth-century romance, Sir Tophas first scorns love before he is caught by it. He ridicules passion by a foolish quarrel with his servant over the physiological origin of love. His servant suggests, "love, sir, may lye in your lunges, and I think it doth, and that is the cause you blow, and are so pursie." Tophas replies, mocking the Elizabethan complimentary sonneteer, "Tush boy! I thinke it but some devise of the Poet to get money."⁶¹ But the caricature goes deeper, and Lyly seems to anticipate for a moment the satiric view of Marston. Conventional conceits of the Petrarchan, or

⁵⁷ *Ibid.*, Act I, scene i, l. 68.   ⁵⁸ *Ibid.*, Act III, scene iv, l. 65.
⁵⁹ *Ibid.*, Act III, scene iv, l. 96.
⁶⁰ Lyly is said by Daniel C. Boughner to have discharged such a "combination of farce and satire . . . upon some aspiring member of the community who mimicked gentlemen and imitated the learned and elaborate forms of the Court" ("The Background of Lyly's Tophas," PMLA, LIV [December, 1939], 973). Boughner indicates the Latin, Italian, and English background of this character. Bond states, in Lyly, *The Complete Works*, that Sir Tophas represents Gabriel Harvey and that Dipsas suggests the quarrelsome Countess of Shrewsbury (III, 98–101).
⁶¹ *Endimion*, Act I, scene iii, ll. 10 *et sqq.*

the Provençal lover are burlesqued in Sir Tophas's description of his passion for Dipsas:

I feele all Ovid "de arte amandi" lie as heavie at my heart as a loade of logges. O what a fine thin hayre hath Dipsas! What a prettie low forehead! What a tall & statlie nose! What little hollowe eyes! What great and goodly lypes! Howe harmlesse shee is beeing toothlesse! her fingers fatte and short, adorned with long nayles like a Bytter! In howe sweete a proportion her cheekes hang downe to her brests like dugges, and her pappes to her waste like bagges! What a lowe stature shee is, and yet what a great foote shee carryeth! [62]

The Woman in the Moone, the last but one of Lyly's comedies which treat the Renaissance complexities of love, has been called "a mirthless and bitter denunciation of woman."[63] Possibly it portrays Lyly's conception of the fickleness of a specific woman, Elizabeth. Indeed, as Feuillerat has pointed out,[64] its original audience could scarcely have failed to think of the queen even if Lyly had conceived the central character in this drama, Pandora, impersonally. Whatever the implied meanings, the import of the play is not limited to them. It contains a somewhat sardonic presentation of lovers' perplexities, which had already been dramatized in Lyly's other plays. The only difference is that here a conflict of attitudes is dramatized as moral allegory. A single woman, Pandora, is sent to Utopia to become the lady of one of the four shepherds who live there in rustic peace. Her response to her wooers is controlled in turn by each of the seven planets. Therefore she represents all the variations of temperament of an actual person in conflict with the shepherds, who voice the sentiments of confirmed idealists. Gunophilus, her servant, makes this clear when he describes his passion in terms of the timeworn

---

[62] *Ibid.*, Act III, scene iii, l. 50. For a parallel with the Italian poet, Berni, see Violet Jeffery, in *John Lyly and the Italian Renaissance*, pp. 100–101: "Lyly's motive is undoubtedly the same as Berni's, to reproduce the exact style of the Bembist poets in love, but to show the ridiculous side of their extravagances, misapplying their favorite epithets, and exaggerating, not beauties, but defects." Cf. Shakespeare's milder satire, Sonnet CXXX, "My mistress' eyes are nothing like the sun."

[63] Violet Jeffery, *John Lyly and the Italian Renaissance*, p. 74.

[64] Feuillerat, *John Lyly*, p. 233.

Lyly's Quarreling Lovers

idea that the first glance of the mistress pierced the heart of the recipient through his eye.

> As I beheld the glory of thy face
> My feeble eyes admiring majestie
> Did sinke into my heart such holly feare
> That very feare amazing every sence,
> Withheld my tongue from saying what I would.[65]

Stesias, whom Pandora under the influence of Sol has chosen as her husband, represents the lover who thinks for a moment that he has realized his idyllic desires. When he has first won Pandora, he cries out:

> O Stesias, what a heavenly love hast thou!
> A love as chaste as is Apolloes tree:
> As modest as a vestall Virgins eye,
> And yet as bright as Glow wormes in the night,
> With which the morning decks her lovers hayre
> O fayre Pandora, blessed Stesias.[66]

Pandora, who has been alternately melancholy, disdainful, raging, chastely coy, is seen in clearest conflict with the romantic ideal envisaged by the shepherds when she is under the influence of Venus. The scorn of this goddess for Pandora's proposed union with Stesias, expressed somewhat in the spirit of the "ars amatoria," is in defiance of all conventional conceits:

> Away with chastity and modest thoughts
> 'Quo mihi fortunam si non conceditur uti?'
> Is she not young? then let her to the world:
> All those are strumpets that are over chaste,
> Defying such as keepe their company.
> Tis not the touching of a womans hand,
> Kissing her lips, hanging about her neck . . .
> That men expect . . .[67]

And Pandora solicits successfully, in turn, the three shepherds she had dismissed to marry Stesias, crying:

---

[65] *The Woman in the Moone*, Act II, scene i, l. 94.
[66] *Ibid.*, Act IV, scene i, l. 37.   [67] *Ibid.*, Act III, scene ii, l. 16.

> A husband? What a folish word is that!
> Give me a lover, let the husband goe.⁶⁸

This is no misogynic tract (as Violet Jeffery, for one, would have it), since the shepherds are as willing to play traitor to Stesias as is Pandora. Like the other comedies, this is a study of the contrasts between the idealized pretensions of lovers' desires and the dismal realizations.

Lyly's Resolution of Controversy

Alexander and Hephestion, Sapho and Mileta, Endimion and Eumenides show how Lyly turns to dramatic use incompatible attitudes toward love already established for Elizabethan thought. But Lyly goes farther in the direction of "love-game comedy." Pairs of lovers in some of his comedies dramatize the intellectual conflict between different ideas of love as a witty duel between a courtier and his lady. In *Campaspe*, for example, there is a mild skirmish of wits between Alexander's successful rival, the painter Apelles, and Campaspe. Apelles is traditionally correct when he suggests to Campaspe that the source of his desire for her is in the glance of her eyes.⁶⁹ As a romantic lover, he believes that she is to be won by a ritual of humble adoration, by "praier, sacrifice and bribes," ⁷⁰ at the shrine of Venus. But he is also sufficiently realistic to wish to possess his lady. In his quarrel with Campaspe he represents the Renaissance attempt to possess its ideal woman, and she represents the attempt to keep love an untouchable ideal. They quarrel first because Campaspe has scornfully rejected Apelles, romantically prostrate before her beauty. He then mocks *her*, suggesting that she is both coy and lustful.

> Mistresse, you neither differ from your selfe nor your sex: for knowing your owne perfection you seeme to dispraise that which men most commend, drawing them by that meane into an admiration, where

---

⁶⁸ *Ibid.*, Act III, scene ii, l. 139.
⁶⁹   "I shall never drawe your eies well,
     Because they blind mine."
     (*Alexander and Campaspe*, Act III, scene iii, l. 1.)
⁷⁰ *Ibid.*, Act III, scene iii, ll. 35 *et sqq.*

feeding them selves they fall into an extasie; your modestie being the cause of the one, and of the other, your affections.[71]

In their second duel of wits Apelles is finally driven to teasing protest that the real Campaspe is incredibly hard to bend to his preconceived ideal: "It is not possible that a face so faire, & a wit so sharpe, both without comparison, should not be apt to love." [72]

Their skirmish has an air of reality. It is presented as if it had arisen from the lovers' desires and had been mutually contrived. It actually draws the lovers together instead of separating them (as such duels had done in *Euphues* and in *The Courtier*). Out of their final witty game of disagreement comes Campaspe's confession of surrender, though she quibbles with Apelles even as he swears the eternal nature of his passion, mocking him with, "That is, neither to have beginning nor ending." But she immediately relents and admits, "but this assure your self, that I had rather bee in thy shop grinding colours, then in Alexanders court, following higher fortunes." [73] Thus these lovers, like Berowne and Rosalind, like Beatrice and Benedick, do work out their conflict of attitudes after a fashion.

But neither Apelles nor Campaspe is the subtle creature of later comedy, neither one personifies an aspect of the quarrel over love with sufficient clarity to make his compromise or betrayal of his point of view dramatically effective. Each acknowledges his acceptance of the other too soon. Furthermore, narrative events impede the climax to their verbal combats. It is Alexander who finally decides their fate, not they themselves. Their union signalizes less an accommodation of common sense to romantic theory than, like the marriages in pastoral romance, an escape into an unashamedly idyllic world. The benediction pronounced over them by Alexander does not settle their quarrel in a way to satisfy either dramatic or comic considerations: "Two loving wormes, Hephestion! I perceive Alexander cannot subdue the affections of men, though he conquer their countries . . . Well, enjoy one another, I give her thee franckly, Apelles." [74]

[71] *Ibid.*, Act III, scene i, l. 8.
[72] *Ibid.*, Act III, scene i, l. 47.
[73] *Ibid.*, Act IV, scene iv, l. 4.
[74] *Ibid.*, Act V, scene iv, l. 127.

In *Sapho and Phao* there is a fragmentary appearance of a sex duel, but it bears no integral relation to the play.[75] Mileta, the vitriolic denouncer of all manifestations of love, falls its momentary victim in the presence of the amorously chivalric Phao. She suggests to him, as she summons him to the bed of Sapho, "Were I sicke, the verye sight of thy faire face would drive me into a sound sleepe." To which Phao replies, in ironic dismissal, "Indeede Gentlewomen are so drowsie in their desires, that they can scarce hold up their eyes for love." She continues to woo him by praising his extreme beauty; to which he retorts, in derision, "Lady, I forgot to commend you first, and leaste I shoulde have over slipped to praise you at all, you have brought in my bewtie, which is simple, that in curtisie I might remember yours, which is singular." [76]

In this exchange of wit Mileta not only repudiates her own convictions, but woos Phao. Their union, however, is never further suggested by Lyly. Like the contention between Fidus and Iffida, this skirmish between Phao and Mileta parts the two antagonists. The suggested solution to the difficulties experienced by the characters in this play does not come from this minor sex duel at all.[77] It is made by Sybilla, whose dramatic purpose is to comment on the nature of love. She cautions Phao, who has asked her advice on the ways of courtesy, not to miss the possession of his lady by following too closely the romantic conventions of courtship. She emphasizes the mutability of that charm which creates love.[78] Her suggestion is to observe in detail the courtly ritual of adoration as a mere means, to the end that he may achieve the less ideal rewards of sensual pleasure. "Love, faire child, is to be governed by arte . . . Looke pale and learne to

---

[75] Bond, in Lyly, *The Complete Works*, II, 272, mentions elements in these plays that are purely "abortive," that serve only a "generally illustrative purpose, and sometimes not even that . . . nothing follows from . . . Mileta's attempt on Phao."

[76] *Sapho and Phao*, Act III, scene iv, ll. 5 *et sqq*.

[77] Eugenua possibly suggests the acceptance of paradox by her comment on Mileta, "Yet we, when we sweare with our mouthes wee are not in love, then we sigh from the heart and pine in love" (*ibid.*, Act I, scene iv, l. 41).

[78] Cf. *ibid.*, Act III, scene i, ll. 100 *et sqq*.

be leane, that who so seeth thee, may say, the Gentleman is in love." [79] Rosalind was to give Orlando the same advice, but not in shrewd earnest.

In *Endimion* Lyly gives the quarreling lovers a more important role in the dramatic action than they had had in either *Campaspe* or in *Sapho and Phao*. The participants, Eumenides and Semele (the one guided by the ideals of romance, the other controlled by an unyielding sense of reality), never meet, but like Beatrice and Benedick they exchange "unseemely and malepart overthwarts" (i.e., repartee).[80] As in *Campaspe*, the lovers' quarrels in *Endimion* bring about no dramatically effective reconciliation. By his fidelity to Semele "the very waspe of all women, whose tongue stingeth as much as an Adders tooth," [81] Eumenides receives a single wish from a fountain for faithful lovers. At the precise moment when he is given opportunity to ask possession of his lady, however, he reverses his attitude and becomes suddenly skeptical of the entire tradition of romance. He becomes acutely aware that Semele is "of all creatures the most froward" and that he has been "of all creatures the most fond." [82] Like the sardonic Fulke Greville, Eumenides (or Sidney) suddenly sees his love as an illusion, as a mere "golden dreame." [83] Therefore he chooses to release Endimion from his spell, and he lets a cynical sense of fact and his affection for his friend triumph over his romantic desires. Benedick, in Shakespeare's *Much Ado*, forced by Beatrice to make a similar choice, turns against his friend. Benedick thus helps to contrive his ultimate union with Beatrice. Eumenides's decision, on the contrary, turns Semele completely against him. The comic delight of a sudden concord of lovers' wills is therefore impossible to achieve

[79] *Ibid.*, Act II, scene iv, l. 55.
[80] *Endimion*, Act III, scene i, l. 16. Bond suggests that Eumenides represents Sir Philip Sidney, and Semele, Lady Rich. See further, *ibid.*, Act III, scene i, ll. 12 *et sqq.* and Act V, scene iii, ll. 205–240.
[81] *Ibid.*, Act V, scene iii, l. 203.   [82] *Ibid.*, Act III, scene iv, l. 60.
[83] *Ibid.*, Act III, scene iv, l. 108. The novelty here is that courtly love is mocked realistically by Eumenides' analysis. In Chaucer's "Knight's Tale," the two friends, Palamoun and Arcite, are eventually shown to be mortal enemies in order to prove the power of "amour courtois."

in this play. It is by the command of Cynthia that Semele grudgingly accepts Eumenides. In this fashion Lyly destroys the dramatic effect of the long anticipated surrender of his lovers.

In Lyly's *The Woman in the Moone* no sex duel appears. This play is far too didactic an allegory for witty repartee to reconcile the inconstant Pandora and the faithful shepherds. Stesias, the courtly bucolic lover whom Pandora has agreed to marry, comes to scorn her when he finds how far she is from his exalted conception of woman. He wishes to destroy Utopia, his rustic garden of love, crying:

> Curst be Utopia for Pandoraes sake!
> Let wilde bores with their tuskes plow up my lawnes,
> Devouring Wolves come shake my tender lambes,
> Drive up my goates unto some steepy rocke,
> And let them fall downe headlong in the sea.
> She shall not live . . .[84]

But Stesias is not allowed to flee Pandora, who represents the reality of passion, or to possess her. He is translated to the moon, where he is destined to follow her always, however repulsive she has become to him as a caricature of the mistress of romance. Shakespeare did better in *As You Like It*, presenting a less bitter, a kindlier, acceptance of the conventional illusions of love.

Only in Lyly's final play,[85] *Love's Metamorphosis*, is the conflict over the nature of love dramatized solely by pairs of quarreling lovers. The foresters in this comedy defend romance and the nymphs treat it with derision. Moreover, Lyly creates the impression that the battle of wits is mutually contrived. Both his lovers and their ladies are presented as if they were conscious that they are playing parts in a game in which neither the pretensions nor the denunciations of love are fully justified. Thus, when alone the foresters Ramis, Silvestris, and Montanus are themselves somewhat skeptical. They are willing to follow the

---

[84] *The Woman in the Moone*, Act V, scene i, l. 244.
[85] Bond gives 1584–1588, as the first date for the composition of this play and its present form as 1599. Thus it is possible to argue that *The Woman in the Moone* is Lyly's final, sardonic presentation of love.

ritual of the enamored courtier, to play at being in love, in order to gain their ladies. They do not disavow the precepts of formalized passion, they merely wish to apply them, somewhat crassly, for their own purposes. As Silvestris states it,

> I doe not thinke Love hath any sparke of Divinitie in him; since the end of his being is earthly. In the bloud he is begot by the fraile fires of the eye, & quencht by the frayler shadowes of thought. What reason have we then to soothe his humor with such zeale, and folow his fading delights with such passion?

And Ramis replies that romance should be accepted with a great deal of reservation, "since it will aske longer labour and studie to subdue the powers of our bloud to the rule of the soule, then to satisfie them with the fruition of our loves, let us bee constant in the worlds errours, and seeke our owne torments." [86]

When their ladies, Nisa, Celia, Niobe, are alone, they spend no time analyzing romance. Nisa is the most scornful of the three in her ridicule of Cupid: "What should he doe with wings that knowes not where to flie? Or what with arrowes, that sees not how to ayme? The heart is a narrow marke to hit, and rather requireth Argus eyes to take level, then a blind boy to shoote at randome." [87] These nymphs are scornfully amused by their wooers' attempts to play the role of lover in the traditional drama of courtship. They read the poems which the foresters have hung on trees, and Nisa comments on their assertions that they suffer the usual physical languishings of love: "they have eaten so much wake-Robin, that they cannot sleepe for love." [88] Niobe indicates the nymphs' share in the contrived, witty sex duels to come, when she argues, "Give them leave to love, since we have libertie to chuse, for as great sport doe I take in coursing their tame hearts, as they doe paines in hunting their wilde Harts." [89]

When these three sets of lovers meet, it is to release the antag-

---

[86] *Love's Metamorphosis*, Act I, scene i, ll. 9 *et sqq.*

[87] *Ibid.*, Act II, scene i, l. 56. Bond speaks of this as satire on the "poets' fine talk about love" (II, 261). Cf. his note (Vol. III, p. 566, ll. 50 *et sqq.*).

[88] *Ibid.*, Act I, scene ii, l. 18.

[89] *Ibid.*, Act I, scene ii, l. 23. See also Act II, scene i, l. 67.

onism that has been carefully built up by the foresters' pretense of accepting idyllic romance and the nymphs' pretense of complete skepticism. Each set of lovers quarrels, in turn, and each of the foresters retires, vanquished in wit, but not in impulse to love. Ramis maintains the immutability of his passion, despite Nisa's scorn, crying after her that he will "practice by denials to bee patient, or by disdaining die, and so be happie." [90] Montanus stresses both his fidelity to Celia and his languishing grief in his petitions to her to "yeelde to love, sweete love." She tempts him into rebuking her for her obdurate pride, and then reduces him to a greater confusion of self-contradiction. He suddenly ceases to be the humble prostrate lover and asserts his independence. But it is only for a moment, and he returns to his pretended humility. Celia dismisses him, crying, "You want wit, that you can be content to be patient." [91] Silvestris, reversing the order of procedure in his conflict with Niobe, begins by suggesting that she is not qualified to play the lady of amorous courtesy. But she soon brings him to despair by her mocking. He begs off, suggesting that when he has but heard her sing he will be content to die, and she replies, "I will sing to content thee."

Even in this final play of Lyly's, however, the lovers do not quite solve their own destinies. Despite their nimble fencing, these characters never come to full dramatic realization. Once more Lyly contrives his denouement by using the device of devine intervention. His foresters are allowed to reach an agreement with the nymphs only by an appeal to Cupid. They offer at his shrine, in evidence of their plight, all the courtier's symbols and symptoms of love.[92] They prevail upon the god to force the nymphs to yield, and therefore the story ends in no swift surrender, in no sudden concord of lovers' conflicting wills to give a comic release to the built-up tension. Lyly himself was aware of this lack, for he makes Silvestris cry, "what joye can there be in our lives . . . when every kisse shall bee sealed with a curse . . . enforcement is worse than enchantment." [93]

[90] *Ibid.*, Act III, scene i, ll. 1 *et sqq.* [91] *Ibid.*, Act III, scene i, l. 72.
[92] *Ibid.*, Act IV, scene i, l. 8. [93] *Ibid.*, Act V, scene iii, l. 14.

Lyly's Quarreling Lovers

There is little comic triumph here, because the play ends in a forced compromise between an idealistic and a realistic attitude. Ramis expresses this play's equivocal conclusion when he suggests that the delights of actual possession will mitigate some of the unpleasant consequences of an inharmonious and forced love. "Let them curse all day," he says, "so I may have but one kisse at night." [94] And to his lady he cries, "O, my sweete Nisa! bee what thou wilt, and let all thy imperfections bee excused by me, so thou but say thou lovest me." [95] But such a terminus does not carry any illusion of momentary belief.[96] Rather it suggests that Lyly regarded the two worlds of romance and real life as irreconcilable. As such, it is more ironic than comic. It may be a revelation of his acute pessimism, but not of his sense of comedy.

In his novel and in his comedies, the play of ideas is like that found in Elizabethan poetry. These comedies represent something new in literature.[97] Lyly did what had not been done before, he brought to the stage the complexities of Elizabethan amorous thought. But even more important than this, Lyly depicts a kind of miraculous adjustment of contradictory theories of love, by a final union of warring lovers. Aesthetically this advances him at once beyond the mere presentation of unsolved dilemma in *The Courtier,* and in Elizabethan poetry. Lyly, however, failed to see all of the comic implications to be derived from a dramatized conflict of attitudes. Drama could do more than relate romantic pretensions to less exalted fact in an incredible and magical fashion. It might lend belief to the resolution that serves to bring the play to an end. Lyly's dramas, therefore, are but a link in the series of literary expressions of the Renaissance love dilemma. They stand somewhere between the recognition

---

[94] *Ibid.,* Act V, scene iii, ll. 19 *et sqq.*
[95] *Ibid.,* Act V, scene iv, l. 136.
[96] Cf. Nisa's final remarks, *ibid.,* Act V, scene iv, l. 133.
[97] Cf. G. P. Baker, in *Cambridge History of English Literature,* V, 127. He describes what he calls a new "high comedy." It consists of "Contrasts, delicately brought out, between the real underlying feelings of the characters and what they wish to feel or wish to be thought to feel, all of this phrased as perfectly as possible . . ."

and analysis of the problems found in *The Courtier* and the comic solution of the problem portrayed in Shakespeare's love-game comedies.

R. Warwick Bond, in his essay on Lyly as a playwright, states that Lyly's importance lies in the fact that he wrote a kind of comedy which Shakespeare imitated. Bond remarks,

> Lyly's farcical scenes are undoubtedly the model for the similar scenes in Shakespeare's early work . . . for the wit contests between Boyet and the French ladies, the Two Gentlemen, Romeo and Mercutio; while he is indebted also to Lyly's example of graceful and witty interchange between ladies and courtiers, nymphs and foresters, for many a gentle and pretty scene between Julia and Lucetta, Portia and Nerissa, Rosalind and Celia, Hero and Ursula, and for the witty war between Benedick and Beatrice, and others.[98]

This is all true, but one must add that what Shakespeare borrowed from Lyly's comedies was not only a method of characterization. Shakespeare also borrowed a method of reducing an intellectual conflict between different ideas of love to the form of a witty verbal combat. In the antagonisms that Lyly dramatizes, the lovers never come completely to life. His characters merely voice current attitudes toward love, whereas Shakespeare's characters express these ideas as if they were their own. It is something, no doubt, that Lyly was able to present in dramatic form the complex love dilemma of which ladies and gentlemen of his age were acutely aware. He developed comedy to the stage where its characters exist not merely to relate a story but also to act out the Elizabethan critical revolt from romance. Yet Lyly never

---

[98] Bond, in Lyly, *The Complete Works*, II, 253. Cf. Violet Jeffery, *John Lyly and The Italian Renaissance*, p. 115: "Lyly's true greatness is of the same type as Shakespeare's: it lies in his method of handling the material ready to his hand." This is sound if one includes attitudes as well as mere narrative material. Cf. further, G. P. Baker, in *Cambridge History of English Literature*, V, 126, "do we not find *Much Ado About Nothing* and *As You Like It*, in their essentials, only developments through the intermediate experiments in *Love's Labour's Lost* and *Two Gentlemen of Verona*, from Lyly's comedies?" But Baker fails to state precisely what these "essentials" are. See also Elmer Edgar Stoll, *Shakespeare Studies*, pp. 157–158.

turns these intellectual materials into high comedy, because his characterization does not entirely grow out of them. Lyly's characters remain strictly under his control, Shakespeare's characters seem to create their own destiny.

· X ·

Conflict in Shakespeare's Sonnets

Lyly had amused his audience by dramatizing some of the obvious improbabilities and incongruities provoked by traditional romance. But he scarcely exceeds the limits of the controversy over love found elsewhere in his age. He adds little to the ideas given to him by his time. He merely adapts them to the stage. Shakespeare, however, in his sonnets to a dark lady,[1] exceeds these limits and presents the sixteenth-century quarrel over the nature of love from a point of view peculiarly his own. This presentation of love in his sonnets is important because it is very like that found in his comedies of courtship. Within the narrow limits of their fourteen lines, he expresses with intensity and candor the highly individualized version of lovers' difficulties which is comic and implicit in his love-game comedies.

Shakespeare expresses the familiar sentiments of the courtly or Petrarchan lover in very few of his sonnets. In Sonnet CXXVIII he elaborates a metaphor in which he wishes he were the nimbly leaping jacks of the spinet his lady is playing, that he might also "kiss the tender inward" of her hand. In Sonnet CXXXII he writes a playful, romantic compliment. He toys with the time-honored conceit of the eye and the heart, concluding that since his mistress' eyes are black, they are mourners for the love sickness caused in him by her heart. In Sonnet CXLV, the lightest of the three, he plays with his mistress' exclamation, "I hate,"

---

[1] It is assumed here that Sonnets 1–126 are addressed to a young man; 127–152 to the poet's mistress. For a discussion of this point see *Shakespeare's Sonnets*, ed. by Tucker Brooke, pp. 17–19.

for the length of the sonnet, closing it with the quick about face,

> "I hate" from hate away she threw,
> And sav'd my life, saying—"not you."

Conversely, in only two sonnets does Shakespeare concern himself with what had been a major problem to Sidney and Drayton —the unreality of the conceits which served to describe the traditional romantic ideal of beauty. In the one (Sonnet CXXVII), Shakespeare suggests that his mistress lacks the fair complexion and golden hair required of the ideal lady of romance.

> In the old age black was not counted fair,
> Or if it were, it bore not beauty's name;
> But now is black beauty's successive heir.

In the other sonnet (Sonnet CXXX), in a line by line analysis, he calls attention to the disparity between his mistress' attractions and those which poetic convention decreed that she should possess. This sonnet is the familiar one beginning, "My mistress' eyes are nothing like the sun."

With these few exceptions,[2] Shakespeare does not give romantic sentiment direct lyric expression in his sonnets. Nor does he present the usual conflict between romance and a new, humanistic skepticism. Moreover, Shakespeare is too objective to react against Petrarchism in the sharply satiric way of Marston and Donne, and he does not try to avoid the difficulties of lovers by following the Renaissance Platonists in spiritualizing love. Least of all does he escape from love by retreating to the sixteenth-century equivalent of monastic morality—Puritanism. The truth is that the majority of his lyrics begin where other Elizabethan poetry leaves off. They both recognize and explain the paradoxical nature of love. They acknowledge in a sardonic fashion the presence of inevitable contradictions in experienced passion. His sonnets record his effort to exploit the conventions of romantic sentiment, but not the idealizing spirit of which they are a product.

[2] Sonnets CXLIII, CXXXV, CXXXVI, the "Will" sonnets, which emphasize the sexuality of love, might also be considered in conflict with romance.

Shakespeare expresses his comprehension of the interplay of an idealizing tendency and cold fact in a number of different ways. In one sonnet (CXXXI) he employs terms of half-complimentary, half-scornful acceptance of his lady's physical imperfections. The poem is a perfectly clear statement of the complementary halves of love. To his "dear doting heart," he says, his lady is "the fairest and most precious jewel." Others have challenged her beauty, he admits, and

> To say they err I dare not be so bold,
> Although I swear it to myself alone.

Therefore, he tells her,

> A thousand groans, but thinking on thy face,
> One on another's neck, do witness bear
> Thy black is fairest in my judgment's place.

A similar perception, that this idealized portrait of his lady is contradicted by the reality of her deeds, is expressed in the sonnet (CL) which opens,

> O! from what power hast thou this powerful might,
> With insufficiency my heart to sway?

There is so much graceful redemption in the "very refuse" of her deeds, he cries,

> That, in my mind, thy worst all best exceeds.

And he concludes, turning the contradictions of love upon himself in derision:

> If thy unworthiness rais'd love in me,
> More worthy I to be belov'd of thee.

In several of his sonnets he further examines the difference between ideal love and the less than ideal reality of his mistress. He uses, in ironic fashion, the old descriptive psychology of passion and its origins in the flame of the eye.[3] Thus he cries,

> O me! what eyes hath Love put in my head,
> Which have no correspondence with true sight.

[3] See Sonnets CXLVIII, CXXXVII, CXXXIX, CXL, CXLI, CXLII, CXLIX.

And he concludes, again in self-mockery, that the eyes of a lover are blinded with his tears of despair. It is they which blur tawdry aspects of his passion till the discrepancy between them and his ideal is all but invisible.

> O cunning Love! with tears thou keep'st me blind,
> Lest eyes well-seeing thy foul faults should find.[4]

Shakespeare uses this same figure of the self-deceptive eye, but more bitterly, more in self-castigation, when he asks of Love,

> Why of eyes' falsehood hast thou forged hooks,
> Whereto the judgment of my heart is tied?[5]

Shakespeare often deliberately turns his back upon Petrarchan conventions. He elaborates in caustic fashion his mistress' departure from the prescribed appearance[6] and behavior of the lady of romance. He cries that he has perjured himself far more than she. She has merely her

> . . . bed-vow broke, and new faith torn,
> In vowing new hate after new love bearing.

But as her lover he has

> . . . sworn deep oaths of thy deep kindness,
> Oaths of thy love, thy truth, thy constancy;
> And, to enlighten thee, gave eyes to blindness,
> Or made them swear against the thing they see;
> For I have sworn thee fair; more perjur'd I,
> To swear against the truth so foul a lie![7]

However, Shakespeare presents most graphically the contradictory impulses that go to form the experience of love, not through ironic use of familiar metaphors of poetry,[8] but by a description of the attraction and repulsion of sexual desire. Thus, in Sonnet CXLVII he exhibits the same wretched consciousness

---

[4] Sonnet CXLVIII. [5] Sonnet CXXXVII.
[6] Sonnet CXLIV. [7] Sonnet CLII.
[8] But note the concluding couplet to Sonnet CXLVII:
> For I have sworn thee fair, and thought thee bright
> Who art as black as hell, as dark as night.

of the power of physical love to destroy an ideal as he did in *The Rape of Lucrece*. The mere sexual impulse

> . . . is as a fever, longing still
> For that which longer nurseth the disease.

He uses the figure of Reason, the physician whose prescription has been ignored, abandoning the lover to incurable dilemma.

> Past cure I am, now Reason is past care,
> And frantic-mad with evermore unrest.

A similar, though more generalized, presentation of the inadequacy of lust either to satiate itself or to come up to its imagined delight is the subject of Sonnet CXXIX. Desire is

> A bliss in proof,—and, prov'd, a very woe;
> Before, a joy propos'd; behind, a dream.

Like Lucretius, like Bembo, Shakespeare here reduces the paradox to its essentials. But he does not, like Lucretius, deny the romantic expectations of love or, like Bembo, deny its carnality. He acknowledges, on the contrary, the irrationality of human passion.

> All this the world well knows; yet none knows well
> To shun the heaven that leads men to this hell.

Most of Shakespeare's sonnets to a dark lady describe in various ways and in varying degrees of derision his understanding of the conflicting forces which form the experience of love. In a few sonnets, however, he goes beyond recognition of these forces to suggest (as did John Donne) that the discordant elements of love must be accepted as essential parts of a unified experience. Shakespeare, in Sonnet CXLII, proposes one way of easing man's disappointment when he discovers that sexual experience is not to be identified with complete spiritual felicity. His lady has questioned his love for her because of his past infidelity. He replies that her own life has not been of the sort to give her the right to criticize his.

> O! but with mine compare thou thine own state,
> And thou shalt find it merits not reproving;
> Or, if it do, not from those lips of thine.

He suggests that they can strike some kind of balance between the dismal fruition of their love and their extravagant hopes only through pity for each other. If she "root pity" in her heart for him, she, in turn, may receive pity from those

> Whom thine eyes woo as mine importune thee.

Otherwise,

> If thou dost seek to have what thou dost hide,
> By self-example mayst thou be denied.

With less mockery, Shakespeare expresses a similar conciliatory idea in Sonnet CLI. He builds up an elaborate phallic metaphor to describe the triumph of sexuality in love despite the knowledge (conscience) that his lady, as well as he, has been a "gentle cheater." The mere recognition of their unillusioned views of each other, their mutual skepticism, does not inevitably destroy his pride in possessing her.

> No want of conscience [9] hold it that I call
> Her "love" for whose dear love I rise and fall.

Shakespeare repeats this propitiatory gesture in a clearer fashion in another sonnet. He first acknowledges the insincerities of both parties to love.

> When my love swears that she is made of truth,
> I do believe her, though I know she lies,
> That she might think me some untutor'd youth
> Unlearned in the world's false subtleties.

Then he concludes that tranquility is best served by a resigned accommodation of oneself both to illusion and to fact.

> O! love's best habit is in seeming trust,
> And age in love loves not to have years told:

---

[9] That is, recognition of reality—"knowledge," "disingenuousness," with an obvious pun on the word, too. Tucker Brooke pairs this sonnet with CXXXVIII as "fruition sonnets."

> Therefore I lie with her, and she with me
> And in our faults by lies we flatter'd be.[10]

It would be difficult to find in any other Elizabethan poet a more frank acknowledgment not only that there are paradoxes involved in love, but also that they define love. In Donne alone is there anything comparable, but in his poetry an intellectual skepticism pervades his attitude of disillusionment, and a philosophic detachment his dispassionate balancing of contradictory impulses. Shakespeare arrives at a conclusion like that suggested by Donne, but usually by an approach that is quite different, by an emotional reaction to experience. In one of Shakespeare's sonnets, however, an intellectual skepticism does triumph. In this one sonnet is found his nearest lyric approach to the comic spirit dramatized by his love-game comedies. He presents his lady with the ironic suggestion that she pretend to be faithful to him, that she merely play the role of romantic mistress.

> If I might teach thee wit, better it were,
> Though not to love, yet, love, to tell me so;—
> As testy sick men, when their deaths be near,
> No news but health from their physicians know.

And the last line of this sonnet, which repeats this concept, does so by echoing familiar courtly love phraseology.

> Bear thine eyes straight, though thy proud heart go wide.[11]

Shakespeare's sonnets are not written outside the Petrarchan tradition, nor do they ignore romantic sentiment. Indeed, as has been seen, he makes constant use of the inherited language of love, with its symbols the eye and the heart.[12] It is merely that in his sonnets he does not use the usual metaphors and conceits as a Petrarchan or as an anti-Petrarchan. He succeeds in evoking the innermost essence of his emotions, and thus can make no easy

---

[10] Sonnet CXXXVIII.   [11] Sonnet CXL.
[12] He protests the "precious phrase by all the Muses fil'd," in Sonnet LXXXV. Tucker Brooke asserts: "the industrious critics who, ignoring them [Shakespeare's statements in Sonnet LXXVI] have sought for resemblances between Shakespeare's sonnets and those of other poets, have ploughed some of the aridest sands of commonplace" (*Shakespeare's Sonnets*, p. 8).

use of conventional materials. He reshapes them, not in rebellion against a romantic attitude, but as part of a sardonic commentary on the contradiction between idealized and experienced passion. The customary Elizabethan poetic conceits fail to convey all that Shakespeare wishes to say about love.[13] He expresses a much more profound understanding of what had hitherto been presented in most sixteenth-century writings as the conflict of a systematized romanticism with reality. The contradictory attitudes and emotions which his sonnets display are presented with so much more apparent conviction that they appear to be not so much a generalized comment on a common problem as a highly personal comment on an individual one.[14]

This fact is illustrated further in a few sonnets [15] which are concerned solely with the attraction and the repulsion of sexual desire. Here the thought seems distant from that usually found in Elizabethan love poetry. But these sonnets are related to the sixteenth century by the fact that they display a mood of bitter recoil from romantic sentiment. Recourse to obscenity is, in fact, a way of making rebellion against one's own ideals seem tolerable. It is an attempt to drown out the insistent voice of hopeless disenchantment. Such erotic blasphemy gives significance, for example, to such a metaphor as the one from Sonnet CXXXV,

> Wilt thou, whose will is large and spacious,
> Not once vouchsafe to hide my will in thine? [16]

By insisting that the physical consummation of love is a gross and undignified act its psychic, intangible import is derided. This descent to the phallic is an attempt to reduce love to its elements and thereby to free oneself from the penalties of a softly idyllic mood which has carried one too far from reality. It is paralleled by all the jealous or frustrated lovers in Shakespeare's plays. It is

---

[13] See especially Sonnets CXXXVII and CXLVIII. These make use of the medieval psychology of the eye as the carrier of love, but in a highly individualized way. It is the eye that is now guilty of fomenting illusion.

[14] This is not to say that only Shakespeare's sonnets present an individual interpretation of Elizabethan amorous thought. It is a matter of degree.

[15] Sonnets CXXIX, CXXXV, CLI.

[16] See Tucker Brooke's note on these lines, *Shakespeare's Sonnets*, p. 338.

Hamlet's treatment of Ophelia, Leontes's of Hermione, and the basis of one of the most harrowing scenes in all literature, Othello's treatment of Desdemona as his whore.[17]

Shakespeare's sonnets mirror lovers' difficulties in a highly individualized fashion. What John Donne was doing intellectually, Shakespeare was doing in a more intuitive way. He was turning the exaggerated conflict between an idealized sentiment and a skepticism engendered by humanistic thought back into an expression of a conflict more fundamental to the human being. More in the spirit of Catullus [18] than in that of Sidney, Shakespeare often appears to be describing the contention between a personally imagined perfection of amorous experience and experience itself. In his sonnets the courtly and Petrarchan symbols of love are partially transmuted. The wheel has nearly come full circle. What began in Provence as a systemized exaltation of love, in Shakespeare's lyrics to a dark lady begins to break down into the confusion inherent in the quarrel between an individual's own imagination and his own experience of reality. In a sense, therefore, the spirit of Shakespeare's sonnets is more integrally related to his tragedies and tragi-comedies than to his love-game comedies.[19] The comedies written during the first decade of his dramatic activity exhibit none of the intensity of emotional consciousness that he reveals in the sonnets. Perhaps, as Professor Tucker Brooke has stated it, Shakespeare withheld the "vital inward part" of himself from these earlier plays. There are indications in *Much Ado*, however, that he was beginning to dramatize some of this vitality. For this play, with all its romantic

---

[17] J. Dover Wilson discusses the resemblance between the "sex nausea" found in the sonnets and that found in the characters in Shakespeare's seventeenth-century plays, in *What Happens in Hamlet*, Appendix D, p. 306. Shakespeare, of course, repudiates mere "lust in action." It is the "heaven that leads men to this hell" (Sonnet CXXIX).

[18] Cf. H. J. C. Grierson, in *The Poems of John Donne*, II, xlii: "to the passion which animates these sensual, witty, troubled poems of John Donne, the closest parallel is to be sought in Shakespeare's sonnets to a dark lady and in some of the verses written by Catullus to or of Lesbia."

[19] Tucker Brooke relates the sonnets and the tragedies in "subtle undertones of common emotion," *Shakespeare's Sonnets*, p. 16.

conventionalities, barely escapes tragedy. Comedy is allowed to triumph only after it has been shadowed by a darker consciousness of the possible fate of its characters. But in such light comedies as *Love's Labour's Lost* and *As You Like It* Shakespeare does present a comic solution to the problem presented in his sonnets.

The relationship between the sonnets and the comedies, then, is that they make use of an identical conception of the nature of love, but treat it in separate ways for two very different purposes. In the one, Shakespeare appraises the disparity between the realities of gross lust, of infidelity, of vanity, and a Renaissance individual's desire for perfection in love. In the other, he does not seek to dramatize a comprehensive analysis of emotions, but to adjust the conflicting elements in Renaissance conceptions of love so that they may give delight. The purpose of his comedy was to make reality and romance appear to reach harmonious adjustment. These sonnets present Shakespeare's vivid insight into what was a problem for him as a man of the sixteenth century. But his first decade of comedies shows the same problem objectified, dramatized in a less profound and a more genial manner. Tucker Brooke relates these two different literary treatments of a common conception when he asks:

Is not the best explanation of this the simple one that Shakespeare's development within the sonnet's scanty plot of ground far outspeeded his development as a dramatist? The poignancy and the immediacy of the feelings he was driven to express in the Sonnets taught him early, I take it, to handle with finality those intenser and more private depths of soul which in his drama were mainly reserved for a later period.[20]

To be sure, the ironic contrast between sex experience and romantic exaltation is given its most complete dramatic expression in *Troilus and Cressida*. But this play belongs to the early seventeenth century, which was turning its attention to satire.[21] His love-game comedy evokes no harsh dissonance from the interplay

[20] *Ibid.*
[21] Cf. Campbell, *Comicall Satyre and Shakespeare's Troilus and Cressida,* ch. vii.

of complementary attitudes toward love. It reconciles almost nonchalantly the contradictions of romance. Its sole purpose is to urge amused acceptance of such unyielding imperfections of experience as were elsewhere denounced in the songs and sonnets of contemporary poets.

· XI ·

SHAKESPEARE'S COMEDIES
OF COURTSHIP

IN SHAKESPEARE's sonnets, as we have seen, he subtracts the idealizing tendency from its courtly and Petrarchan expressions and treats it as a distinct and necessary force in the experience of love. In his love-game comedies he describes this tendency more conventionally and in terms of traditional romance. His lovers, whose wit combats are part of the basic dramatic structure of these plays, keep their quarrels pretty well within the limits of the controversy as it had been expressed in *Astrophel and Stella,* in *The Courtier,* in Lyly's court comedies. What Shakespeare adds to this established pattern of conflict is the illusion that his lovers have not only solved their own amorous difficulties but those of the age. They have defined love for their Elizabethan audience as the process of adjustment between romance and reality which they have acted out in their skirmishes. At the point in the play where they surrender to each other, their excesses of idealism and skepticism, which are the essential ingredients of love, are seen in a moment of perfect balance.

Although Shakespeare makes his most comically effective use of love as this battleground of conflicting elements in his love-game comedies, these elements (alone or in conflict) do appear elsewhere in his romantic comedies and farces. In *Midsummer-Night's Dream* and in *Twelfth Night,* where lovers' ideal wishes triumph, there is an occasional intrusion of a salty skepticism.[1] In

---

[1] The thesis of H. B. Charlton's lectures, *Shakespearian Comedy,* is that the mere bringing of romance to the stage lent it a comic realism. See especially pp. 33–34. Thomas H. McNeal argues (in "The Tyger's Heart Wrapt in a

the first of these plays the rustics' presentation of "Pyramus and Thisbe" serves as a parody on the half-serious, romantic entanglements of the lovers, and Titania's fondling of Bottom the Weaver is a momentary caricature of their raptures. Likewise, in *Twelfth Night* Sir Andrew Aguecheek's wooing of Olivia is an absurd and mocking contrast to the courtly passion of Duke Orsino.[2]

In *The Comedy of Errors* and *The Taming of the Shrew* the basic unreality of romantic conventions is exaggerated into farce.[3] In the one, incidental comedy is derived by showing how far from the idyllic pretensions of courtiers are the infelicities of a domesticated passion. Adriana is the wife whose husband has apparently been unfaithful to her. She applies the standards of romantic fiction to an actual predicament and protests to her sister Luciana against the behavior of married lovers, "Why should their liberty than ours be more?"[4] Luciana replies that Adriana has a false conception of the proper relationship between the sexes. Far from being a servant either to love or to a wife, a man is master of both. A woman's love must be humble and patient. Antipholus, therefore, should be the "bridle" of Adriana's will. But Adriana is concerned with the disparity between the worship she once had received from Antipholus and her present lack of it. She is as unwilling to be pleased with Luciana's outmoded ideas of the position of woman as she is to resign herself to the unpleasantness of fact. She questions her own power to maintain her former exalted position.

> His company must do his minions grace
> Whilst I at home starve for a merry look.

Player's Hide," *Shakespeare Association Bulletin*, XIII [January, 1938], 30–39), that *Midsummer Night's Dream*, along with Sonnet CXXX, is in part a satire on Greene's *A Most Rare Dream*. This latter is a late version of the medieval love-vision.

[2] For example, *Twelfth Night*, Act III, scene i, ll. 96 *et sqq.*, in which Auguecheek is taken in by Viola's strained use of poetic conceits.

[3] Cf. H. B. Charlton, *Shakespearian Comedy*, p. 102. *The Taming of the Shrew*, "does not mirror an Elizabethan facing and grappling with the dilemmas of Elizabethan man; it is not therefore comic drama, it is farce. It succeeds, not by its representation, but by its distortion of life."

[4] *The Comedy of Errors*, Act II, scene i, l. 10.

> Hath homely age the alluring beauty took
> From my poor cheek? [5]

Not entirely in the farcical spirit of the rest of the play is her exclamation to Antipholus of Syracuse, whom she supposes to be her husband.

> The time was once when thou unurg'd wouldst vow
> That never words were music to thine ear,
> That never object pleasing in thine eye,
> That never touch well welcome to thy hand,
> That never meat sweet-savour'd in thy taste,
> Unless I spake, or look'd, or touch'd, or carv'd to thee.[6]

Adriana remains baffled to the end, crying out finally, in her bewilderment, "My heart prays for him, though my tongue do curse." [7]

It is not in the province of farce to solve any problems for its characters, and Adriana's efforts to close the gap between lovers' vows and lovers' infidelity plays no part in the denouement. Similarly, the warring ideas in *The Taming of the Shrew* are carried to no conclusion. Petruchio boisterously disdains the usual languishings and ecstasies demanded of the romantic courtier.[8] The worldly satisfactions that he seeks are far away from those of the conventional Lucentio. Petruchio insists that

> . . . wealth is burden of my wooing dance,
> Be she as foul as was Florentius' love,
> As old as Sibyl, and as curst and shrewd
> As Socrates' Xanthippe, or a worse,
> She moves me not, or not removes, at least
> Affection's edge in me . . .

---

[5] *Ibid.*, Act II, scene i, l. 87. [6] *Ibid.*, Act II, scene ii, l. 117.
[7] *Ibid.*, Act IV, scene ii, l. 28.
[8] Charlton suggests that this play is "Shakespeare's first recoil from romance" (*Shakespearian Comedy*, p. 45). He further states (*ibid.*, p. 96) that in this play Shakespeare took "the brutal rollicking temper of classical comedy which knew not love," and imposed it "as the ruling air on a story which comprises nothing but the incidents of courtship. Love becomes a matter of business, not of sentiment."

> I come to wive it wealthily in Padua;
> If wealthily, then happily in Padua.[9]

But Petruchio's conception of love achieves no triumph over the courtly, Petrarchan ideal. No conflict of attitudes takes place in his heart. His difficulties are entirely external and objective and cease to exist as soon as his shrewish wife surrenders. Hence these romantic and farcical plays of Shakespeare, though clearly reflecting antagonistic notions of love, make no attempt to reconcile them.

Two Gentlemen of Verona is Shakespeare's first play in which a reconciliation of lovers is given full dramatic treatment. This drama therefore forms a kind of intermediate link between his farces and the romances, on the one hand, and his love-game comedies, on the other. There is no witty sex duel in *Two Gentlemen of Verona;* at its termination a conflict of attitudes comes to rest. This play is rather one of romantic adventure in which two friends pursue the same mistress. The love-conflict here (aside from incidental and obvious parody of Petrarchan sentiments in the figure of Thurio) is double. It is based first of all on the "question," dramatized in Lyly's *Endimion,* of the relative value of love and friendship. Secondly, the conflict is between a courtly conception of passion and a realistic if perfidious one. Valentine, as his name suggests, is the proper amorist, a man who seeks the sublime experience of love. Like Troilus in Chaucer's poem, Valentine follows the conventional rules of romance. After a short period in which he jeers at all fanciful sentiment [10] he becomes a convert. He lapses into melancholy, he sighs, he cannot eat. He confesses to Proteus:

> I have done penance for contemning love;
> Whose high imperious thoughts have punish'd me
> With bitter fasts, with penitential groans,
> With nightly tears . . .[11]

---

[9] *The Taming of the Shrew,* Act I, scene ii, l. 68.

[10] *Two Gentlemen of Verona,* Act I, scene i.

[11] Cf., *ibid.,* Speed's description, Act II, scene i, l. 19. Valentine's confession to Proteus, II-iv-130.

In contrast to Valentine, Proteus rashly denies both the ideal of friendship and that of love. When Silvia refuses him as her lover, Proteus recoils from *fine amor* to flout it.[12] Expressing, curiously, the same frustration as that voiced by John Donne, in *Loves Deitie*,[13] Proteus cries out against the obdurate Silvia:

> O, 'tis the curse in love, and still approv'd
> When women cannot love where they're belov'd.[14]

His cynical contempt for established ideals of friendship and passion forms the chief dramatic interest in the play. Proteus's attempt to force Silvia to yield to his desire comes as the logical result of his repudiation of convention. He forces an unpleasant reality into Valentine's unworldly behavior, as did Euphues in Lyly's novel in an effort to seduce Philautus's mistress. Yet Valentine's fidelity to courtly conventions is so abject that he refuses to believe his friend's treachery. Wishing that Proteus's attempt to force Silvia were an illusion, he shuts his eyes and ears to this manifestation of his friend's gross licentiousness, crying "How like a dream is this I see and hear!" [15] In an effort to preserve the ideals of his unsubstantial world, Valentine goes so far as to offer Silvia to the repentant Proteus. This triumph of romantic friendship over crass faithlessness brings the discordant attitudes dramatized in this play into a final harmony, for Proteus is reclaimed. The mutual reconciliation of friends and lovers, which rounds out the narrative, at the same time suggests that the ideals of romance and friendship can persist in spite of momentary triumphs of physical passion.[16]

---

[12] He also expresses a disrespect for Petrarchan conceit, *ibid.*, Act III, scene ii, l. 73.

[13] *The Poems of John Donne*, ed. by Grierson, I, 54.

[14] *Two Gentlemen of Verona*, Act V, scene iv, l. 43.

[15] *Ibid.*, Act V, scene iv, l. 26.

[16] This play's conclusion is often found unpalatable by critics. Charlton suggests, in *Shakespearian Comedy*, p. 43, that Valentine "turns the world from its compassionate approval [of romance] to a mood of skeptical questioning . . . Shakespeare's first attempt to make romantic comedy had only succeeded in so far that it had unexpectedly and inadvertantly made romance comic."

Shakespeare's
First Love-Game Comedy
LOVE'S LABOUR'S LOST

In *Love's Labour's Lost* Shakespeare presents a quarrel over the nature of love dramatized for the first time in the fashion inaugurated by John Lyly.[17] In this play Shakespeare derives comedy from a simple and overt use of the contradictions between romantic courtesy and the actual behavior of ladies and gentlemen. Opposing points of view are personified by lovers and their mistresses, who quarrel with each other with an ingenuousness very like that of the foresters and the nymphs of Lyly's *Love's Metamorphosis*.

Love's Labour's Lost, however, is not entirely preoccupied with the relationship between realistic passion and Petrarchan conventions of thought and feeling. First of all, it satirizes the attempt of the King of Navarre and three courtiers to become anchorites for the sake of knowledge, to substitute an ascetic intellectualism for more normal pursuits. *Love's Labour's Lost* is thus a comment on the folly of a philosophic contempt for worldly pleasures. In addition, Shakespeare may have singled out members of the "School of Night," Elizabethans interested in new scientific theories of the universe, as specific targets for ridicule. Miss Yates [18] has brought together evidence to show the many similarities between characters in this play and actual people of the sixteenth century. Berowne, for example, is seen to be a kind of parody of the anti-Petrarchan attitude of the Italian philosopher Giordano Bruno. Bruno had expressed his scorn of romantic love in his dedication to Sidney of his book *De gli eroici furori*. Bruno regarded the amorous devotions of courtiers as absurd, because he felt that the intellectual "fury" of an active mind was so much more admirable.[19] Preoccupation with the

---

[17] For a general summary and comment on the debt of *Love's Labour's Lost* to John Lyly see O. J. Campbell, "*Love's Labour's Lost* Restudied," in *Studies in Shakespeare, Milton and Donne*, pp. 20–21.
[18] Yates, *A Study in "Love's Labour's Lost."*
[19] *Ibid.*, pp. 104–105; see also Miss Yates's *John Florio, the Life of an*

exaggerated delights of sexual passion was vile and ignoble when the mind could be freed to contemplate things more profound. Whether Shakespeare's play is in part a satire of real people or not, it is at least a mocking of human vanity, which seeks to escape the actual operation of emotion. For after their first glimpse of attractive women these courtiers from Navarre turn easily from philosophy to the pursuit of love.

It is only after the courtiers have given up asserting that they are men of contemplation that they turn into posturing Petrarchans. They are immediately ridiculed for this second folly by the dissenting courtier of Navarre, the perspicacious, plain-speaking Berowne. He has a double function in the play. He is at once an individual, with his own love problems to solve, and a matter-of-fact commentator on the incredible sentiments which his peers have chosen to accept as valid. Berowne's particular difficulty is that he is caught by a desire to experience romance, and at the same time he senses that it cannot exist on the idyllic level at which it is usually described. Alexander and Sapho, in Lyly's comedies, had escaped their difficulties by a final revolt from love, whereas Berowne's predicament is more nearly that of an actual Renaissance courtier. For this reason he is more credible than Lyly's characters. Berowne is brought finally to acknowledge that he cannot elude the claims of romance, even though he recognizes its insubstantial nature. He reveals the conflict taking place in his personality when he sends Costard with a furtive sonnet to Rosaline and then turns his scorn upon himself:

> And I,
> Forsooth, in love! I, that have been love's whip;
> A very beadle to a humorous sigh.[20]

Italian in Shakespeare's England, pp. 104–108, 118–123. Cf. Boulting, *Giordano Bruno, His Life, Thought, and Martyrdom*, pp. 96–97: "Bruno wished to put before Sidney and the world a higher form of adoration; he would substitute devotion to the imperishable beauty of wisdom for the courtly service of mere perishable charms." Berowne also mocks the scientific spirit of Bruno, *Love's Labour's Lost*, Act I, scene i, ll. 88 *et sqq.*

[20] *Ibid.*, Act III, scene i, l. 183.

Berowne is a cynical amorist, a Mercutio caught by what he has most often flouted. Love, he notes, is not all sentiment. Cupid is not only "regent of love-rimes . . . the annointed sovereign of sighs and groans." [21] He is also the god of the palpable reality of sexual desires, the

> Dread prince of plackets, king of codpieces,
> Sole imperator and great general
> Of trotting 'paritors . . .[22]

It is not enough that Berowne has become a "corporal" of Cupid's field. Even the actual object of his love falls far short of accepted Elizabethan standards of beauty and virtue. He protests the irony that despite his sense of reality, it has been his fate among the three ladies

> . . . to love the worst of all;
> A wightly wanton with a velvet brow,
> With two pitch balls stuck in her face for eyes;
> Ay, and, by heaven, one that will do the deed
> Though Argus were her eunuch and her guard:
> And I to sigh for her! . . .[23]

His only escape from his own inconsistencies is to juggle them into a momentary state of equilibrium. He concludes this feat with the comment,

> Well, I will love, write, sigh, pray, sue, and groan:
> Some men must love my lady, and some Joan.[24]

In his second role, that of cynical commentator [25] on the fatuous posturings of his fellow courtiers, Berowne links their unworldly sentiments to tawdry fact. He prepares them for confusion by revealing to the lovers, and to the audience, the actual nature of their conceptions. This disclosure is staged adroitly.

---

[21] *Ibid.*, Act III, scene i, l. 191.   [22] *Ibid.*, Act III, scene i, l. 205.
[23] *Ibid.*, Act III, scene i, l. 205. See John, *Elizabethan Sonnet Sequences*, p. 141: "For although both the plays and the sonnets contain many striking descriptions of conventional beauty, Shakespeare seems to have recognized fully their limitations and to have satirized them even while employing them."
[24] *Love's Labour's Lost*, Act III, scene i, l. 214.
[25] *Ibid.*, especially Act IV, scene iii.

Berowne, hidden in a tree, overhears in turn, the King, Longaville, and Dumaine file past reading love sonnets. Having muttered almost a line by line rebuttal of all stereotyped conceits contained in this poetry, Berowne descends from his perch to challenge the pretensions of his fellows to their faces. He cries out:

> O! what a scene of foolery have I seen,
> Of sighs, of groans, of sorrow, and of teen;
> O me! with what strict patience have I sat,
> To see a king transformed to a gnat.[26]

In derision he asks each the physiological source of all the languishing love—agony that has been put into rhyme:

> . . . O! tell me, good Dumaine,
> And, gentle Longaville, where lies thy pain?
> And where my liege's? all about the breast:
> A caudle, ho! . . .[27]

Lovers' difficulties are further emphasized by the fact that Berowne, too, can be unmasked. The skeptic in his turn has his own romantic aspirations jeered at.[28] However, he is ready to defend himself, and Rosaline. As for falling in love, he explains,

> We cannot cross the cause why we were born.[29]

And as for the dark complexioned Rosaline, she was

> . . . born to make black fair
> Her favour turns the fashion of the days.[30]

Berowne, who had attempted to accede to his own romantic desires and to force his peers to do likewise, brings the intellectual struggle to the point of comic truce at the end of this scene. The king acknowledges Berowne as an interpreter of love and thus gives dramatic emphasis to his rationalization of romantic inconsistencies. All the courtiers having originally sworn not to fall in

---

[26] *Ibid.*, Act IV, scene iii, l. 163.

[27] *Ibid.*, Act IV, scene iii, l. 171. Some editors prefer the folio reading "candle." A "caudle" for their love-sickness seems the obvious requirement, and is the 1598 quarto reading.

[28] *Ibid.*, Act IV, scene iii, ll. 229 *et sqq.*

[29] *Ibid.*, Act IV, scene iii, l. 218.   [30] *Ibid.*, Act IV, scene iii, l. 261.

love, the king asks for an explanation of their behavior.[31] It is forthcoming in the most familiar passage in *Love's Labour's Lost*.[32] Here, in a neat juggling of traditional love psychology, the skeptical Berowne proves to his audience and to himself that it is wrong not to be in love.

> . . . for not looking on a woman's face,
> You have in that forsworn the use of eyes,
> And study too, the causer of your vow;
> For where is any author in the world
> Teaches such beauty as a woman's eye? [33]

The courtiers accept this ironic and comic defense of their behavior. They see now that the only thing left for them to do is to win the ladies.

The sharp wit of the Princess of France and her three attendant ladies serves (like that of the nymphs in Lyly's *Love's Metamorphosis*) to discipline the exaggerated ardors of these lords. But Shakespeare characterizes his ladies more skilfully than Lyly characterized his nymphs. There is an air of reality about them, as if the attitudes they dramatized were a part of their character, not merely a dramatist's way of rendering specific general ideas of the day. For example, the princess' intolerance of all affected sentiment is suggested in the first words she speaks to her attendant, Lord Boyet. He has automatically paid the gallant respects of courtier to lady and is rewarded by having his mere complimentary phrase snubbed.

> Good Lord Boyet, my beauty, though but mean,
> Needs not the painted flourish of your praise:
> Beauty is bought by judgment of the eye,
> Not utter'd by base sale of chapmen's tongues.
> I am less proud to hear you tell my worth
> Than you much willing to be counted wise
> In spending your wit in the praise of mine.[34]

Likewise, the audience is allowed to discover that the princess and her attendant ladies, though not unwilling to be wooed, are

---

[31] *Ibid.*, Act IV, scene iii, l. 284. [32] *Ibid.*, Act IV, scene iii, ll. 289–365.
[33] *Ibid.*, Act IV, scene iii, l. 309. [34] *Ibid.*, Act II, scene i, l. 13.

consciously realistic where love is concerned. Each praises the courtier whom she is to meet at Navarre so highly that the princess berates them, saying,

> God bless my ladies! are they all in love,
> That every one her own hath garnished
> With such bedecking ornaments of praise? [35]

The princess cautions her ladies not to squander their wit among themselves.

> Good wits will be jangling; but, gentles, agree.
> This civil war of wits were much better us'd
> On Navarre and his book-men, for here 'tis abus'd.[36]

Following her advice, the ladies accept the gifts and the sonnets of their wooers half in delight, half in derision. Their action has been anticipated by the audience and is therefore dramatically credible.[37] Rosaline comments that if the portrait which her lover has presented in his lyric actually describes her,

> I were the fairest goddess on the ground.[38]

In like spirit, Katharine notes that Dumaine has sent her

> Some thousand verses of a faithful lover:
> A huge translation of hypocrisy,
> Vilely compil'd, profound simplicity.[39]

From the point of view of the ladies, therefore, the courtiers, whose poetic compliments were too grossly exaggerated to please, deserve to be disciplined. Vanity can be wounded by overpraise. The courtiers, in Rosaline's words, are "fools to purchase mocking so." [40]

Further dramatic justification for the wit-lashing by which the princess and her ladies-in-waiting bring their lovers to submission is found in the fact that these lovers first attempt to woo by trickery. They visit their mistresses disguised as Muscovites.

---

[35] *Ibid.*, Act II, scene i, l. 77.   [36] *Ibid.*, Act II, scene i, l. 223.

[37] Contrast *Love's Metamorphosis*, Act I, scene ii, ll. 18 *et sqq.* Here the nymphs act as mere mouthpieces for satire.

[38] *Love's Labour's Lost*, Act V, scene ii, l. 36.

[39] *Ibid.*, Act V, scene ii, l. 50.   [40] *Ibid.*, Act V, scene ii, l. 59.

The ladies being forewarned, mask themselves and exchange favors to beguile their suitors into protesting love to the wrong party. The princess emphasizes the culpability of the lords and so lends added credibility to the sex duels. She comments on the masking, as Rosaline had commented on the poetry,

> They do it but in mocking merriment;
> And mock for mock is only my intent.[41]

When the king and his men come to pay final and open court, it is to "jangle" wits until by this means they win their ladies.[42] Three of the courtiers are quickly vanquished by sharp-tongued abuse; so it is left for Berowne and Rosaline to carry on the supreme battle of wits.[43] Having defended without success his efforts to behave in the fashion prescribed by romantic love,[44] Berowne reverses his tactics and disavows, point by point, all the formal ritual of courtesy. He swears that henceforth he will never

> ... come in visor to my friend,
> Nor woo in rime, like a blind harper's song,
> Taffeta phrases, silken terms precise,
> Three-pil'd hyperboles, spruce affectation,
> Figures pedantical; these summer flies
> Have blown me full of maggot ostentation:
> I do forswear them; and I here protest,
> By this white glove,—how white the hand, God knows—
> Henceforth my wooing mind shall be express'd
> In russet yeas and honest kersey noes.[45]

At this point in the love-game comedy as written by Lyly a supernatural being would step in and, by making the reluctant ladies each take a lover, force an ironic termination of the antagonisms which the play had dramatized. In *Love's Labour's Lost,* however, the component elements of character, narrative, and attitude are fused. A reconciliation of conflicting ideas had already

---

[41] *Ibid.,* Act V, scene ii, l. 139.
[42] Berowne has already had a preliminary skirmish with Rosaline (*ibid.,* Act II, scene ii).
[43] *Ibid.,* Act V, scene ii, ll. 374-431.
[44] *Ibid.,* Act V, scene ii, l. 396.   [45] *Ibid.,* Act V, scene ii, l. 405.

been prepared for in the play itself by Berowne's exposure (in Act IV) of the ironies and paradoxes of romance. Furthermore, since the characters in this comedy are sufficiently well delineated to give the dramatic illusion that they create their own difficulties, it would be incongruous to have such difficulties solved by an outside agent. In the denouement of Shakespeare's play the only resemblance to Lyly is that the announcement of the death of the princess' father gives a sudden and unexpected turn to the narrative. But this event serves the purpose of tempering the festive spirit engendered by the wit-combats, of calling a halt to jest, and of forcing a clear-cut decision on the part of the ladies wooed.

Hence the lovers become serious for a few moments in order to lend an air of conviction to the conciliatory gestures to be made by both sides. The princess asks the king to excuse the overbold and "liberal opposition" of her ladies, although she defends them.

> We have receiv'd your letters full of love:
> Your favours, the embassadors of love;
> And, in our maiden council, rated them
> At courtship, pleasant jest, and courtesy,
> . . . and therefore met your loves
> In their own fashion, like a merriment.[46]

This speech gives the lords the necessary chance to speak "honest, plain words" [47] about their love. Shorn of romantic ostentation, first by their ladies' wit, then by the new somber note that forbids jest, the king pleads for himself and his fellows.

> Now, at the latest minute of the hour
> Grant us your loves.[48]

But the princess refuses to enter into any sudden, unrealistic "world-without-end" bargain with romance. The lovers are all accepted only on condition that each does a year's penance to prove a love more durable than that illustrated by their wooing.

In this comedy, the first of his comedies of courtship, Shake-

---

[46] *Ibid.*, Act V, scene ii, l. 785. [47] *Ibid.*, Act V, scene ii, l. 761.
[48] *Ibid.*, Act V, scene ii, l. 795.

speare has contrived to present both the appeal and the incongruities involved in the Elizabethan traditional ritual of wooing. The first four acts are devoted largely to an exposition of the conflicting attitudes the lovers and their ladies will personify in the sex duels in the final act. The comic acceptance of contradictory elements in love is presented by the courtiers, who having first rejected love, with the aid of Berowne, acknowledge it. Comic acceptance is further dramatized by the courtiers as they endeavor to reach an agreement with their ladies. By such means the cynicism voiced by Berowne and the teasing perpetrated by the ladies are brought into harmonious balance with the idyllic love championed by the king, Dumaine, and Longaville. The darkening of the last scene by an allusion to death lends credibility to the final (if somewhat equivocal) reconciliation, in which even Berowne,

> ... a man replete with mocks;
> Full of comparisons and wounding flouts,[49]

has found it necessary to make overt concession to fancy.

As You Like It

In *Love's Labour's Lost* Shakespeare presents the sixteenth-century quarrel over romance by following closely the dramatic devices and situations which Lyly had used in his court comedies. In *As You Like It* the pattern which Lyly devised is no longer obtrusive. The witty skirmish between the wooer and his lady, for example, is no longer a set tableau, but has become a way of revealing character. Moreover, in Shakespeare's second [50] love-game comedy the pretensions of lovers are those found in Renaissance pastoral romances and dramas.[51] Shakespeare's play

---

[49] *Ibid.*, Act V, scene ii, l. 851.
[50] Second for the purpose of studying Shakespeare's dramatic treatment of the Elizabethan love dilemma. Chronologically it may well follow *Much Ado*.
[51] Cf. Walter W. Greg, *Pastoral Poetry and Pastoral Drama*, pp. 337–338: "The idea of pastoral current among the playwrights, and no doubt among the audience too, was largely derived from such novels as the 'Arcadia,' and, as we have seen, the tradition of these works was one rather of polite chivalry and of courtly adventure than of pastoralism proper."

turns Lodge's story [52] of rustic adventure and love-making into comedy by parodying the bucolic version of romantic love. The quarreling couples in this play are once removed from those of *Love's Labour's Lost*, who mock what may well have been the beliefs and practices of actual Elizabethan courtiers. Such discipline as exaggerated fancy receives in the Forest of Arden has less tangible objects. Here Shakespeare does not derive comedy directly from the courtly and Petrarchan ideals of the age, but from these ideals as they had been adopted and sentimentalized by the Renaissance Arcadian garden of love.[53]

In *As You Like It* Shakespeare was following what is, according to W. W. Greg, the one "constant element in the pastoral as known to literature." [54] From the time of Theocritus this tradition had depicted a conscious simplicity and ingenuousness in contrast to a more complex, more sophisticated actuality. Whereas the chief purpose of such Elizabethan pastoral romances as those written by Sidney and by Lodge was to create a Renaissance garden of love where a reader's idealizing tendency could luxuriate, that of Shakespeare's drama was not. He approaches Arden in a matter-of-fact mood and makes it, however pretty and desirable, also incongruous and therefore comic.

He does this in two ways. In the first place, the narrative events of *As You Like It* allow its principal characters to escape from the harsh world of normal life, where they have been dispossessed, into the tranquility of the forest where the good duke has translated the "stubbornness of fortune into so quiet and so sweet a style." [55] It is only in Arden, one is made aware, that an

---

[52] Lodge, *Rosalynde, Euphues Golden Legacie.*

[53] Greg notes that in the prologue to Tasso's *Aminta*, Amore is introduced in "pastoral disguise, escaped from the care of his mother, who would confine his activity to the courts, and intent on loosing his shafts among the nymphs and shepherds of Arcadia," *Pastoral Poetry and Pastoral Drama*, p. 185; cf. further, p. 191, "not a little of the convention at least of chivalrous love survives in the debased Arcadian love of the sentimental pastoral." Cf. Fraunce's *The Countesse of Pembrokes Yvychurch*, an adaptation of Tasso's play. If Shakespeare was influenced by Tasso, it was probably through this translation.

[54] *Pastoral Poetry and Pastoral Drama*, p. 4.

[55] *As You Like It*, Act II, scene i, l. 19.

unpropertied youth turned wrestler could meet and woo the outcast daughter of a duke. It is only here that retribution, followed by forgiveness, overtakes all evil. An obvious contradiction underlies the whole play, as its title indicates. It is the difference between the "working day world" [56] of villainy and delusion and that rustic world, perfected by the Renaissance imagination, where one could "fleet the time carelessly as they did in the golden world." [57]

Secondly, and more important for his comic purpose, Shakespeare peoples Arden both with disenchanted malcontents and wits and characters derived from conventional figures in other pastoral romances who are a parody on their literary origins. Orlando is willing to follow the routine behavior proper to a rustic Petrarchan, but he must first take lessons from Rosalind in the art of languishing. Silvius likewise follows the customary pattern of love too literally and becomes absurd. Both Audrey, a caricatured portrait of an actual milkmaid, and Phebe, an exaggeration of the uncommonly chaste Arcadian heroine, serve as additions to the general mockery of bucolic conventions.

The contradictions between Arden and normal scenes of Elizabethan endeavor are made apparent in *As You Like It*, however, by dramatic devices more engaging than mere mimicry of literary types. The interactions of its various characters are equally illuminating. The rustic shepherd Silvius, for example, in his pursuit of Phebe, is not allowed to be merely an overly correct Arcadian.[58] His sentimental desires are not much less credible than those of Montanus in Lodge's *Rosalynde*, or those of Pyrocles in Sidney's *Arcadia*. Indeed, if it were not for the astute analysis which he receives at the hands of his fellows,

---

[56] *Ibid.*, Act I, scene iii, l. 12.

[57] *Ibid.*, Act I, scene i, l. 126. Cf. Fraunce's translation of the chorus on the "Golden Age" from Tasso's *Aminta*. The idea is considered with levity by Shakespeare in *As You Like It*, indirectly, by Jaques's and by Touchstone's disapproval of Arden. Other Elizabethan uses of the phrase "golden world" are listed by J. Leon Lievsay, in "Shakespere's 'Golden World,'" *Shakespeare Association Bulletin*, XIII, No. 2 (April, 1938), 77-86.

[58] Cf. Greg, *Pastoral Poetry and Pastoral Drama*, p. 412: "Phebe and Silvius represent the polished Arcadians of pastoral tradition."

Silvius would be little more than the ingenuous, highly stereotyped, love-sick youth which the pastoral romance had derived from Petrarchan and courtly literature. But the kind of mystical passion that he wishes to encompass is brought to earth by everyone to whom he appeals. The old man, Corin, suggests that he be less in love if he wish to gain his mistress.[59] Touchstone jeers at Silvius, recalling his own enchantment when he kissed "the cow's dugs" that his mistress' "pretty chopped (i.e., chapped) hands had milked."[60] Rosalind, with sharp logic, points out to Silvius that he is in love with an idea, not with the unattractive Phebe.

> 'Tis not her glass, but you, that flatters her;
> And out of you she sees herself more proper
> Than any of her lineaments can show her.[61]

For the purpose of further emphasizing the conventionally romantic nature of his passion, the shepherdess whom he pursues, Phebe, personifies the froward indifference that cannot love where it is sought. She analyzes realistically and derisively all the symbolic conceits which her wooer has used to express his attachment.

> Thou tell'st me there is murder in mine eyes;
> 'Tis pretty, sure, and very probable,
> That eyes that are the frail'st and softest things,
> Who shut their coward gates on atomies,
> Should be call'd tyrants, butchers, murderers![62]

However, Phebe herself is not merely the embodiment of the "extravagant and conventional 'pudor' which forms one of the most abiding features of the pastoral drama."[63] She is also, in

---

[59] *As You Like It*, Act II, scene iv, l. 22.

[60] *Ibid.*, Act II, scene iv, l. 49.

[61] *Ibid.*, Act III, scene v, l. 54. See further, Act IV, scene iii, l. 23, Act IV, scene iii, l. 66.

[62] *Ibid.*, Act III, scene v, ll. 10 *et sqq.*

[63] Greg, *Pastoral Poetry and Pastoral Drama*, p. 189. He suggests that the Renaissance pastoral's interest in chastity begins with Silvia in Tasso's *Aminta* ("Phillis" in Fraunce's *Yvychurch*). The type is repeated in Amarilli in Guarini's *Pastor Fido*. The chaste nymph is everywhere in Lyly's comedies and is ridiculed in *Love's Metamorphosis* by the foresters' attempts to win the foolishly hesitant nymphs. The character survived in Fletcher's *Faithful Shep-*

part, a parody of the unwilling shepherdess of Arcadia. Her attitude toward Silvius is much like that of the Phoebe in Lodge's story. But her ostentatious chastity, like the ardor of Silvius, is ridiculed by Rosalind, who turns a critical eye on silly, obtuse reluctance, remarking,

> . . . I must tell you friendly in your ear,
> Sell when you can; you are not for all markets.
> Cry the man mercy; love him; take his offer.[64]

Both Touchstone and Jaques serve to bring out the contrasting elements of love. Jaques, the melancholy observer of the insignificance of being alive, who finds even Arden impossible to live in,[65] who jeers at Orlando's love for Rosalind,[66] sums up the cynic's contempt for the practices of the traditional amorist. In his derisive, thumbnail sketch of man's entrances and exits on the world's stage the lover occupies the third act.

> . . . And then the lover,
> Sighing like a furnace, with a woful ballad
> Made to his mistress' eyebrow.[67]

Touchstone, who, like Jaques, finds Arden unpleasant,[68] dramatizes a much more genial caricature of romance. In his solicitation of Audrey he mimics the passionate shepherd of literary

---

herdess, and in Milton's *Comus*. The reluctant girl is also found in Greek romances, but for a different purpose. Her innocence is prolonged to tease the reader, not held up for admiration. See Wolff, *Greek Romances in Elizabethan Prose Fiction*, pp. 127–136.

[64] *As You Like It*, Act III, scene v, l. 59. For other Elizabethan ridicule of Phoebe, see Greg, *Pastoral Poetry and Pastoral Drama*, p. 113n (verses from "Tarlton's News out of Purgatory"). Both Donne's imitation of Marlowe's *Passionate Shepherd* and Raleigh's supposed reply treat this subject with the levity found in Shakespeare's Phebe.

[65] *Ibid.*, Act II, scene v, l. 49, Act V, scene iv, ll. 191, 202.

[66] *Ibid.*, Act III, scene ii, ll. 277 *et sqq.*

[67] *Ibid.*, Act II, scene vii, l. 147. Jaques presents almost too bitter a point of view for light comedy. Professor Oscar James Campbell suggests that he "signalizes Shakespeare's first participation in the satiric movement, which after 1599 began to capture English comedy," and that Jaques is an unfavorable comment upon it (see "Jaques," in *Huntington Library Bulletin*, No. 8, October, 1935, p. 102).

[68] *Ibid.*, Act II, scene iv, l. 16.

tradition and also lightly ridicules the highly imagined ideals of poets. He tells her that he wishes the gods had made her poetical, since "the truest poetry is the most feigning." He concludes:

> . . . thou swearest to me
> thou art honest [i.e., chaste]; now if thou wert a poet I
> might have some hope thou didst feign.[69]

The presentation of pastoral romance at cross purposes with the cynicism of Jaques and Touchstone, moreover, is incidental enrichment to the central conflict of attitudes dramatized by Orlando and Rosalind. This pair of lovers, about whom the action of the play pivots, have escaped the court to find themselves in idyllic Arden. They both fall in love, according to custom, at first sight. But Orlando, who is stricken speechless and begins to languish in the fashion proper to a Chaucerian or Petrarchan lover, is, as was Silvius, disciplined not only by the lady he pursues but also by the commentators Touchstone and Jaques. The one is content to taunt Orlando by a caricature of his first poetic appeal to his lady.

> If a hart do lack a hind,
> Let him seek out Rosalind.
> If the cat will after kind,
> So be sure will Rosalind (etc.) [70]

Jaques, however, jeers at Orlando's enamored posturings almost to a quarrel. He expresses his contempt for all the youthful ideals which Orlando cherishes, by dubbing him "good Signior love" and asking:

> I pray you, mar no more trees
> with writing love-songs in their barks.[71]

---

[69] *Ibid.*, Act III, scene iii, ll. 21–29.   [70] *Ibid.*, Act III, scene ii, l. 108.
[71] *Ibid.*, Act III, scene ii, l. 277. Lovers had been ridiculed before for leaving messages or verses for their mistresses, in Lyly's *Love's Metamorphosis* (Act I, scene iii) and in *Love's Labour's Lost* (Act IV, scene iii; Act V, scene ii). This latter scene is also in imitation of one in Greene's *Orlando Furioso* (see *As You Like It*, ed. by Sir Arthur Quiller-Couch and John Dover Wilson, p. 134*n*). But where Greene's hero acts in a mad fury of love, Shakespeare's Orlando acts in mockery of it. Shakespeare chose his hero's name, possibly, to make parody more complete. In Lodge's story Montanus carves both

Rosalind, who has escaped into Arden disguised as the young page Ganymede, keeps her identity hidden for the dramatic purpose of taunting the extravagances displayed by Orlando. She is a more subtle compound of realism and fancy than was Rosaline of *Love's Labour's Lost*. She shares with Berowne a subjective knowledge of the contradictions of love, but differs from him in that such knowledge is no problem to her. She can be skeptical and in love at the same time. Although she carries a recollection of the "burrs" and the "briers" [72] of the outside world with her into Arden, she does not dramatize the malcontented attitude of Jaques.[73] She does not point out the illusions of love to dispel them. Rather, she has an affection for the absurdities of romantic wooers and encourages these absurdities in Orlando. She herself accepts Orlando only after she has forced him to be the awkward personification of the traditional courtier.

The wit combats in *Love's Labour's Lost*, except those between Berowne and his lady, were rather one-sided; the courtiers were always put to flight. This unequal division of verbal skill is further emphasized in *As You Like It*. Rosalind keeps in check Orlando's efforts to exalt her as the object of his passion by exposing the differences between him and the lover as described by an Elizabethan sonneteer. She mocks him by pointing out that the marks of such a one are:

A lean cheek, which you have not; a blue eye and sunken, which you have not . . . Your hose should be ungartered, your bonnet unbanded, your sleeve unbuttoned, your shoe untied, and everything about you demonstrating a careless desolation.[74]

---

a beech and a pine tree in honor of Phoebe, and Rosader (Shakespeare's Orlando) makes use of a myrtle tree for the same purpose. See Townsend Rich, *Harington and Ariosto; a Study in Elizabethan Verse Translation*, pp. 110–111: "Ariosto, in describing Angelica writing her own and her lover's names on trees, treated the action as a matter of course, while Sir John made the girl out a silly fool."

[72] *As You Like It*, Act I, scene iii, ll. 12, 17.

[73] This contrast is clearly made by her remark to Jaques: "I had rather have a fool to make me merry than experience to make me sad: and travel for it too!" (*ibid.*, Act IV, scene i, l. 28).

[74] *Ibid.*, Act III, scene ii, l. 397.

Orlando's inadequate and comic defense here, as in subsequent controversy, is his simple bewilderment. All he can do is to swear to his passion "by the white hand of Rosalind." [75]

All the unpleasant realities of love with which Rosalind taunts Orlando act to balance his excessively romantic point of view. But they are so expressed that Orlando does not need to deny them. Both he and the audience ascribe them, not to Rosalind, but to Ganymede. She suggests that the actual woman he thinks so idyllic (much as Lyly had described Pandora in *The Woman in the Moone*) is:

... changeable, longing and liking; proud, fantastical, apish, shallow, inconstant, full of tears, full of smiles, for every passion something, and for no passion truly anything.[76]

She tells him, when he comes too late to his appointment, that she "had as lief be wooed of a snail," because "he brings his destiny with him." [77] That is, the horns of a cuckold. And Orlando can manage only an ingenuous protest: "Virtue is no hornmaker; and my Rosalind is virtuous." [78]

Romantic sentiment almost emerges unscathed in *As You Like It*. Such is Shakespeare's art that witty contentions appear to be primarily a means of presenting Orlando and Rosalind courting each other. Only secondarily and by implication are their quarrels an expression of conflicting elements in Elizabethan thought about love. Such conflict as takes place in Arden may threaten romantic or pastoral notions with reality, but never ridicule them in the (comparatively) harsher fashion found at the Court of Navarre. The witty sex duel by which Lyly sought to analyze and to adjust the Renaissance complexities of love is still the dramatic method by which Shakespeare presents Orlando and Rosalind. But they are an intentionally individualized

---

[75] *Ibid.*, Act III, scene ii, l. 419.

[76] *As You Like It*, Act III, scene ii, l. 437. Cf. Rosalind's attack on the important heroes of romance, *ibid.*, Act IV, scene i, l. 97, and on the notion that one can die of love. Orlando remains skeptical of such realism. See also *ibid.*, Act IV, scene i, l. 151.

[77] *Ibid.*, Act IV, scene i, l. 54.

[78] *Ibid.*, Act IV, scene i, l. 65.

version of the undifferentiated lovers in Lyly's plays, and their quarrels partake of the lyric spell of Arden.

In *Love's Labour's Lost* the derisive princess and her ladies nearly destroy the aspirations of their wooers. But a final introduction of death serves to reconcile the quarreling couples to each other and to love itself. In *As You Like it,* on the other hand, the ultimate reconciliations between bickering lovers are almost too easily made. Hence, to forestall a universal triumph of romance Shakespeare allows the forces of cynicism, roaming Arden, to remain articulate. The two sturdy realists, Touchstone and Jaques, do not succumb to the illusions of the pastoral world. They remain unconverted, and they stay outside the universal reconciliations to comment on them, to balance the romance in Arden with the reality of the "working-day world." Touchstone, dragging his Audrey after him, tempers the exalted mood of the final scene when he remarks to the prince:

> I press in here, sir, amongst the rest of the
> country copulatives, to swear, and to forswear,
> according as marriage binds and blood breaks.
> A poor virgin sir, an ill-favoured thing sir,
> but mine own.[79]

And Jaques's estimation of the several sets of lovers serves as a similar link with actuality.

> There is, sure, another flood toward, and
> these couples are coming to the ark.[80]

Jaques passes a final sardonic comment on the marriages of Silvius and Touchstone. He suggests the sexual fulfillment of the one and the probable unpleasantness of the other.[81] Finally, as a benediction, Hymen presents a jocular wedding song which adds a final touch of discipline to bring into balance the conflict of romance and fact found in this play. It sets free the ultimate comic conviction that the contradictions between Arden and Lon-

---

[79] *Ibid.,* Act V, scene iv, l. 57.
[80] *Ibid.,* Act V, scene iv, l. 35.
[81] *Ibid.,* Act V, scene iv, ll. 197–198.

don are really separate aspects of a larger reality which includes them both:

> Wedding is great Juno's crown:
> O blessed bond of board and bed!
> 'Tis Hymen peoples every town;
> High wedlock then be honored.[82]

[82] *Ibid.*, Act V, scene iv, l. 148.

·XII·

COMEDY OF COURTSHIP
IN *Much Ado about Nothing*
AND SATIRE OF COURTSHIP IN
Troilus and Cressida

ROMANTIC sentiment had been disciplined by Berowne and by the ladies of *Love's Labour's Lost* and had been parodied by Touchstone, Jaques, and Rosalind, in *As You Like It*. In Shakespeare's final love-game comedy, *Much Ado about Nothing*, romance is shadowed for the first time by the threat that an attempt to adapt it to everyday reality could lead to an outcome not in the least comic. The paradoxes and contradictions which Shakespeare had hitherto presented in a rather light mood are dramatized in *Much Ado* for the first time in a more derisive spirit. Some of the harsher results of mutability of love, which Shakespeare expressed in his sonnets, begin to appear in drama.

He brings a new note of a deeper concern with the opposed elements of love into *Much Ado*. The fickle loyalties of the chief characters in the play are no longer merely comic and gay. These men and women change their amorous convictions, not, as before, according to chance or to whim, but chameleon-like and according to the shifting of circumstances in which they are caught. The central narrative event in this play is the trick whereby the innocent Hero is made to appear as a lascivious wanton. Claudio, for whom she has been the incarnation of all "soft and delicate desires,"[1] is a kind of romantic Orlando brought face to face with

---

[1] *Much Ado*, Act I, scene i, l. 313.

dismal fact. His rebuff is sufficiently brutal to force the whole play to the verge of tragedy. The embodiment of his love is transformed in his eyes from "the sweetest lady that ever I looked on" [2] to "this rotten orange," [3] who is more vile

> Than Venus, or those pamper'd animals
> That rage in savage sensuality.[4]

Claudio himself is changed from the spokesman for the spirit of romantic love, ready to tire all hearers "with a book of words," [5] to a cynical flouter of all love.[6] It is as if in *As You Like It* Rosalind had suddenly faced Orlando as the intemperate creature she had jestingly said she was. The conflict had been an intellectual one in Shakespeare's other love-game comedies, an amused acknowledgment that passion is not all gossamer. In *Much Ado* the complementary half of romance is what appears to be desperate fact.

If Claudio's blighted love affair were all of *Much Ado*, this play would carry the satiric implications of *Troilus and Cressida* and *Measure for Measure*. The light touch necessary to temper this effect and to counterbalance Claudio's delusion is given by the bickerings and wit skirmishes of Beatrice and Benedick. It is their quarrels, ultimately stilled by their marriage, which, like those of the lords and the ladies of *Love's Labour's Lost* and of Orlando and Rosalind of *As You Like It*, make *Much Ado* a love-game comedy. For this purpose the progress of their romance neatly parallels that between Claudio and Hero, only in reverse order. Like Claudio, they are tricked; but it is from a mutual antagonism into love. The scene in which Hero is pilloried is preceded by the events which bring about the capitulation of Beatrice and Benedick and followed by the first acknowledgment of love by this pair. Hence the comedy involved in exposing these antiromantic pretenders acts to mitigate the bitterness of Claudio's collapse as the languishing lover.

Beatrice and Benedick do not serve merely as a comic contrast

---

[2] *Ibid.*, Act I, scene i, l. 196.
[3] *Ibid.*, Act IV, scene i, l. 32.
[4] *Ibid.*, Act IV, scene i, l. 60.
[5] *Ibid.*, Act I, scene i, l. 317.
[6] Cf. *ibid.*, Act V, scene i, *passim*.

to the unpleasant events of this play, however. Their own falling in love is an equally ironic (if comic) acknowledgment of the paradoxical nature of love. If it is incongruous that what should have been an immutable sentiment to Claudio is shattered by an apparent exhibition of his lady's robust appetite, it is equally incongruous that adepts in the mocking denial of sentiment should be destroyed by it. Benedick had expressed himself concerning love, in general:

> . . . till all graces be in one woman, one woman shall not come in my grace.[7]

Specifically, he had said of Beatrice's sharp wit, "I cannot endure my Lady Tongue." [8] More elaborately, he had commented:

> I would not marry her, though she were endowed with all that Adam had left him before he transgressed.[9]

Likewise, Beatrice had confessed that she would never marry until "God make men of some other metal than earth," [10] asking further:

> Would it not grieve a woman to be over-mastered with a piece of valiant dust? to make an account of her life to a clod of wayward marl? [11]

But the vehemence of these denials, like Claudio's firm romantic convictions, is merely the prelude to their reversal, the preparation for their defeat. Benedick is tricked into overhearing that Beatrice has entered into the desperate, conventionally medieval love-sickness for him. Leonato confesses that his daughter, Hero, is "sometimes afeard she will do a desperate outrage to herself." [12] Immediately this former misogynist recollects that Beatrice has all the virtues that he has so recently denied her, and he succumbs to all he has jeered at, crying:

[7] *Ibid.*, Act II, scene iii, l. 31.
[8] *Ibid.*, Act II, scene i, l. 285.
[9] *Ibid.*, Act II, scene i, l. 260.
[10] *Ibid.*, Act II, scene i, l. 63.
[11] *Ibid.*, Act II, scene i, l. 64.
[12] *Ibid.*, Act II, scene iii, l. 169.

Comedy and Satire of Courtship

> They say the lady's fair: 'tis a truth
> I can bear them witness; and virtuous: 'tis so,
> I cannot reprove it; and wise, but for loving me:
> by my troth, it is no addition to her wit, nor no
> great argument of her folly, for I will be horribly
> in love with her.[13]

In a like manner, when Beatrice is made to overhear that Benedick has nothing left but to "consume away in sighs, waste inwardly" [14] with a secret passion for her, she, too, surrenders to romance, saying:

> . . . Benedick, love on; I will requite thee,
> Taming my wild heart to thy loving hand:
> If thou dost love, my kindness shall incite thee
> To bind our loves up in a holy band;
> For others say thou dost deserve, and I
> Believe it better than reportingly.[15]

The metamorphosis in the relationship between Benedick and Beatrice is given dramatic emphasis through its contrast to the alterations in Claudio's attitude toward love. But the elements of love remain the same. Before Hero has been maligned, Benedick expresses his scorn for all the ritual of courtship (after the fashion of such other realistic commentators as Berowne and Jaques) by mocking Claudio. Concerning Claudio's exaggerated praise of Hero, Benedick says: "I can see yet without spectacles, and I see no such matter." [16] Furthermore, Benedick unwittingly suggests Claudio's coming disillusionment by stating the conventional joke that the marriage of lovers is the deceiving of husbands.

> Is't come to this, i' faith: Hath not
> the world one man but he will wear his cap with
> suspicion?—an thou wilt needs
> thrust thy neck into a yoke, wear the print of it.[17]

---

[13] *Ibid.*, Act II, scene iii, l. 250.
[14] *Ibid.*, Act III, scene i, l. 78.
[15] *Ibid.*, Act III, scene i, l. 111.
[16] *Ibid.*, Act I, scene i, l. 198.
[17] *Ibid.*, Act I, scene i, l. 207.

After Benedick's conversion to love, however, he, in turn, is mocked by his former victim, Claudio. The cynic and the romantic lover have changed places, though the attitude each represents merely has a new spokesman. It is now Benedick whose head will wear the "savage bull's horns," with

> . . . text underneath, "Here dwells Benedick the married man!" [18]

It is now Benedick whom Don Pedro describes derisively to Claudio.

> What a pretty thing man is when he goes in his doublet and hose, and leaves off his wit! [19]

An ironic, rather than the hitherto merely comic, contrast gives vitality to the conflicting points of view expressed by the characters of *Much Ado*. But Shakespeare further enlarges the suggestive power of this play. He creates the illusion that Beatrice and Benedick have been quarreling over the nature of love before they were involved in the particular circumstances of this play. Their conflict is presented as one of long standing. Beatrice's first speech with the messenger mocks Benedick even before he has appeared on the scene. Leonato then explains the relationship of these two.

> You must not, sir, mistake my niece. There is a kind of merry war betwixt Signior Benedick and her: they never meet but there's a skirmish of wit between them.[20]

Beatrice indicates an earlier contention with Benedick when she refers to a meeting with him previous to the action in which she is now concerned. In their last exchange, she says,

> . . . four of his five wits went halting off, and now is the whole man governed with one! so that if he have wit enough to keep himself

---

[18] *Ibid.*, Act V, scene i, l. 190.   [19] *Ibid.*, Act V, scene i, l. 207.
[20] *Ibid.*, Act I, scene i, l. 62.

Comedy and Satire of Courtship

   warm, let himself bear it for a difference between himself and his horse.[21]

This sort of reference to events outside the narrative scope of the play [22] forces the audience to believe in the quarrel of these lovers immediately; whereas in *Love's Labour's Lost* the first four acts were necessary to make credible the wit contests of the fifth. Beatrice and Benedick are fully developed at the beginning of the play. Hence, in so far as their worldly wisdom makes concession to romance, their reconciliation is given a more than comic significance: it is linked to the world outside the theater. Having seemed to exist before the play began, these characters project themselves into the future, after the play is over.[23] The very artistry of such dramatization tends to obscure the use which Shakespeare makes of contrasting aspects of love in *Much Ado*. Because Beatrice and Benedick have been made so real, they seem to be involved merely in a personal problem. Actually, their conflict is that of the age, completely individualized.

   Beatrice and Benedick are highly self-conscious. The wooers in Shakespeare's other love-game comedies who follow the versifying routine of courtship are mocked by their ladies because their lyrics are so poor. But the lovers of *Much Ado* serve as their own critics. Benedick complains that though he is more in love than Leander and Troilus, yet he cannot express his passion in rhyme. The best he can do is to pair off "lady" and "baby," "scorn" and "horn," "school" and "fool." He concludes, ". . . no, I was not born under a riming planet, nor I cannot woo in festival terms." [24] He uses the stereotyped conceits of the day, not as elsewhere in Shakespeare to have their validity challenged, but merely to tease Beatrice. Thus, he says to her, "I will live in thy heart, die in thy lap, and be buried in thy eyes; and moreover I will go with thee to thy uncle's." [25] Likewise Beatrice is not so much conscious of the disparity between senti-

---

[21] *Ibid.*, Act I, scene i, l. 67.
[22] Cf. further, *ibid.*, Act I, scene i, ll. 30, 38, 89, 123; Act II, scene i, l. 289.
[23] Thus we speak of a "benedict," but not of a "berowne."
[24] *Much Ado*, Act V, scene ii, l. 40.   [25] *Ibid.*, Act V, scene ii, l. 108.

ment and reality as she is of her own awkwardness in the presence of such sentiment. This fact is illustrated when she asks him, in jest, "for which of my good parts did you first suffer love for me?" Benedick's reply severs the two completely from all of Shakespeare's other dueling couples. He says, " 'Suffer love,' a good epithet! I do suffer love indeed, for I love thee against my will." [26] Unlike the characters in *Love's Labour's Lost* and in *As You Like It,* Beatrice and Benedick remain as shrewdly enlightened creatures of the Renaissance after they have agreed to marry as they were before.

Quiller-Couch suggests that in this play the principal characters deceive themselves, but not the audience. The latter is meant to be more omniscient than they, to be able to say of Beatrice, following her conversion, " 'Aha! dear lady, you didn't take *us* in!' " [27] Furthermore, their sex duel is to be considered "only a bright prelude to the victory of love and a permanent treaty of peace." [28] If one examines *Much Ado* with greater sobriety, however, one sees that the precise opposite is true. Beatrice and Benedick remain as shrewdly enlightened after they have agreed to marry as they were before. Benedick, indeed, equivocates even as he asks the Friar to marry him.[29] He acknowledges his own paradoxical behavior when one of his halting sonnets is produced, exclaiming, "A miracle! here's our own hands against our hearts. Come, I will have thee; but, by this light, I take thee for pity." [30] The union of these two evokes comic delight by asking the audience to view inherently warring elements in love in a state of momentary rest. Expediency, not peace, has triumphed. Benedick's statement to Beatrice, "Thou and I are too wise to woo peaceably," [31] is a fitting summary of the implications to be drawn from their particular courtship.

Shakespeare improved Lyly's method of dramatizing Renais-

---

[26] *Ibid.*, Act V, scene ii, ll. 67–71.
[27] Quiller-Couch ed., Introduction to *Much Ado about Nothing*, p. xvii.
[28] Quiller-Couch quotes Dowden (*ibid.*, p. xx).
[29] *Much Ado*, Act V, scene iv, l. 20.
[30] *Ibid.*, Act V, scene iv, l. 91.   [31] *Ibid.*, Act V, scene ii, l. 76.

sance conflicting notions of love in ways which have been shown for *Love's Labour's Lost* and *As You Like It*. In *Much Ado* Shakespeare asks his audience to involve itself with some of the more sober implications to be derived from his conception of love. In the first place, the conciliatory acts of the quarreling lovers are brought about by their involvement in more substantial occurrences than those found in *Love's Labour's Lost* and in *As You Like It*. In the second place, Benedick and Beatrice are Shakespeare's additions to the story he chose to dramatize.[32] The main narrative events are not enacted by them as they are by the lords and ladies of Navarre and Orlando and Rosalind of Arden. Rather, Benedick and Beatrice are, like such other Shakespearean characters as Philip the Bastard, Mercutio, and Falstaff, amusing and interesting in themselves. This does not mean that their sex duel is less concerned with the emotional problems of the age, but rather that it gives added vitality to these problems.

Claudio's entanglement presents in a harsh and derisive manner the ironies and paradoxes involved when Elizabethan romantic sentiment sought fulfillment in the actual world of the sixteenth century. Shakespeare cannot push lovers' difficulties farther in this direction without completely destroying comedy. Thereafter, when Shakespeare treats the same conflict as that presented in *Much Ado*, he makes use of it either for satire or for tragedy. There is no comic and comforting reconciliation of romantic pretense with actual fact in the quarrels between the various lovers of *Measure for Measure* or in the travesty of romance acted out by Troilus and Cressida. Othello's very effort to accept Desdemona as something less than ideal involves him in a violent subjective conflict which leads to her murder and his suicide. Even in *Antony and Cleopatra*, where the two central characters are as skeptical, as cynically knowing, as it is possible to be, it is their vain attempt to balance lovers' exaltations

---

[32] Though, to be sure, they become the most interesting characters in the play. Thus Charles I's copy of the second folio has "Benedick and Beatrice" as a subtitle, inserted in his own writing (Introduction to *Much Ado about Nothing*, ed. by Sir Arthur Quiller-Couch, p. xii).

with practical necessity that leads to their deaths.[33] The significance of *Much Ado* lies in the fact that it dramatizes opposed elements in Elizabethan (and in Shakespeare's) amorous thought in as comprehensive a fashion as was possible for comedy. It suggests as effective a resolution of these elements as comedy could make.

Although Shakespeare intensifies the conflict over love in *Much Ado*, the play remains a comedy. He keeps it ultimately comic by bringing into final balance complementary aspects of love. In *Troilus and Cressida*, written at the beginning of the seventeenth century, Shakespeare makes use of contradictions in love for another purpose. This play, as the recent study by Professor Campbell makes clear,[34] is written in the satiric manner suggested by the "comicall satyre" of Jonson and Marston. It is both more mocking and more didactic than *Much Ado*. It makes use of lovers' illusions to serve a more serious purpose. The genial spirit of comedy has altogether vanished. In this play of the Trojan War Shakespeare asks his audience to regard the ideals of a romantic suitor as a cloak for his sexual desires. Troilus is a young libertine who regards himself as a chivalric lover, while actually merely seeking an assignation with his mistress, Cressida. She is a wanton who cannot actualize the lady of romance for him. The gap between the lovers' simulated idealism and their frank exhibitions of physical passion is too great to be rendered comic. The discord sounded in Troilus by his pretense makes him an object of wry laughter. Therefore this play cannot end with romantic illusions neatly balanced by mundane fact. Its lover reaps the reward of his own folly and becomes an object of pity or contempt. The comedy of courtly or Petrarchan lovers awkwardly seeking acceptance in a world of reality has vanished. In Shakespeare's play of the Trojan War the ideals of traditional

---

[33] G. Wilson Knight, in *The Imperial Theme*, p. 325, comments on *Antony and Cleopatra:* "There is a violent, sometimes a harsh, realism in *Antony and Cleopatra*. Human love is battered, weary, yet divine. These opposing aspects we view alternately. It is the opposition of our own lives . . . Every negation in the play is subservient to the total unity."

[34] Campbell, *Comicall Satyre and Shakespeare's "Troilus and Cressida."*

romance are made absurd in a man avid merely for sex experience.

Troilus apes the fashionable language and attitudes fixed by convention for the courtly or Petrarchan wooer. His ostensible philosophy is not unlike that expressed by Berowne.[35] Troilus, in the opening scene of this play, proclaims himself to be languishing in traditional fashion. He assures Pandarus that his ineffectiveness as a warrior is due to the fact that he is in love:

> . . . I am weaker than a woman's tear,
> Tamer than sleep, fonder than ignorance,
> Less valiant than the virgin in the night,
> And skilless as unpractis'd infancy.[36]

But in the act of uttering these words, Troilus becomes much more ironically his own victim than Berowne. In Shakespeare's age the very name of the goddess adored by Troilus, "Cressida," had become a byword for an unchaste woman.[37] The incongruity between Troilus's chivalric attitude and its object would be apparent at once to an Elizabethan audience. Moreover Troilus's pose deceives no one but himself. All see that he seeks no ineffably ennobling experience of passion. He may speak as if he were weak from the oppressively ideal nature of his love. But that is part of the irony. His go-between, Pandarus, is a real "pandar" and presents conclusive evidence of the actual quality of Troilus's desires. This friend continually whets Troilus's appetite and makes no concession to the exalted sentiments the latter has claimed. According to Pandarus, who is amused by Troilus's attempt to be romantic, Cressida exists to be devoured like a cake. But her lover must have patience and stay the "heating of the oven, and baking," the "cooking too," or he may burn his lips.[38] Pandarus concludes his sly advice with a list of suggestive metaphors, enticing Troilus with the reality of Cressida's physical attractions.

---

[35] *Love's Labour's Lost*, Act IV, scene iii, ll. 289–365.
[36] *Troilus and Cressida*, Act I, scene i, l. 9.
[37] See William Witherle Lawrence, *Shakespeare's Problem Comedies*, pp. 149–154. See also Campbell, *Comicall Satyre*, pp. 191–195.
[38] *Troilus and Cressida*, Act I, scene i, ll. 13–28.

Shakespeare suggests an unpleasant quality of sickness in Troilus's obsession with sex by making him continue to speak of his enslavement by Cressida as if he were the victim of a noble love. He feels it necessary to keep his attachment to this wanton the secret and clandestine affair that high-born love was in courtly poetry. Thus Troilus confesses to Pandarus his anguish lest he betray his lady:

> I have—as when the sun doth light a storm—
> Buried this sigh in wrinkle of a smile;
> But sorrow, that is couch'd in seeming gladness,
> Is like that mirth fate turns to sudden sadness.[39]

Pandarus's reply destroys Troilus's presumptuous rhetoric by again telling the lover just what he really wants to hear. He cuts through the young man's flow of words, which merely hide the impatience of his desire, to tease his appetite still more: "An her hair were not somewhat darker than Helen's—well, go to, —there were no more comparison between the women." [40] Cressida is his kinswoman, Pandarus explains in mock apology, and he is too modest to praise his own goods; "but I would somebody had heard her talk yesterday, as I did; I will not dispraise your sister Cassandra's wit, but . . ." [41] At the end of this scene between the libertine and his solicitor Troilus cries out:

> O gods! how do you plague me.
> I cannot come to Cressid but by Pandar;
> And he's as techy to be woo'd to woo
> As she is stubborn-chaste against all suit.[42]

But Pandarus had given no indication that he had any wish other than to bring the lovers together. And Cressida, as an Elizabethan would have known, is something less than "stubborn-chaste."

The fact that Troilus is the victim of his own self-deceit is obvious in all the love scenes of the play. The object of his passion characterizes herself very quickly. She is one who is restless

[39] *Ibid.*, Act I, scene i, l. 39. [40] *Ibid.*, Act I, scene i, l. 43.
[41] *Ibid.*, Act I, scene i, l. 47. [42] *Ibid.*, Act I, scene i, l. 99.

Comedy and Satire of Courtship

under any kind of idealizing, amatory or otherwise. She has the capacity to see only the tawdry quality of her own personality in everyone else. Thus, in reply to Alexander's praise of Ajax as a "very man 'per se'" who stands alone, she exhibits her own gross insolence. She suggests that all men stand alone,

> . . . unless they are drunk,
> Sick, or have no legs.[43]

She is unmistakably crude in her simulations of the traditional modesty proper to the lady worshiped by the courtly lover. Her pretense is a calculated coquetry, pleasing to Troilus, but essentially hypocritical. Chaucer's Criseyde tests the sincerity of her lover's passion by not yielding to him at once. Shakespeare's Cressida withholds herself from Troilus as shrewd teasing. She confesses that her lover is attractive.

> Yet hold I off. Women are angels, wooing:
> Things won are done; joy's soul lies in the doing:
> That she belov'd knows nought that knows not this:
> Men prize the thing ungain'd more than it is.[44]

It has been aptly observed that Cressida's second lover, Diomede, "is a much more suitable mate for her than Troilus was, for he is a cynical realist, without the romantic ideals which she must try to actualize."[45]

Shakespeare presents Troilus as one who has an imbalance in his nature between an idealizing tendency and a crassly sensual appetite that cannot be eradicated. Troilus is utterly incapable of adjusting these disparate conceptions of love. Before he possesses Cressida, he whips himself into an ecstasy of anticipatory pleasure. Campbell describes this feat in the following way: "Troilus is beset with the sexual gourmet's anxiety lest the morsel which he is about to devour will be so ravishing that thereafter he will lose his sense of nice distinctions in sexual experience."[46] After he loses Cressida to the solicitations of Diomede, Troilus finds her behavior incredibly treacherous and unideal. In his confusion

---

[43] *Ibid.*, Act I, scene ii, ll. 15–18. [44] *Ibid.*, Act I, scene ii, l. 310.
[45] Campbell, *Comicall Satyre*, p. 215. [46] *Ibid.*, p. 212.

somehow the Cressida of his fanciful imagination is the only "real" person. Hence his cry,

> But if I tell how these two did co-act,
> Shall I not lie in publishing a truth?
> Sith yet there is a credence in my heart,
> An esperance so obstinately strong,
> That doth invert the attest of eyes and ears.[47]

He almost refuses to accept the disillusionment which is forced upon him.

In *Love's Labour's Lost* and *As You Like It* the clash of opposed attitudes toward love arouses only light-hearted laughter. In *Much Ado* the laughter is shadowed by graver issues. But in *Troilus and Cressida,* as in Shakespeare's sonnets, the interplay of the conflicting elements in love is not a jocular one. In the sonnets Shakespeare often mocks himself for confusing sexual desire with notions of romantic perfection. In *Troilus and Cressida* he depicts Troilus's stubborn and conscious [48] lack of insight with a like intensity of derision. What, then, is the import of this play? Comedy derived from the absurdity of lovers' posturings has given way to satire and to intense mockery. In this play, where practices of adepts in sensuality are ridiculed, something seems to be suggested concerning the nature of love itself, apart from fashionable Elizabethan ideals. The import seems to be that an amorous idealist is always incompletely satisfied by his experience of passion. Troilus expresses this idea when he attempts to analyze his love for Cressida. He remarks, "This is the monstruosity in love, lady, that the will is infinite, and the execution confined, that the desire is boundless, and the act a slave to limit." [49] Shakespeare had commented on this inadequacy of experience before, in his sonnets. In *Troilus and Cressida* he dramatizes the indignity of the consummation of desire in the light of the idealism which men associate with love.

It is true that Shakespeare's satiric treatment of Troilus, in this

---
[47] *Troilus and Cressida,* Act V, scene ii, 1. 115.
[48] Cf. *ibid.,* Act III, scene ii, ll. 81–88.
[49] *Ibid.,* Act III, scene ii, ll. 85–88.

play, was in part predetermined by a changed conception of these Trojan lovers. Cressida was not considered a courtly lady by Elizabethans, but a harlot. In Shakespeare's *King Henry the Fifth* Pistol illustrates her metamorphosis when he remarks,

> . . . to the spital go,
> And from the powdering-tub of infamy
> Fetch forth the lazer kite of Cressid's kind.[50]

As Lawrence suggests, "Elizabethans would have jeered at a pure and noble Cressida." [51] Therefore Troilus's love for her in Shakespeare's play had perforce to be ironic. It is also important to remember that the seventeenth-century audience had begun to be interested in more substantial treatments of human passions than those found in Shakespeare's earlier comedies. He may well have had this fact in mind when he wrote *Troilus and Cressida*. From a romantic's point of view, this play may seem a sorry terminus to the cheerful presentation of lovers' affectations found in *As You Like It*. An early seventeenth-century audience may have thought that Shakespeare's Trojan lovers represented a highly intelligent, if mocking, analysis of familiar attitudes. But the stern treatment these lovers receive is not wholly explained by making the dramatist either the victim of an Elizabethan conception of Cressida or of a changed audience. His choice of story, as Campbell has pointed out, was not entirely fortuitous.[52]

On the basis of Professor Campbell's investigations it is safe to say that *Troilus and Cressida* represents Shakespeare's conscious effort to write in the newly satiric fashion inaugurated by Jonson and Marston. Why may one not add, that such a play would tap reservoirs of feeling which the love-game comedy could not reach? The fact that the mood of this play is like that found in his sonnets lends credence to such a hypothesis. In both

[50] *King Henry the Fifth*, Act II, scene i, ll. 78–80.
[51] *Shakespeare's Problem Comedies*, p. 152.
[52] *Comicall Satyre*, p. 194: "Where could Shakespeare find a fable better adapted to his continuation of that combination of excoriation and derision of sexual indulgence which the satirist had made a literary fashion?"

he analyzes the contradictions in love found in his comedies. But in his satiric drama and in his poems he treats lovers' problems in a sardonic way that would be interesting to a sophisticated audience [53] willing to think about the graver aspects of passion. It has been remarked that many critics find it very difficult to admit that Shakespeare gave the love story an intentionally derisive treatment.[54] Yet, as we have seen, love is often presented by other Elizabethans as a contradictory, somewhat desperate affair. Shakespeare was necessarily concerned with the contemporary scrutiny of the complex relationship between mere desire and fashionable ideals of love. Why cannot one concede that he was able to bring to a brilliant, dramatic focus a satiric presentation of the dark side of passion? The love story in *Troilus and Cressida* is a frank depiction of elemental conflicts within the human mind. Since Shakespeare's sonnets and his love-game comedies show that he had long been aware of these conflicts, it is difficult to consider their appearance in *Troilus and Cressida* as in any way a novel departure. The mocking point of view from which he surveys Troilus may have satisfied the taste of his day, or merely that of a special audience. Surely it also reflects the deeper tides of his own emotions.

[53] Lawrence, *Shakespeare's Problem Comedies*, p. 127, states that "it seems unlikely that the whole acid picture of the hollowness of artificial romantic love would ever have been painted to please a court which loved to affect and practice submission to such conventions. It is far more probable that Shakespeare wrote the play for a special audience of the more sophisticated sort." Cf. Campbell, *Comicall Satyre*, pp. 191–195. See also Peter Alexander, "Troilus and Cressida, 1609," in *The Library*, 4th series, Vol. IX (1929), 267–286.

[54] Campbell, *Comicall Satyre*, pp. 207–209; cf. *ibid.*, "The Quandary of the Critics," pp. 187–191, for a summary of conflicting opinions concerning the import of the play.

·XIII·

The Right Promethean Fire

WHAT is meaningful, historically, in Shakespeare's comedies of courtship is that they resolve a quarrel over the nature of love which had been current in English literature for about four centuries. What is significant in these plays in terms of human experience as a whole is that they dramatize a conflict which is a fundamental part of love itself. Chaucer, and most of the writers of Shakespeare's age, it is true, describe this conflict by means of the special formulae of their times, treating it as if it were the peculiar offspring of troubadour speculations at cross purposes with a Pauline asceticism, for example—or of Petrarchism with Ovid's notions of love. However, in the lyrics of Donne and in the sonnets of Shakespeare, which were written outside this fairly fixed orbit of contemporary literary minds, lovers' difficulties are seen to be created not entirely by conventionalized attitudes. Rather they are often provoked by an individual's tendency to imagine an ideal fulfillment of passion in terms of his own personality and beyond the limitations set by his own experience. In Shakespeare's love-game comedies, although the boundaries of the lovers' quarrels are fixed by the familiar stereotyped attitudes of the day, these lovers are sufficiently individualized for their skirmishes likewise to resolve not only the particular problem of the age but also the universal one.

This is not to say that Shakespeare's love-game comedies are a final revelation of all amorous wisdom. His lovers adjust their difficulties too easily, for one thing. In these comedies he carefully maneuvers their attitudes which have created dramatic tension toward a moment of balance. The state of equilibrium reached at the conclusion of these plays is, of course, a product of the writer's artistry rather than the inevitable occurrence it is made to appear. Such moments would be rare in the world outside the theater (as Francis Bacon implies in his essay "Of Love"). But caught up by the imitation of life unfolding on the stage, the audience would have its appetite aroused for this final moment of resolution, perhaps recognizing the writer's trick even at the moment of fulfillment, but accepting the deceit with pleasure.

The game can be played otherwise and for different effects. On the one hand, the point at which the elements of love reach balance can come too early, as in *Othello*.[1] This moment when the idyllic and the actual are in perfect harmony, when, as Othello phrases it, if one could but die, " 'Twere now to be most happy," cannot remain static in real life or in drama. The elements that go to make this moment, as they recede from each other, bring violence and catastrophe. On the other hand, the point of balance can remain just out of reach to give us another kind of play, as in *Troilus and Cressida*. And here we are left with our teeth on edge by the dramatist's satiric sketch of man's humiliating folly.

This spectacle of the interplay of imagined ideal and commonplace (or worse) reality has drawn comment from men remote from the medieval and sixteenth-century controversy over the nature of love. Ovid's sophisticated wit in the *Ars amatoria* must have had point in its own time because there were men who took their passion somewhat more seriously than he did. Lucretius recognizes the elements of the essential quarrel in his analysis of love at the end of the fourth book of his long philosophical poem, *De rerum natura*. He describes this interplay as the disastrous struggle to seize what most men find unattainable, to grasp an impalpable image even in the act of possession: "Sic in amore Venus simulacris ludit amantis nec satiare queunt spectando corpora coram."[2] And in his verses to Lesbia, Catullus has set down for all time the revulsion of the idealist from the world of common sense fact.

---

[1] *Othello*, Act II, scene i, ll. 185 *et sqq.*
[2] Lucretius, *De rerum natura*, Bk. IV, ll. 1101 *et sqq.*

Catullus, to be sure, did not have at hand the phrases which the medieval and Renaissance poets brought together to describe love. He had no system of metaphors associated with the picture of a man in adoration before a shrine,[3] no symbols of worship and prostration into which he could translate his experience. He was initiating an idea. The words he uses to describe the abstract quality, the idealization of *amor*, the illusion of escape from commonplace delight, are therefore personal. He takes his metaphors either from a sharp denial of *amor* as a measurable commodity or from a comparison of it to the unselfish affection of a parent. Thus it is,

> illa Lesbia, quam Catullus unam
> plus quam se atque suos amavit omnes [4]

or

> dilexi tum te non tantum ut vulgus amicam
> sed pater ut gnatos diligit et generos.[5]

That is, his own imagination suggested to him a "romantic" conception of love which was to become in courtly and Petrarchan poetry the conventional one. He strove, through the impulses of sex, to possess the dancing illusion that Lucretius had warned led to frenzy. Catullus found that his only escape was to accept the prevailing realistic sentiment of his day. Now that his Lesbia has proved to be the mocking "simulacrum" of Lucretius, she has become more seductive, but of less importance.

> nunc te cognovi: quare etsi impensius uror,
> multo mi tamen es vilior et levior.
> qui potis est? inquis. quod amantem iniuria talis
> cogit amare magis, sed bene velle minus.[6]

---

[3] See Lee's listing of Shakespeare's use of the word "idolatry" in *Shakespeare's Sonnets*, p. 24. Medieval poets, influenced in large measure by worship of the Virgin, ascribed this form of divine adoration to actual women. E. K. Rand (*Ovid and His Influence*, p. 153) expresses this Renaissance conflict between medieval ideal and realistic interpretation of "love" in terms of Plato and Ovid. "These two," he says, "battle hard for the soul of every poet of the coming (Renaissance) centuries who sang of love."

[4] Carmen LVIII.   [5] Carmen LXXII.
[6] *Ibid.*

If a man with Catullus's intensity of feeling seeks to transmute desire into impalpable ideal and fails, he will fall back into frenzied frustration. This was the fate of the Roman lyricist, just as it was of many Elizabethan poets. Catullus, with what has been called the conciseness of inimitable genius,[7] illustrates the dilemma of the defeated spirit for all time in his paradoxical epigram:

>Odi et amo. quare id faciam, fortasse requiris.
>nescio, sed fieri sentio et excrucior.[8]

The special contribution to the understanding of love which the medieval and Renaissance controversy made was that it gave tangible form to the universal process of psychological adjustment (or maladjustment) between lovers. Catullus's reaction to his predicament remains personal. Writers of the Middle Ages and of the Renaissance established a language by which a normal idealizing tendency could be expressed and set boundaries within which the difficulties of lovers could be explored. The danger of idealizing love was balanced in the Middle Ages by the *fabliaux*, on the one hand, and by clerical satire and exhortation, on the other. In the Renaissance this danger was checked by a healthy skepticism (partly in imitation of Ovid) and by recourse to Platonism. At the level of its most conventional expression this quarrel over romance may not appear to have had any significance beyond the tenets it expounded. But from the point of view of the present moment, even its conventional expression can be seen to mirror an intellectual and emotional problem not limited by the way in which a particular age made it concrete and definite.

For Shakespeare, as for most of his contemporaries, the right Promethean fire was romantic love. His first comedy of courtship, *Love's Labour's Lost*, as Charlton remarks,

>broadly indicates what features of man's contact with the world were, for Shakespeare's day, the crucial and decisive moments of his mortal existence. . . . The sixteenth-century dramatist, depicting the dilemma and the triumph of life, was mainly moved to discover man

---

[7] K. P. Harrington, *Catullus and His Influence*, p. 36.
[8] Carmen LXXXV.

achieving happiness or sorrow through his relationship with woman, through his liability to love.[9]

Shakespeare's distinction in dealing with the fundamental problem provoked by his century's all-consuming interest is that he suggested a way by which the pretensions of medieval romance and lovers' actual fulfillments can be accepted as related aspects of experience. He isolated and exhibited as understandable the incongruities and paradoxes acknowledged by other Renaissance men and women in love. He formulated the comic method of the sex duel which was followed by later and diverse writers such as Fletcher, in *The Wild-Goose Chase,* Congreve, in *The Way of the World,* and Shaw, in *Man and Superman,* in describing contentious aspects of love of other times.

The age in which the love-game comedies of Shakespeare were written, indeed, is in no sense unrelated to the present. The sixteenth century is not a long-vanished era that has left only obscure traces to tantalize the mind. The contradictory aspirations and desires which make articulate the Renaissance obsession with the systematized ideal of courtly love can still be described and assessed with accuracy because they are not so very different from our own. We are both the victims and the benefactors of the Elizabethan attempt to rationalize and to secularize romantic love. Yet one of the astonishing aspects of our literary criticism is that it has rather generally tended to slight this fact. Critics who would not deny the importance of contemporary literature as a repository for the intellectual preoccupations and perturbations that haunt the present often refuse to consider that of the sixteenth century important save as a study in poetic techniques and dramatic fashions. It has sometimes been forgotten that the aesthetic value of literary expression is enhanced by the historical and psychological importance of the problem concerned. The Elizabethan reaction to its medieval romantic heritage, which has been shown to be revealed in its sonnets and comedies, has frequently been slighted because more palpably measurable elements were at hand.

[9] *Shakespearian Comedy,* p. 101.

The analytic methods employed in numerous comparative studies of Renaissance sonnet sequences, for example, often serve, not to elucidate, but to obscure the primary import of such poetry. Because it can be demonstrated that Elizabethan Petrarchans borrowed many of their conceits from foreign models, and because there is little evidence that these poets always described intensely personal experiences, many scholars choose to read their lyrics merely as formal literary exercises.[10] The implication is that attitudes and conceptions expressed in poetry are to be measured either by the originality of metaphor or by the actuality of events transcribed. Such a procedure ignores the importance of what a poet says, because he makes use of a highly dramatic method and a traditional language of love. In an attempt to analyze the materials out of which a sonnet was constructed, critics often forget that the author of the poem had something he wished to communicate to his audience. That his subject matter and his words were not entirely individual means no more than that as a man of his time he was naturally concerned with what his age generally thought important. The Elizabethan amorous poet did not attempt to reproduce experience, but to appraise it. The meaning of his poetry lies, not in the degree to which he departs from the conventions of his lyric, but in the amount of penetration he brings to his analysis of Renaissance conceptions of love.

It is evident that sixteenth-century poets wrote in the rather stereotyped literary fashion that was acceptable to their contemporaries. One must not for this reason slight the content of such poetry. To accept the critical verdict that there are "very few instances of real love passion among the Elizabethan sonneteers"[11] is to signify no more than that they were writing about

---

[10] Sir Sidney Lee, in his Introduction to *Elizabethan Sonnets*, I, cviii, remarks that the love described in the Elizabethan sonnet "was nearly always feigned." See also his essay, "The Impersonal Aspect of Shakespeare's Art," in *Elizabethan and Other Essays*, pp. 90 ff. He has been the most prominent twentieth-century critic to emphasize the traditional and the borrowed elements in these lyrics to the exclusion of all else. A survey of the critical quarrel over the significance of the Elizabethan sonnet is found in the Appendix to *The Sonnets of Shakespeare*, ed. by Raymond Macdonald Alden, pp. 377–416.

[11] Purcell, *Sidney's Stella*, p. 99.

a passion which they did not experience at the moment of writing, but of which they were not necessarily ignorant. Insensibility, imaginative obtuseness, is the fault in sonnet sequences, as elsewhere in literature, where significance is lacking. To label the progressively realistic treatment of sentiment, that culminates in the lyrics of John Donne, a fashionable exercise in literary form, is to neglect content for artifice. The importance of Elizabethan poetry is not that it is a special kind of syllabic legerdemain. And the critic who expects Shakespeare's sonnets to stand or fall by the ascertainable identity of his "dark lady" or by the number of conceits that he borrowed must, perforce, ignore the evocative intensity of his analysis of love.

There is a point of view which seeks to place Elizabethan dramatic expression apart from the concerns of its time in a like manner, to isolate it as "art." Professor Stoll, for example, denies that Shakespeare's comedies dramatize any peculiarly Elizabethan problem.[12] He would have literature generally and Elizabethan and Restoration comedy in particular reflect the taste of a time, unmotivated by the time itself. Literature, he suggests,

> is, of course, not life, neither history nor material for history, but a scroll whereon are traced and charactered the unfettered thoughts of writer and reader,—a life within a life, fancy somewhat at odds with fact. But by critics and historians this is often forgotten—"to pass from the art of a time to the time itself," says Wilde, "is the great mistake that all historians commit." [13]

Such aesthetic theory is based upon two palpable delusions. In the first place, it makes use of the romantic notion of art for its own sake, existing within an aesthetic void, rather than art in relationship to audience. The thoughts of writer and reader, indeed, are fettered precisely by the concerns of the time in which they are transcribed, or else they pass into the limbo of nonsense. In the second place, merely because Shakespeare's lovers behave in a conventional way, somewhat at odds with fact, merely because Restoration husbands, generally, may have been less

---

[12] Stoll, *Shakespeare Studies*, ch. ii, "Literature and Life."
[13] *Ibid.*, p. 39.

callous than those found in its comedies, does not indicate that these dramatic representations exhibit nothing but the vagaries of sixteenth- and seventeenth-century taste. The amount of "realism" in a piece of writing depends upon the imaginative habits of its audience, depends upon what materials are necessary to create an illusion of belief for them. What Professor Stoll finds contrary to fact in Elizabethan comedy is the medieval code of love, which to the Renaissance audience was synonymous with love itself.[14] Though this systematized ideal is not literally pictorial, it is certainly one of the most significant aspects of the taste of the time.

Literary expression, as Francis Bacon noted, may tend "to satisfy the mind with the shadows of things when the substance cannot be obtained," [15] but surely such "shadows" cannot be segregated from the period that called them forth. Shakespeare's love-game comedy and Elizabethan love poetry hold the mirror up to contemporary attitudes, to the delusions and the desires of the sixteenth-century lover. If such dramatic exposition of the intellectual and emotional material of the age does not serve, at least in part, to express and to characterize it, one wonders what does. Merely the clothes it wore, the vehicles that transported it, the buildings it raised? It may be said that literature is concerned with the aspirations that motivate an era rather than with the actions of its individuals. But this is not to say that an aesthetic pattern fails to reflect the period in which it is written merely because its characters embody these aspirations. To hold with such a point of view would be to ignore the fundamental import of written expression. The question is not whether the speech, the action, the motivating forces of the characters in the love-

---

[14] Cf. Lisle Cecil John, *Elizabethan Sonnet Sequences*, p. 83, "The modern reader who . . . finds himself unmoved by the distressing symptoms brought forth as proof of the poet's unswerving devotion, must occasionally remind himself that such analyzing and attitudinizing were familiar enough to the average Elizabethan. Sighing, melancholy, analytical lovers were not only the heroes of their romances and pastoral fiction but trod the boards realistically enough upon the Elizabethan stage."

[15] Bacon, *The Works*, ed. by Spedding, Ellis, and Heath, Bk. II, ch. xiii: "Of the Dignity and Advancement of Learning," IV, 315.

game comedies of Lyly and Shakespeare are duplicates of those that would be found in the last two decades of the sixteenth century. It is not whether Sidney's sonnet sequence is a transcript of his passion for a particular woman—a passion which, "in reality," would have to be evanescent, changeable from moment to moment. The question is with what comprehension and understanding the important antagonism between an idealized sentiment and a skeptical criticism of it was re-created first in the poetry and then in the comedies of the Elizabethan Renaissance.

As we have seen, a study of the conflict that presents itself in sixteenth-century English literature is more than an elucidation of the verbal borrowings and the literary fashions that were used to enthrall and to amuse an Elizabethan audience. Viewed in large perspective, it is a partial representation of the attempt to formulate a consistent philosophy of love from medieval inconsistencies. It is a fragmentary expression of that insight into the actual consequences of belief which we consider characteristic of the modern world. The disintegration of the thought patterns of an essentially theocratic society was taking place during the whole of the sixteenth century and continued into the seventeenth. Conceptions vital to this old society were losing established place and giving way more and more to the secular ideas and attitudes which were the offspring of a resurgent, humanistic criticism. Thus, the ever increasing incredulity with which the sixteenth century regarded its heritage of romance is but one of many reflections of a new age.

The aesthetic advance, from the first appearance of amorous conflict in the poetry of Wyatt to its dramatic exposition in Benedick and Beatrice, is therefore important historically. It indicates the emergence of an awareness of fact as a test for the conventionalized ideals of courtly or Petrarchan love. More generally, it suggests the progressive rationality of the Renaissance, its slow but persistent reassessment of the medieval, formalized ideals of all aspects of life. The most widely divergent conceptions of love for the Middle Ages were represented by asceticism, on the one hand, and by the system of courtly love on the other.

Both were isolated from the highly imperfect nature of "l'homme moyen sensuel." But in certain Elizabethan comedies which mirror the changing attitudes of the sixteenth century, as Professor Charlton suggests, the "gross ponderable facts of a very material world swept the symbol of an outworn ideal from off the face of the earth." [16] In *Much Ado*, for example, what would have been the characteristics of a shrew in the Middle Ages, in Beatrice have become those of a realistic and witty court lady. And what would have been the philosophy of a monk in the Middle Ages, a cry to avoid the snares of the flesh, in Benedick has become a skeptical criticism of the pretensions of romance. The love-game comedy pushed our comprehension of love beyond the boundaries of literary formulae. By revealing that the incongruities of a traditional ennoblement of love can be viewed as comic it brings to a close one phase of the Elizabethan reevaluation of its heritage of amorous sentiment. This amused resignation before the elements of love is one segment of the new world.

[16] Charlton, *Shakespearian Comedy*, p. 34.

Bibliography

Alexander, Peter, Troilus and Cressida, 1609. The Library, fourth series, 1929, Vol. IX.

Andreas Capellanus, The Art of Courtly Love, *ca.* 1184; tr. by John Jay Parry. New York, 1941.

Anglade, Joseph, Les Troubadours. 3d ed. Paris, 1922.

Ascham, Roger, The English Works of; ed. by William Aldis Wright. Cambridge, 1904.

Augustine, Saint, The City of God (De civitate Dei); tr. by John Healey, 1610. Edinburgh, 1909. "Ancient and Modern Library of Theological Literature."

—— Confessions; tr. by William Watts, 1631. London, 1912. "Loeb Classical Library."

—— Select Letters; tr. by James Houston Baxter. London, 1930. "Loeb Classical Library."

Bacon, Francis, Essays, and Colours of Good and Evil; ed. by William Aldis Wright. London, 1879.

—— The Works; ed. by James Spedding, Robert Leslie Ellis, and Douglas Denan Heath. London, 1858.

Baskerville, Charles Read, "Taverner's *Garden of Wisdom* and the Apophthegmata of Erasmus," *Studies in Philology*, Vol. XXIX, No. 2 (April, 1932).

Bédier, Joseph, Les Fabliaux. 5th ed. Paris, 1925.

Bercher (Barker), William, The Nobility of Women, 1559; ed. by R. Warwick Bond. London, 1904. Roxburghe Club.

Boughner, Daniel C., "The Background of Lyly's Tophas," PMLA, Vol. LIV (December, 1939).

Boulting, William, Giordano Bruno, His Life, Thought and Martyrdom. London, 1917.

Brooke, Charles Frederick Tucker, The Tudor Drama. Cambridge, Mass., 1910.

Brooke, Fulke Greville, first Baron, Caelica; ed. with introduction by Una Ellis-Fermor. Newton, 1936.

Brooke, Fulke Greville, Certaine Learned and Elegant Workes of the Right Honorable Fulke, Lorde Brooke, Written in his Youth and Familiar Exercise with Sir Philip Sidney. London, 1633.
—— Sir Fulke Greville's Life of Sir Philip Sidney, 1652; Introduction by Nowell Smith. Oxford, 1907. "Tudor and Stuart Library."
—— The Works in Verse and Prose complete; ed. by the Rev. Alexander B. Grosart. 4 vols. Blackburn, 1890.
Brown, Carleton, "Mulier est hominis confusio," *Modern Language Notes*, Vol. XXXV (1920).
—— "The Prologue of Chaucer's Lyf of Seint Cecile," *Modern Philology*, Vol. IX (July, 1912).
Brown, Carleton, ed., English Lyrics of the XIIIth Century. Oxford, 1932.
—— Religious Lyrics of the XIVth Century. Oxford, 1924.
Bush, Douglas, Mythology and the Renaissance Tradition in English Poetry. Minneapolis, 1932.
Calvin, John, Commentary on the Epistles of Paul the Apostle to the Corinthians; tr. by John Pringle. Edinburgh, 1848–1849. "Calvin Translation Society."
Cambridge History of English Literature, The. Vols. III, V. Cambridge, 1930.
Cambridge Medieval History, The. Vol. VI. Cambridge, 1929.
Camden Society Publications; ed. by Samuel Tymms. Vols. XLIX–L. London, 1850.
Campbell, Oscar James, "Jaques," *Huntington Library Bulletin*, No. 8, October, 1935.
—— "*Love's Labour's Lost* Restudied," in Studies in Shakespeare, Milton and Donne, New York, 1925. University of Michigan Publications; Language and Literature, Vol. I.
—— Comicall Satyre and Shakespeare's *Troilus and Cressida*. San Marino, Calif., 1938. "Huntington Library Publications."
Catholic Encyclopedia, The. Vol. I. New York, 1913.
Catullus, Caius Valerius, The Poems: tr. by F. W. Cornish. London, 1912. "Loeb Classical Library."
Chamard, Henri, Les origines de la poésie française de la Renaissance. Paris, 1920.
Chambers, Sir Edmund Kerchever, Sir Thomas Wyatt and Some Collected Studies. London, 1933.
—— and F. Sidgwick, comps., Early English Lyrics. London, 1922.

Chapman, George, Ovids Banquet of Sence. 1595.
Charlton, Henry Buckley, Shakespearian Comedy. London, 1938.
Chaucer, Geoffrey, The Complete Works; ed. by Fred Norris Robinson. "Students' Cambridge Edition." Cambridge, 1933.
Colet, John, An Exposition of St. Paul's Epistle to the Romans; ed. with introduction by J. H. Lupton. London, 1873.
―――― Letters to Radulphus on the Mosaic Account of Creation; ed. with introduction by J. H. Lupton. London, 1876.
―――― Two Treatises on the Hierarchies of Dionysius; ed. with introduction by J. H. Lupton. London, 1869.
Cooper, Clyde Barnes, Some Elizabethan Opinions of the Poetry and Character of Ovid. Menasha, Wisc., 1914.
Coulton, G. G., Medieval Panorama; the English Scene from Conquest to Reformation. New York and Cambridge, 1938.
Craig, Hardin, The Enchanted Glass; the Elizabethan Mind in Literature. New York, 1936.
Crane, William Garrett, Wit and Rhetoric in the Renaissance; The Formal Basis of Elizabethan Prose Style. New York, 1937.
Croll, Morris W., The Works of Fulke Greville. Philadelphia, 1903.
Cross, Tom Peete, and William Albert Nitze, Lancelot and Guenevere; a Study on the Origins of Courtly Love. Chicago, 1930.
Curry, Walter Clyde, Destiny in Chaucer's *Troilus*. PMLA, Vol. XLV (1930).
Daniel, Samuel, Poems and a Defence of Ryme; ed. by Arthur Colby Sprague. Cambridge, Mass., 1930.
Dante Alighieri, The *Vita nuova*, with Rossetti's Version; ed. by H. Oelsner. London, 1908. "The King's Classics."
Dodd, William George, Courtly Love in Chaucer and Gower. Boston, 1913.
Donne, John, The Poems; ed. by Herbert J. C. Grierson. 2 vols. Oxford, 1912.
Dow, Blanche Hinman, The Varying Attitudes toward Women in French Literature of the Fifteenth Century: the Opening Years. New York, 1936.
Dowden, Edward, Shakespere; a Critical Study of His Mind and Art. London, 1875.
Drayton, Michael, Ideas Mirrour; Amours in Quatorzains. London, 1594.

Drayton, Michael, Minor Poems; ed. by Cyril Brett. Oxford, 1907. "Tudor and Stuart Library."
——— The Works; ed. by J. William Hebel. Oxford, 1931–1933.
Dunbar, William, The Poems; ed. by John Small. Edinburgh and London, 1893. "Scottish Text Society [Publications]."
Einstein, Lewis David, The Italian Renaissance in England. New York, 1913.
——— Tudor Ideals. London, 1921.
Eliot, Thomas Stearns, Selected Essays, 1917–1932. London, 1932.
Elyot, Sir Thomas, The Bankett of Sapience, 1542.
——— The Boke of the Governour; ed. by H. H. S. Crofts from the 1531 edition. London, 1883.
——— The Defence of Good Women. London, 1540.
Emerton, Ephraim, Desiderius Erasmus of Rotterdam. New York, 1899.
Encyclopedia Britannica, The. 14th ed. Vol. VIII. New York, 1929.
Encyclopedia of Religion and Ethics, The; ed. by James Hastings. Vol. I. New York, 1926.
England's Helicon; ed. by Hyder Edward Rollins. Cambridge, Mass., 1935.
Erasmus, Desiderius, The Colloquies; tr. by N. Bailey, ed. by the Rev. E. Johnson. London, 1878.
——— A Ryght Frutefull Epystle . . . in Laude and Prayse of Matrymony; tr. by Rychard Taverner. London, 1530.
Fansler, Dean Spruill, Chaucer and the *Roman de la Rose*. New York, 1914.
Feuillerat, Albert, John Lyly; contribution à l'histoire de la Renaissance en Angleterre. Cambridge, 1910.
Fletcher, Jefferson Butler, Literature of the Italian Renaissance. New York, 1934.
——— The Religion of Beauty in Woman. New York, 1911.
——— "A Study in Renaissance Mysticism: Spenser's *Fowre Hymnes*," PMLA, Vol. XXVI (1911).
Fowler, Earle Broadus, Spenser and the System of Courtly Love. Louisville, 1934.
Fraunce, Abraham, The Countesse of Pembrokes Yvychurch. London, 1591.
Furnivall, Frederick J., ed. Ballads from Manuscripts. 2 vols. London, 1868–1872. "Ballad Society [Publications]."

Grasset, Pierre, "Faillite de l'amour courtois," *Mercure de France*, Vol. CCXCII (June, 1939).
Greene, Robert, The Plays and Poems; ed. by J. Churton Collins. Oxford, 1905.
Greg, Walter W., Pastoral Poetry and Pastoral Drama; a Literary Inquiry with Special Reference to the Pre-Restoration Stage in England. London, 1906.
Grierson, Herbert J. C., The Background of English Literature. London, 1925.
Guevara, Antonio de, Libro aureo de Marco Aurelio; tr. by Lord Berners, 1535, as The Golden Boke of Marcus Aurelius; ed. by José Maria Galvéz Oliváres. Berlin, 1916.
Hammond, Eleanor Prescott, English Verse between Chaucer and Surrey. Durham, N.C., 1927.
Harington, Sir John, Nugae antiquae, 1598; ed. the Rev. Henry Harington, 1779. London, 1779.
Harrington, Karl Pomeroy, Catullus and His Influence. New York, 1927.
Harrison, John Smith, Platonism in English Poetry of the Sixteenth and Seventeenth Centuries. New York, 1930.
Hawes, Stephen, The Passetyme of Pleasure; ed. by William Edward Mead. London, 1928. "Early English Text Society [Publications]."
Hazlitt, W. Carew, ed. Remains of the Early Popular Poetry of England. London, 1864–1866.
Henry VIII, The Letters; selected and ed. by Muriel St. Clare Byrne. London, 1936.
Heywood, John, A Play of Love, 1533. London, 1909. "The Tudor Facsimile Texts."
Hinckley, Henry Barret, "The Debate on Marriage in the *Canterbury Tales*," PMLA, Vol. XXXII (1917).
History of Patient Grissel, The; ed. by J. Payne Collier. London, 1841. "Percy Society Publications," Vol. III.
Hoby, Sir Thomas, tr., The Book of the Courtier, 1561; introduction by Sir Walter Raleigh. London, 1900. "Tudor Translations," No. 23.
Holmes, Urban Tigner, Jr., A History of Old French Literature. New York, 1937.
Huizinga, Johan, The Waning of the Middle Ages. London, 1927.

Jacobs, Henry Eyster, A Study in Comparative Symbolics, The Lutheran Movement in England during the Reigns of Henry VIII and Edward VI, and Its Literary Monuments. Philadelphia, 1890.

Jaques de Vitry, The Exempla or Illustrative Stories from the *Sermones Vulgares* of; ed. by Thomas Frederick Crane. London, 1890. "Folk Lore Society [Publications]."

Jeanroy, Alfred, La Poésie lyric des troubadours. Toulouse and Paris, 1934.

Jeffery, Violet May, John Lyly and the Italian Renaissance. Paris, 1928. "Bibliotheque de la Revue de Littérature Comparée, Tome 53."

Jerome, Saint, Select Letters; tr. by F. A. Wright. London, 1933. "Loeb Classical Library."

—— The Perpetual Virginity of the Blessed Mary; contra Jovinianum. New York, 1893. Nicene and Post-Nicene Fathers, 2d series, ed. by Philip Schaff and Henry Wace.

John, Lisle Cecil, Elizabethan Sonnet Sequences. New York, 1938.

Jones, Howard Mumford, and Philip Schuyler Allen, The Romanesque Lyric. Chapel Hill, N.C., 1928.

Jonson, Ben, Ben Jonson's Conversations with William Drummond of Hawthornden; ed. by R. F. Patterson. London, 1923.

Juvenal, Juvenal and Persius, Satire VI; tr. by G. G. Ramsay. London, 1918. "Loeb Classical Library."

Kilgour, Raymond Lincoln, The Decline of Chivalry as Shown in French Literature of the Late Middle Ages. Cambridge, Mass., 1937.

Kirby, Thomas A., Chaucer's *Troilus;* a Study in Courtly Love. University, La., 1940.

Kittredge, G. L., "Chaucer's Discussion of Marriage," *Modern Philology*, Vol. IX (1912).

Knight, George Wilson, The Imperial Theme. London, 1931.

—— "Lyly," *Review of English Studies*, Vol. XV (April, 1939).

Knox, John, The First Blast of the Trumpet against the Monstrous Regiment of Women, 1558; Introduction by Edward Arber. London, 1878. "English Scholars' Library," No. 2.

Krutch, Joseph Wood, Comedy and Conscience after the Restoration. New York, 1924.

La Tour-Landry, Geoffroy de, The Book of the Knight of La Tour-

Landry, Comp. for the Instruction of His Daughters; ed. by Thomas Wright. London, 1868. "Early English Text Society [Publications]."

Lawrence, William Witherle, Shakespeare's Problem Comedies. New York, 1931.

Lawson, Alexander, ed. The Kingis Quair; and The Quare of Jelusy. London, 1910.

Lee, Sir Sidney, Elizabethan and Other Essays. Oxford, 1929.

—— ed.; Elizabethan Sonnets. Westminster, 1904.

—— The French Renaissance in England. New York, 1910.

Legouis, Emile, Edmund Spenser. Paris, 1923.

—— and Louis Cazamian, A History of English Literature. New York, 1931.

Lewis, Clive Staples, The Allegory of Love. Oxford, 1936.

Lievsay, J. Leon, "Shakespere's 'Golden World.'" *Shakespeare Association Bulletin*, Vol. XIII, No. 2 (April, 1938).

Lodge, Thomas, Rosalynde, Euphues Golden Legacie. London, 1590.

Lounsbury, Thomas Raynesford, Studies in Chaucer. 2 vols. New York, 1892.

Lowes, John Livingston, "Chaucer and the 'Miroir de Mariage.'" *Modern Philology*, Vol. VIII (1910).

Lucretius, De rerum natura; tr. by W. H. D. Rouse. London, 1924. "Loeb Classical Library."

Luther, Martin, Table Talk; tr. by William Hazlitt. London, 1872.

—— Autobiography; comp. from letters by John Parker Lawson. 1863.

—— Letters. Selected and tr. by Margaret Currie. New York, 1908.

Lyly, John, The Complete Works; ed. by R. Warwick Bond. Oxford, 1902.

Lynche, Richard, Poems by Richard Linche, Gentleman, 1596; ed. by the Rev. Alexander B. Grosart. Blackburn, 1877.

McNeal, Thomas H., "*The Tyger's Heart Wrapt in a Player's Hide.*" *Shakespeare Association Bulletin*, Vol. XIII (January, 1938).

Mancinus, Dominicus, The Mirrour of Good Manners, 1523; tr. by Alexander Barclay. The edition of 1570. Manchester, 1885. "Spenser Society Publications."

Mannyng, Robert, of Brunne, Robert of Brunnes "Handlyng synne." 1303; ed. by Frederick James Furnivall. London, 1901. "Early English Text Society [Publications]."

Map, Walter, Master Walter Map's Book, de nugis curialium (Courtier's Trifles); Englished by Frederick Tupper and Marbury Bladen Ogle. London, 1924.

Marlowe, Christopher, Marlowe's Poems; ed. by L. C. Martin, in The Works and Life of Christopher Marlowe, General editor R. H. Case, Vol. IV. London, 1931.

—— The Works; ed. by A. H. Bullen. 3 vols. London, 1885.

Marston, John, The Metamorphosis of Pigmalions Image and Certain Satyres. London, 1598.

—— The Plays; ed. by H. Harvey Wood. 3 vols. Edinburgh, 1934.

—— The Works; ed. by A. H. Bullen. London, 1887.

Matulka, Barbara, The Novels of Juan de Flores and Their European Diffusion. New York, 1931.

Maulde la Clavière, Marie Alphonse René de, The Women of the Renaissance; tr. by George Herbert Ely. London, 1900.

Meres, Francis, *Palladis Tamia*, Wits Treasury, London, 1598; ed. by Joseph Haslewood, in Ancient Critical Essays. London, 1811–1815, Vol. II.

Michel, Dan, Dan Michel's Ayenbite of Inwit, 1340; ed. by Richard Morris. London, 1866. "Early English Text Society [Publications]."

More, Sir Thomas, Sir Thomas More's Utopia; tr. by Ralph Robinson, 1551; ed. by Robert Steele. London, 1908. "King's Classics," No. 40.

Morgan, Lucy Ingram, The Renaissance Lady in England. Berkeley, 1932. Unpublished dissertation, University of California.

Mott, Lewis Freeman, The System of Courtly Love, Studied as an Introduction to the *Vita nuova* of Dante. New York, 1896. Reprint, 1924.

Neilson, William Allen, The Origins and Sources of the "Court of Love." Boston, 1899.

—— and K. G. T. Webster, eds., Chief British Poets of the Fourteenth and Fifteenth Centuries. Cambridge, Mass., 1916.

Nicoll, Allardyce, British Drama. London, 1925.

Niebuhr, H. Richard, The Social Sources of Denominationalism. New York, 1929.

Ovid, The Art of Love and Other Poems; tr. by J. H. Mozely. London, 1929. "Loeb Classical Library."
—— Fasti; tr. by Sir James George Frazer. London, 1931. "Loeb Classical Library."
—— Heroides and Amores; tr. by Grant Showerman. London, 1914. "Loeb Classical Library."
—— Metamorphoses; tr. by Frank Justus Miller. London, 1916. "Loeb Classical Library."
—— Tristia, Ex ponto; tr. by Arthur Leslie Wheeler. London, 1924. "Loeb Classical Library."
Owl and the Nightingale, The; ed. by J. W. H. Atkins. Cambridge, 1922.
Owst, G. R., Literature and the Pulpit in Medieval England. Cambridge, 1933.
Pasquier, Etienne, Le monophyle; tr. by Geffray Fenton as "Monophylo . . . a Philosophicall Discourse and Division of Love," 1572.
Passetyme of Pleasure, The; ed. by William Edward Mead. London, 1928. "Early English Text Society [Publications]."
Patch, Howard Rollins, On Re-reading Chaucer. Cambridge, Mass., 1939.
Pearson, Lu Emily, Elizabethan Love Conventions. Berkeley, 1933.
Peele, George, The Works; ed. by A. H. Bullen. London, 1888.
Petit de Julleville, L., ed., Histoire de la langue et de la littérature Française. Vols. I–II. Paris, 1896.
Phillip, John, The Play of Patient Grissell (1565–66); ed. by Ronald B. McKerrow and W. W. Greg. London, 1909. Malone Society Reprints.
Phoenix Nest, The, 1593; ed. by Hyder Edward Rollins. Cambridge, Mass., 1931.
Piaget, A. "La Belle Dame sans Merci et ses imitations," *Romania*, Vol. XXX (1901), and Vol. XXXIII (1904).
Pricke of Conscience, The (Stimulus conscientiae); ed. by Richard Morris. Berlin, 1863. "Philological Society [Publications]."
Purcell, James Mark, Sidney's Stella. New York, 1934.
Quatrefoil of Love, The; ed. by Sir Israel Gollancz and Magdalene M. Weale. London, 1935. "Early English Text Society Publications."
Rand, Edward Kennard, Ovid and His Influence. New York, 1928.

Rare Triumphs of Love and Fortune, The, 1589; ed. by W. W. Greg. Oxford, 1930. Malone Society Reprints.
Raysor, Thomas Middleton, ed., Coleridge's Shakespearean Criticism. 2 vols. London, 1930.
Read, Conyers, The Tudors. New York, 1936.
Reich, Emil, Woman through the Ages. 2 vols. London, 1908.
Renwick, W. L., Edmund Spenser. London, 1925.
Rerum britannicarum medii aevi scriptores, No. 21, Vol. VIII. London, 1861–1891.
Rich, Townsend, Harington and Ariosto; a Study in Elizabethan Verse Translation. New Haven, 1940.
Robb, Nesca Adeline, Neoplatonism of the Italian Renaissance. London, 1935.
Romance of the Rose; Englished by Frederick S. Ellis. Temple Classics. New York, 1900.
Root, Robert Kilburn, The Poetry of Chaucer. Revised ed. Cambridge, Mass., 1934.
Ross, Woodburn O., ed., Middle English Sermons. London, 1940. "Early English Text Society [Publications]."
Rougement, Denis de, Love in the Western World; tr. by Montgomery Belgion. New York, 1940.
Schelling, Felix E., Elizabethan Drama, 1558–1642. 2 vols. Boston and New York, 1908.
Scott, Mary Augusta, The Book of the Courtyer. PMLA, Vol. XVI (1901).
Shakespeare, William, As You Like It; ed. by Sir Arthur Quiller-Couch and John Dover Wilson. Cambridge, 1926.
―――― Much Ado about Nothing; ed. by Sir Arthur Quiller-Couch and John Dover Wilson. Cambridge, 1923.
―――― The Sonnets; ed. by C. Knox Pooler. London, 1931. "Arden Shakespeare."
―――― The Sonnets; ed. by Raymond Macdonald Alden. Boston and New York, 1916.
―――― Sonnets; ed. by Tucker Brooke. New York, 1936.
―――― Sonnets; a Reproduction in Facsimile; ed. by Sir Sidney Lee. Oxford, 1905.
―――― The Works; ed. by W. J. Craig. New York, 1906. "Oxford Shakespeare."

Siciliano, Italo, François Villon et les thèmes poétiques du moyen âge. Paris, 1934.
Sidney, Sir Philip, Correspondence of Philip Sidney and Hubert Languet; ed. by William Aspenwall Bradley. Boston, 1912. Humanists' Library Series.
—— The Complete Works; ed. by Albert Feuillerat. 4 vols. Cambridge, 1922–1926. "Cambridge English Classics."
Skeat, Walter William, ed., Chaucerian and Other Pieces. Oxford, 1897.
Skelton, John, The Complete Poems of John Skelton, Laureat; ed. by Philip Henderson. Southampton, 1931.
Smith, George Gregory, ed., Elizabethan Critical Essays. Oxford, 1904.
Spenser, Edmund, Shepherd's Calendar; ed. by W. L. Renwick. London, 1930.
—— The Poetical Works. 3 vols. Volume I, Spenser's Minor Poems; ed. by Ernest de Sélincourt. Oxford, 1910.
—— The Works; a Variorum Edition; ed. by Edwin Greenlaw, Charles Grosvenor Osgood, Frederick Morgan Padelford. Vols. I–VI. Baltimore, 1932–1938.
Steiner, Arpad, "The Identity of the 'Count' in Andreas Capellanus' *De Amore*," *Speculum*, Vol. XIII (1938).
Stoll, Elmer Edgar, Art and Artifice in Shakespeare; a Study in Dramatic Contrast and Illusion. Cambridge, 1933.
—— Poets and Playwrights. Minneapolis, 1930.
—— Shakespeare Studies. New York, 1927.
—— Shakespeare's Young Lovers. New York, 1937.
Surrey, Henry Howard, earl of, The Poems; ed. by Frederick Morgan Padelford. Seattle, 1928. "University of Washington Publications in Language and Literature." Vol. V.
Symonds, John Addington, Wine, Women and Song, Medieval Latin Student Songs. London, 1925.
Tatlock, J. S. P., "Chaucer and Wyclif," *Modern Philology*, Vol. XIV (September, 1916).
—— "The Epilog of Chaucer's *Troilus*," *Modern Philology*, Vol. XVIII (April, 1921).
—— "Interpreting Literature by History," *Speculum*, Vol. XII (July, 1937).

Taylor, Henry Osborn, The Medieval Mind; a History of the Development of Thought and Emotion in the Middle Ages. London, 1927.
Tenison, Eva Mabel, Elizabethan England. 10 vols. Royal Leamington Spa, 1933–1937.
Thorndike, Ashley H., English Comedy. New York, 1929.
Tofte, Robert, Laura; the Toyes of a Traveller, or the Feast of Fancie. London, 1597.
Tottel's Miscellany; ed. by Hyder Edward Rollins. 2 vols. Cambridge, Mass., 1928–1929.
Villon, François, The Complete Works; tr. by J. U. Nicolson. New York, 1931.
Vives, Juan Luis, Instruction of a Christen Woman; tr. by Rychard Hyrde. London, 1541.
Voretzsch, Karl, Introduction to the Study of Old French Literature; tr. by Francis M. Du Mont. New York, 1931.
Ward, Charles, Frederick, The Epistles on the *Romance of the Rose* and Other Documents in the Debate. University of Chicago, 1911.
Watson, Foster, Vives and the Renascence Education of Women. London, 1912.
Wells, John Edwin, Manual of Writings in Middle English. New Haven, 1916.
Wilson, John Dover, John Lyly. Cambridge, 1905.
—— What Happens in Hamlet. Cambridge, 1935.
Wilson, Mona, Sir Philip Sidney. London, 1931.
Wilson, Robert (?), Fair Em; ed. by W. W. Greg. London, 1593. "Malone Society Reprints," London, 1927.
Wilson, Violet, Society Women of Shakespeare's Time. London, 1924.
Wolff, Samuel Lee, Greek Romances in Elizabethan Prose Fiction. New York, 1912.
Wood, Mary Morton, The Spirit of Protest in Old French Literature. New York, 1917.
Woodward, William Harrison, Desiderius Erasmus concerning the Aim and Method of Education. Cambridge, 1904.
Wright, Frederick Adam, Fathers of the Church. London, 1928.
—— Feminism in Greek Literature from Homer to Aristotle. London, 1923.

Wright, Louis Booker, Middle-Class Culture in Elizabethan England. Chapel Hill, N.C., 1935.
Wright, Thomas, ed., A Selection of Latin Stories. London, 1843. "Percy Society Publications."
—— ed., The Latin Poems Commonly Attributed to Walter Mapes. London, 1841.
Wiat, Sir Thomas, The Poems; ed. by A. K. Foxwell. London, 1913.
Wyat, George, Extracts from the Life of the Virtuous, Christian and Renowned Queen Anne Boleigne; *ca.* 1600. London, 1817.
Wyatt, Sir Thomas, The Poetry; introduction by E. M. W. Tillyard. London, 1929.
Wyclif, John, Select English Works; ed. by Thomas Arnold. Oxford, 1869–1871.
Yates, Frances A., John Florio; the Life of an Italian in Shakespeare's England. Cambridge, 1934.
—— A Study in *Love's Labour's Lost*. Cambridge, 1936.

Index

Adriana in *The Comedy of Errors*, 186 f.
Alençon, Duc d', 158
Alexander and Campaspe (Lyly), 3, 157 f., 164
Allegorical meanings in Lyly's plays, 156 ff., 162, 168
Amores (Ovid), 25, 28, 35
Amoretti (Spenser), 89, 98, 126
Andreas Capellanus, 33, 35, 40, 43, 45, 65, 82
Anglade, Joseph, quoted, 44
Antoine de la Salle, 75
Antony and Cleopatra (Shakespeare), 215
Arcadia (Sidney), 7, 148, 156, 200
Arcadian pastoral love, 199
Ariosto, 11, 13, 17
Aristocratic class, courtly love the product of, 38; efforts to adjust medieval tradition to facts of life, 123
Arraignment of Paris (Peele), 2
Ars amatoria (Ovid), 19, 32, 35, 134, 224
Arte honeste amandi, De (Andreas Capellanus), 33, 45, 65
Ascetic idealism, of medieval church fathers, 9, 35-38, 42, 83; St. Paul's repudiation of life of the senses the basis for, 35; shift from, in lyrics of Wyatt, 69; theologians' re-evaluations, 85-88; *see also* Church
Ascham, Roger, 112
Astrophel and Stella (Sidney), 94, 95, 145, 185; conflict in, 130-32
As You Like It (Shakespeare), 14, 23, 79, 99, 168, 183, 220; direct source for, 2; significance, 14; the second love-game comedy: its pastoral setting, 198; analyzed, 198-207
Augustine, Saint, 51, 85, 86; ascetic idealism, 36, 37

Bacon, Francis, 1, 7, 16, 224, 230
"Baite, The" (Marlowe, Donne's metamorphosis), 146
Balade, A . . . (Lydgate), 70
Banquet of Sence (Chapman), 25
Barclay, Alexander, 108, 110
Bastard of Coucy, 75
Batchelars Banquet, The, 84
Beatrice, Dante's, 37, 89
Beatrice and Benedick in *Much Ado about Nothing*, 120, 209 ff.
Beaufort, Lady Jane, 70
Bédier, Joseph, 41
Belle Dame sans Merci, La (Chartier), 74, 78, 82, 128
Bembo, Cardinal, 90, 91, 99, 132, 134, 141, 148, 178; analysis of Platonic love in *Il cortegiano*, 117 ff.
Benedick and Beatrice in *Much Ado about Nothing*, 120, 209 ff.
Benivieni's Platonism, 99
Bercher (or Barker), William, 110, 113
Bernarde, M., in *The Courtier*, 114, 115
Bernart de Ventadorn, 33, 40
Berowne in *Love's Labour's Lost*, 191 ff.
Boccaccio, Giovanni, 84
Boke of the Governour (Elyot), 108
Boleyn, Anne, 103, 105 f., 109, 129
Bond, R. Warwick, quoted, 172
Book of the Courtier, The (and Chaucer), 10 (*see under Cortegiano, Il*)
Book of the Duchess (Chaucer), 48

Book of the Knight of La Tour-Landry, 40
Boucicault, Jean le M. (marshal of France), 74
Bourgeois gentilhomme (Molière), 15
"Bowre of Blis" destroyed by Spenser, 7, 94
Bromyard, John, 52
Brooke, Tucker, 14, 182; quoted, 183
Bruno, Giordano, 190
Bucolic romances and dramas, 198 ff.
Bush, Douglas, 19, 32*n*

Caelica (Greville), 133
Calvin, John, 1, 36, 83, 85, 110; marriage, 88
Camilla, character in *Euphues*, 151 ff.
Campaspe, *see Alexander and Campaspe*
Campbell, Oscar James, 216, 221
Canterbury Tales (Chaucer), 38, 51 ff. *passim;* "Marriage Group" sequence, 54, 60 ff. *passim*
Cardenal, Peire, 44, 89
Caricature of the lover's woes, 161, 200
Castiglione, Baldassare, 1, 10, 17, 83, 111, 154; analysis of love, 111-22; *see his Cortegiano, Il*
Catullus, 8, 20, 96, 102, 182; revulsion of idealist from the world of common sense fact, in verses to Lesbia, 224 ff.; initiation of an idea: originality, 225
Cecilia, Saint, 40, 51
Celia in *Love's Metamorphosis,* 169 f.
Cents ballades, 75
Chambers, E. K., 71, 73, 128
Chapman, George, 11, 22; use of Ovid, 24 f., 26
Charlton, Henry Buckley, quoted, 226, 232
Chartier, Alain, 75; *La Belle Dame sans Merci,* 74, 78, 82, 128
Chastity, medieval lyrics in praise of, 37; in marriage, 51
Chaucer, Geoffrey, 10, 18, 23, 32, 38, 39, 41, 77, 82, 84, 91, 97, 223; importance as expositor of medieval attitudes, 9, 47, 101; varied attitudes toward love, 9, 10, 47-53; presentation of amorous controversy, 47-68; use of conflict, 54-60; literary artistry: objective and impartial attitude, 54; attempt to resolve conflicting attitudes, 60-65
Chevalier de la Charrette (Chrestien de Troyes), 33, 41, 43, 45
Choice, rational, 92
Chrestien de Troyes, 33, 41, 43, 45, 48, 64
Christian asceticism, *see* Ascetic idealism; Church
Christian doctrine, Platonism as an explanation of, 90
Christine de Pisan, 75; criticism of *Roman de la Rose,* 44, 66; new direction of interest in love given by: focus of her attack, 74; poem made part of English critical appraisal, 76
Church, ascetic philosophy and its attitude toward love, 9, 35, 36 ff., 83; movement away from harsh idealism, 38; clergy's conceptions of masculine sovereignty, 41, 84; attitude rarely challenged, 43; Chaucer's references to tenets of, 51; theologians' re-evaluations of ascetic doctrines, 85-88; marriage of clergy, 85, 87, 88; danger of idealizing love balanced by, 226
City of God (St. Augustine), 36
Clanvowe's *The Cuckoo and the Nightingale . . . ,* 78
Classes, those appealed to by courtly and by sensual love, 38, 71
Claudio in *Much Ado about Nothing,* 208 ff.
Clergy, *see under* Church
Cligès (Chrestien de Troyes), 33, 64
Coleridge, Samuel Taylor, 14
Colloquies (Erasmus), 86 f.
Comedies, *see* Love-game comedies
Comedy of Errors, The (Shakespeare), 186

Index

Commentaries on Isaiah (Calvin), 84
Complaint of Mars (Chaucer), 59
Complaint of the Black Knight . . . (Lydgate), 76, 77
Complaint to His Lady (Chaucer), 48
Complaint unto Pity (Chaucer), 48
Conduct books, *Il cortegiano* adopted by Elizabethans, 83, 111-22; early Tudor books, 107-11
Congreve, William, 3, 227
Contra Jovinianum (St. Jerome), 38, 62
Coronet for His Mistresse Philosophie (Chapman), 25
Cortegiano, Il (Castiglione), 1, 17, 107, 123, 124, 127, 131, 144, 145, 146, 165; the book of manners adopted by Elizabethans, 83; characters, and analysis of love in, with excerpts, 111-22
Coulton, G. G., quoted, 68
Courtesy evaluated, 109
Courtier, The, see *Cortegiano, Il*
Courtly love, ritual and its demands, 8, 34 f., 96; medieval importance, 9; rare in writings of Romans, 20; origin of concept: ideal of, the basic factor in controversy about passion, 32; stages in development of, 33, 65 ff.; product of aristocratic class, 38; why easily prey for skeptics, 43; French writers' re-examination, and debate about, nature of, 44, 66; most bitter critic and most subtle foe, 65; whether a secularized, practicable version possible, 67; re-examination in fifteenth-century literature, 71, 73-81; Renaissance adaptations and re-evaluations, 82-102; by theologians, 85-88; by Platonists, 89-96; marital adaptation, 98 ff.; Renaissance attempts to actualize theories of, 103-22; conceptions in early Tudor conduct books, 107-11; analysis in *Il cortegiano*, 111-22; tradition of, as elaborated in the sonnets, 123 (*see* Sonnets); *see also* Love; Love-game comedies; Troubadours
Court of Love, 80
Courtship, ideal and comic compared, 5
Cresseid, Testament of (Henryson), 71
Cressida, *see* Shakespeare's *Troilus and Cressida*
Criseyde, *see* Chaucer's *Troilus and Criseyde*
Cuckoo and the Nightingale, The . . . (Clanvowe), 78

Daniel, Samuel, 125, 126, 127
Dante, and Beatrice, 37, 89, 90, 91; compared with Sidney, 95; poetic doctrines of Provence developed by, 124
Dark lady, Shakespeare's sonnets to, 174, 178, 182
Débat de deux amans, Le (Christine de Pisan), 74, 79
Defence of Good Women (Elyot), 109
De gli eroici furori (Bruno), 190
Delia (Daniel), 126
De rerum natura (Lucretius), 20, 224
Deschamps's *Miroir de mariage*, 38
Desdemona, character in *Othello*, 182, 215
Devereux, Penelope (Lady Rich), 106, 107, 160, 167*n*
Diella (Linche), 136
Dissuasio Valerii ad Rufinum philosophum . . . (Map), 37
Divorce in *Utopia*, 87
Domenichi, Lodovico, 110
Donne, John, 1, 8, 9, 18, 67, 129, 137, 138, 146, 147, 148, 149, 175, 178, 189, 229; Renaissance mind at its subtlest represented by, 141; solution of lovers' difficulties, 141-44, 223; attitude and method in poetry of Shakespeare and, 180, 182
Dowden, Edward, 14
Drama, psychological dilemma that could be used in, 146; always sug-

Drama (*Continued*)
  gested by sonnet, 147; of Lyly appraised, 171; its importance, 172
Drayton, Michael, 144, 148, 149, 175; satire in Marston and, 137-41
Dumaine in *Love's Labour's Lost*, 193 ff.
Dunbar, William, 71, 79

"Ecstasy, The" (Donne), 143
Eleanor of Aquitaine, 33, 40, 65
Elizabeth, Queen, 84, 105, 106, 107, 110; Lyly's masked references to, 156, 157, 158, 160, 162
Elizabethan poetry, *see* Sonnets
Elizabethan Renaissance, *see* Renaissance
Elyot, Sir Thomas, 108-10, 112, 113, 120, 121
Endimion (Lyly), 5, 19, 159-62, 167, 188
Epistre au Dieu d'Amours (Christine de Pisan), 44, 66, 74; Hoccleve's *Letter of Cupid* a translation of, 76
Epithalamion (Spenser), 91, 98
Erasmus, 38, 85; views expressed in his *Colloquies*: its influence, 86 f.
Escape literature, love-game comedies as, 6, 7
Essays (Bacon), 1
Eumenides, in Lyly's *Endimion*, 160, 167
Euphues . . . (Lyly), 3, 82, 165, 189; analysis of: significance, 148-56
Experience, whether the ritual of courtesy could be embodied in, 44, 65, 68, 74; as a criterion by which to judge preconceived ideals, 95; in Shakespeare's sonnets, 177, 182, 183; his treatment of the inadequacy of, 220; way by which pretensions of medieval romance, and actual fulfillments, can be accepted as related aspects of, 227; poets did not attempt to reproduce, but to appraise it, 228; *see also* Realism

Fabliaux, 41, 43, 83, 226; defined: medieval literary examples of sensualism, 39; portraits of women in, 53, 85
Faerie Queene (Spenser), 1, 10, 17, 92, 95, 98, 126
Fasti (Ovid), 22
Feuillerat, Albert, 11, 162
Ficino, Marsilio, 90
Fidus, character in *Euphues*, 152 ff.
Fifteenth century, sharp break in literature between Middle Ages and Renaissance, 69; traditional attitudes, 69-73; re-examination of courtly love in literature of, 73-81
Fletcher, Jefferson B., 91
Fletcher, John, 11, 227
Flower and the Leaf, 70
Fowre Hymnes . . . (Spenser), 89, 90, 91, 93
France, re-examination of, and debate about, the nature of love, 44, 66, 74
"Franklin's Tale" (Chaucer), 60, 65, 66, 83, 98
French literature, farces, 38; inherent incompatibility of the three ways of regarding love made explicit for, in *Roman de la Rose*, 47
French troubadours, *see* Troubadours

Galahad, Sir, 37
Gallathea (Lyly), 156n
Gallus, 20
Gascoigne, tr. of Ariosto, 11
George a' Greene . . . (Greene), 2
Gerson, Jean, 74
Golden Boke of Marcus Aurelius, The, 110n
"Golden Book" (Theophrastus), 62
Golden Legend, 37, 43, 70
Golden Targe, The (Dunbar), 79
Goliardic verse, 43; defined: medieval literary examples of sensualism, 39
Gollancz, Sir Israel, 42
Gonzaga, Lord Cesar, in *The Courtier*, 114, 115
Gosson, Stephen, 18, 84

Index

Grail story, 37, 70
Grasset, Pierre, quoted, 44*n*
Greene, Robert, 2, 12
Greg, W. W., 199
Greville, Fulke, 7, 135, 136, 141, 144, 167; realism of, 132-35
Grierson, Herbert J. C., 143
Griselda, 41, 84, 103, 104
Guevara, Antonio de, 110, 113
Guillaume de Lorris, 33, 48, 52, 73; portion of *Roman de la Rose* by, 45, 47
Guillaume de Tignonville, 74
Guinizelli, Guido, 89

Hall, Joseph, 1, 7
Hamlet (Shakespeare), 121, 182
Hawes, Stephen, 70
Henry VIII, 104, 105
Henryson, Robert, 71
Hero and Leander (Marlowe), 21, 27, 32; Ovid's influence on, 22-24
Hero in *Much Ado about Nothing*, 208 ff.
Heroides (Ovid), 20, 23, 35
Heywood, John, 2
Hoby, tr. of *Il cortegiano*, 1, 107, 111, 122
Hoccleve, Thomas, 71, 76
Human conduct, interest in, during Renaissance, 1
Humanism, 67, 92; love-game comedies nourished from forces of, 7; first artistic manifestations, 69; attitude toward love, of humanists within the church, 85 ff. *passim*; its attempt to accommodate romantic love to the new woman, presented by *Il cortegiano*, 111

Iffida, character in *Euphues*, 152 ff.
Idea, sonnets to (Drayton), 137
Ideal, imagined: age-old comment about interplay of reality and, 224 ff.
Idealism, *see* Ascetic idealism
"Indifferent, The" (Donne), 142

Instruction of a Christen Woman (Vives), 104
Italian sources, 17, 152*n*
Italy, Renaissance influence spreading from, 101; aristocrats' efforts to adjust a medieval tradition to the facts of life, 123

James I of Scotland, 70
Jaques in *As You Like It*, 202 ff.
Jean de Meung, 40, 43, 48, 54, 58, 65, 101; portion of the *Roman de la Rose* by, 38, 45, 47, 66; focus of Christine de Pisan's attack, 74
Jeffery, Violet, 164
Jehan de Condé, 39
Jerome, Saint, 38, 40, 51, 52, 56, 62, 85, 86, 87, 88; attitude toward women and love, 36; toward marriage, 56
John, Lisle Cecil, quoted, 230*n*
John of Bromyard, 37
Jonson, Ben, 216, 221
Joseph in mystery plays, 38, 43
Julian, Lord, in *The Courtier*, 114 ff.
Juvenal, 35

Kate in *The Taming of the Shrew*, 84
Katharine, Queen, 104, 105, 106
Kilgour, Raymond L., 75
King Henry the Fifth (Shakespeare), 221
Kingis Quair by James I, 69, 98, 99
Kittredge, G. L., 64
"Knights Tale" (Chaucer), 48, 53, 54, 58, 76, 82, 96, 97, 167*n*
Knox, John, 1, 110
Krutch, Joseph Wood, 3*n*, 15

Lancelot and the Grail, 37
Langlois, Ernest, 45
Latinate writers, 4, 19 f., 35, 224 ff., *see also* names, *e.g.*, Ovid
Lawrence, William Witherle, 221; quoted, 222
Leander, *see* Hero and Leander

"Leave me ô Love . . ." (Sidney), 89, 132
Lee, Sir Sidney, 228*n*
Legend of Good Women (Chaucer), 51, 57, 65, 66, 97
Leicester, Earl of, 160
Lesbia, poems of Catullus to, 8, 224 ff.
Letter of Cupid, a tr. by Hoccleve, 76
Lewis, C. S., 98, 102
Libertine conception of love, *see* Sensual love
Libro aureo (Guevara), 110
Linche, Richard, 136, 139
Literary expression of Elizabethan poets and dramatists, 227 ff.
Lodge, Thomas, 199, 200, 202
Longaville in *Love's Labour's Lost*, 193 ff.
Looking Glass, A . . . (Greene), 2
Love, incongruities of action during, 2; treatment by Latinate writers, 4, 18 ff., 224 ff.; development of amorous controversy in Middle Ages and Renaissance, 8, 9, 18, 32-46, 65-68, 226 (*see also* Middle Ages; Renaissance); the several attitudes toward love, 32 ff.; conflict between heavenly and earthly love presented as debate, 41; Chaucer's presentation of controversy, 47-65, 66; his attempt to resolve conflicting attitudes, 60-65; clash between sacred and profane, continued in fifteenth-century writings, 70; love became a quarrel between the ideal and the psychologically possible, once the social and emotional equality of the sexes was assumed, 120; when sentiment became a subject for logical analysis: expressions of new consciousness of emotional difficulties, 122; involved, subjective analysis of, 123 (*see* Sonnets); conception of, basic in all Elizabethan poetry, 124; emergence of a new philosophy of, in poetry of Donne, 143; how Shakespeare's love-game comedies resolve four-century quarrel over nature of, 223 ff.; tangible form given to universal process of psychological adjustment between lovers, 226; *see also* Courtly love; Love-game comedies
Love at first sight, 23, 50, 70, 130
Love-game comedies, Shakespeare's, 1-17, 185-222 (*see entries under* Shakespeare); type of wit and mockery developed in, 1; dramatic method, 2-6; a form of "escape" literature, 6; as conceived or anticipated by Lyly, 3, 152, 156, 164; intellectual substance, 6-10; significance, 10-17; marriage as target for, 100; emergence of a new philosophy of love, 143; conflicting ideas in Elizabethan sonnets and in comedy, 144-47; emotional turmoil, or psychological need, satisfied dramatically by, 144; Shakespeare's nearest lyric approach to comic spirit dramatized by, 180; what is meaningful, historically, and significant, in them, 223 ff.; they held the mirror up to contemporary attitudes, 230; and pushed our comprehension of love beyond the boundaries of literary formulae, 232; *see also* Courtly love; Shakespeare
"Lovers Infiniteness" (Donne), 142
Loves Deitie (Donne), 189
Love's Labour's Lost (Shakespeare), 4, 5, 13, 14, 82, 183, 213, 220, 226; direct source for, 2; significance, 14; the first love-game comedy: a satire of real people? 190; analyzed, 191-98, 199, 204, 206
Love's Metamorphosis (Lyly), 3, 5, 168-71, 190, 194
Luciana in *The Comedy of Errors*, 186
Lucilla, character in *Euphues*, 149 ff.
Lucrece, *see Rape of Lucrece*
Lucretius, 20, 132, 134, 178, 224, 225
Luther, Martin, 1, 85, 86; marriage of, and views on marriage, 88

Index

Lydgate, John, 70, 72, 76, 77
Lyly, John, 11, 13, 19, 82, 83, 122, 146, 174, 188, 189, 194, 214; Shakespeare's indebtedness to, 2, 172, 198; love-game comedy as conceived or anticipated by, 3, 152, 156, 164; critics' opinions about comedies of, 10 f., 14; sources, 11, 152*n*; purely local value of comedies when seen as social satire, 13; reasons for his place in history of English literature, 17; first Elizabethan to see that opposed attitudes in love quarrel could be used for new purpose, 148; its possibilities explored in his novel *Euphues*, 148-56; allegorical significance of the characters, 156 ff., 162, 168; contending attitudes in comedies, 156-64; his resolution of controversy, 164-73; something new in literature repesented by work of: limitations in his drama, 171; his true greatness of the same type as Shakespeare's, 172*n*; their work compared, 172 f., 190, 191, 194, 196, 205, 214; where his importance as a playwright lay, 172

Malory, Sir Thomas, 37, 70
Man and Superman (Shaw), 227
Mancinus Dominicus, 108
Manners, book of, adopted by Elizabethans, 83; see *Cortegiano, Il*
—— comedies of, 68; beginnings, 1; love-game comedies as, 4, 14, 66
Map, Walter, 37, 40, 65, 88
Marie de Champagne, 33
Marlowe, Christopher, 19, 21, 25, 27, 32, 146; Ovid's influence on *Hero and Leander*, 22-24, 26
Marriage, regarded as inconsistent with love, 8; chastity in, 51; Chaucer's treatment of, in his "Marriage Group," 54 ff. *passim*; accepted by Jerome because it produced virgins, 56; question of, for clergy, 85, 87, 88; marital adaptation of courtly love, 96-101; important difficulties left untouched by, 99; as target for love-game comedy, 100
Marston, John, 1, 7, 11, 15, 22, 27, 142, 144, 148; use of Ovid, 25 f.; satire in Drayton and, 137-41, 216, 221
Masculine sovereignty, 41
Measure for Measure (Shakespeare), 6, 99, 209, 215
Merchant of Venice (Shakespeare), 6, 7, 14
Meres, Francis, 18
Metamorphoses (Ovid), 20, 28
Midas (Lyly), 156*n*
Middle Ages, three attitudes around which sex conflict revolves, 8; Chaucer's importance as expositor of attitudes, 9, 47, 66; importance of courtly love to, 9; origins of amorous controversy: Ovid and his influence, 18-31; amorous controversy in literature, 32-46; ideal of courtly love, origin and theories, 32-35; ascetic idealism, 35-38; misogynic attitude, 35 f., 38; courtly love the product of the aristocratic class, 38; realism and its appeal to the socially inferior, 38-39; the three ways mutually incompatible, 39; literary expressions of conflict, 39-46, 65 ff.; conventional setting, 42, 49; conflict between Christian asceticism and realistic criticism, rare, 42; difference between mind, then and later, 68; Renaissance adaptations and re-evaluations of medieval attitudes, 82-102; by theologians, 85-88; Platonic adaptation, 89-96; marital, 96-101; how the most widely divergent conceptions of love were represented: Elizabethan reaction to its heritage, 231
Midsummer Night's Dream (Shakespeare), 6, 99, 185
Mileta, character in *Sapho and Phao*, 159, 166

"Miller's Tale" (Chaucer), 9
Miroir de mariage (Deschamps), 38
Mirrour for Magistrates, The, 1
Mirrour of Good Manners, The (Mancinus Dominicus), 108
Misogynic attitude, 35 f., 38, 71 f., 83, 110
Mockery and wit, type found in love-game comedies, 1, 6
Molière, 15
"Monks Tale, Prologue of the" (Chaucer), 52, 55
Montanus in *Love's Metamorphosis*, 168 ff.
Morals, Renaissance preoccupation with, 1; Elizabethan code, 100; outstanding study of manners and, 112
More, Sir Thomas, 85; views of, in *Utopia*, 87 f.
Morte d'Arthur (Malory), 37, 70
Mother Bombie (Lyly), 156n
Mott, Lewis F., 33
Mountjoy, Penelope Devereux's relations with, 107
Much Ado about Nothing (Shakespeare), 4, 12, 14, 82, 83, 155, 156, 167, 182; direct source for, 2; significance, 14, 216; similarity between contention in *The Courtier* and, 120; Shakespeare's third and final love-game comedy: how it differs from the others, 208; a derisive comedy of courtship: analyzed, 208-16, 232; mood like that of the sonnets, 208, 220, 221; reality of the characters the very artistry of dramatization: their conflict that of the age, individualized, 213
Mumming at Hertford (Lydgate), 72
Mystery plays, 39, 43, 84

Nicoll, Allardyce, 14
Niobe and Nisa in *Love's Metamorphosis*, 169 ff.
Noah in mystery plays, 39; wife, 84
Nobility of Women, The, 110

Norfolk, *The Courtier* denounced by, 112
Novels, *see* Prose
"Nun's Priest's Tale" (Chaucer), 54
Nut Brown Maid, 72, 85

"Of Love" (Bacon), 224
Of Weddid Men and Wifis (Wyclif), 85
Orlando in *As You Like It*, 200 ff.
Othello (Shakespeare), 182, 215, 224
Ovid, 11, 13, 94, 134, 139, 143, 224, 226; extent of influence upon sixteenth-century writers, 18-32; notions of sex, 19, 20; type of realism, 20; influence on Marlowe, 22-24; Chapman's and Marston's use of, 24-26; influence on Shakespeare, 26-31; amorous poetry governed by psychology of attack and retreat, 31; influence upon troubadour poets, 34
Owl and the Nightingale, The, 41, 65
Owst, G. R., 84

Padelford, Professor, 98
Pain and Sorrow of Evil Marriage, The, 84
Pallavicino, Lord Gaspar, in *The Courtier*, 112 ff.
Pandarus, character in *Troilus and Cressida*, 217 ff.
Pandora in *The Woman in the Moone*, 162 f., 168
Parliament of Fowls (Chaucer), 59
Passetyme of Pleasure (Hawes), 70
Passion, *see* Sensual love
Pastoral romances and dramas, 198 ff.
Paul, Saint, repudiation of the life of the senses, and its influence, 9, 35 ff.
Pearson, Lu Emily, 136
Peele, George, 2
Pembroke, Mary, Countess of, 126
Personal experience, *see* Experience; Realism
Petit Jehan de Saintré (Antoine de la Salle), 75
Petrarch, 32, 84, 90, 113, 115, 123;

Index

source of, and influence upon, English sonnet, 123 ff. *passim*
Petrarchism, 8, 19, 67, 68, 124 ff. *passim*, 228; and Platonism terms for same sentiment, 91; self-analysis, 128; much of poetry in tradition of, is dramatic, 144; Shakespeare's treatment of the conventions of, 174-82 *passim*; parody of Bruno's anti-Petrarchan attitude, 190
Petruchio in *The Taming of the Shrew*, 187
Phao, see *Sapho and Phao*
Phebe in *As You Like It*, 200 ff.
Philantus in *Euphues*, 150 ff.
Philosophy of love, new: emergence of, in Donne's poetry, 143
Pia, Lady Emilia, in *The Courtier*, 112 ff.
Pigmalion's Image (Marston), 25, 26, 27
Plato, 35
Platonism, 17, 175; adaptation of courtly love, 89-96; as an explanation of Christian doctrine, 90; same sentiment as Petrarchism, 91; idealism as used by Spenser and Sidney, 94; Bembo's analysis of Platonic love, in *Il cortegiano*, 117 ff.; Platonic ideal love of the sonneteers, 124 ff. *passim*; recourse to, a check to danger of idealizing love, 226
Play of Love, A (Heywood), 2
Pleasant Quippes for Upstart Newfangled Gentlewomen (Gosson), 84
Pooler, C. Knox, 27
Propertius, 20
Prose romances, Elizabethan, 148*n*; Lyly's *Euphues*, 148-56
Proteus in *Two Gentlemen of Verona*, 188 f.
Provence, lyrics of, 16, 43; developed by Dante, 124
Psychological adjustment, marriage a process of, 100; tangible form given to universal process of, between lovers, 226

Psychological need satisfied dramatically by love-game comedies, 144, 146
Psychological significance of the comedies, 15

Quatrefoil of Love, 42
Quiller-Couch, Sir Arthur T., 214

Raleigh, Sir Walter, 146
Ramis in *Love's Metamorphosis*, 168 ff.
Rape of Lucrece, The (Shakespeare), 178; Ovid's influence, 27, 29-31, 32
Rare Triumphs of Love and Fortune, The, 2
Realism, in medieval drama, 38 f.; opposed ethics of monk and courtier challenged by, 40; why direct conflict rare, 42; Wyatt the first to protest against neglect of reality, 129; Sidney's movement in direction of, 130, 131; Fulke Greville's, 133-35; movement toward skepticism, 135, 136; extent of comment about interplay of imagined ideal and commonplace reality, 224 ff.; see also Experience
Remedia amoris (Ovid), 19
Renaissance, interest in human conduct, 1; pursuit of love in literature of, 4; intense interest in nature of love a part of new rationalism, 9; Ovid's influence upon attempt to synthesize conflicting attitudes, 19; relationship between conceptions familiar to Middle Ages and, illustrated by study of Chaucer, 47, 66; contrasts in, and development of, those conceptions, 65-68; adaptations and re-evaluations of medieval attitudes, 82-102; theologians' re-evaluations of ascetic doctrines, 85-88; Platonic adaptation of courtly love, 89-96; marital adaptation, 96-101; attempts to actualize theories of courtly love, 103-22; in conduct books, 107-11; in *Il cortegiano*,

Renaissance (*Continued*)
111-22; social and emotional equality of the sexes assumed: effect upon quarrel about love, 120; movement of literary taste toward seventeenth-century skepticism, 135, 136; pastoral romances and dramas, 198 ff.; growing interest in more substantial treatments of human passions, 221; relation to the present time and its literature, 227; Elizabethan reaction to its medieval romantic heritage, 227, 231; aesthetic theory about Elizabethan dramatic expression, 229
Restoration drama, 3*n*
Rich, Lady, *see* Devereux, Penelope
Rich, Lord, 107
Ridicule, real people as targets for, 190
Robinson, Professor, 48
Roman de la Rose, 19, 33, 40, 44, 54, 58, 97, 100; Jean de Meung's portion, 38, 45, 47, 66; most memorable literary expression of conflicting points of view, 44; Christine de Pisan's criticism of, 44, 66, 74; Guillaume de Lorris's portion, 45, 47
Roman poets, 19 f., 35, 224 ff.; *see also names, e.g.,* Ovid
Romeo and Juliet (Shakespeare), 100
Ros, Sir Richard, 78
Rosalind in *As You Like It*, 200 ff.
Rosaline in *Love's Labour's Lost*, 191 ff.
Rosalynde . . . (Lodge), 200
Royden, Matthew, 24

Saints, austere behavior, 37, 43
Salamacis in Ovid's *Metamorphoses*, 27, 28
Sapho and Phao (Lyly), 158 f., 166 f.
"Sapience," Spenser's personification of divine beauty, 94
Satire, in Elizabethan poetry, 137-41, 146, 183; Lyly's satirical caricature, 161; *Troilus and Cressida* a satire of courtship, 215, 216-22

Schelling, Felix E., 11
"School of Night" individuals satirized, 190
"Second Nun's Tale" (Chaucer), 51, 54
Sensual love, realistic view of, 9; Ovid's conception of, 19, 20 (*see also* Ovid); differences in treatment by Shakespeare and Ovid, 27 ff.; Renaissance treatment of, governed by internal conflict, 31; triumph of libertine notions a dismal one: the courtly ideal the central and basic factor, 32; attempt to localize literary expression of, 38; important examples in *fabliaux* and goliardic verse, 39, 53; clash between extreme viewpoints made articulate in various ways, 40; rarely advocated before the Reformation, 43; Spenser's conception of a wisely tempered passion, 91 ff.; denied much significance, 108; in sonnets of Shakespeare, 176, 177 f., 181, 220; in his *Troilus and Cressida*, 216 ff.
Sentiment became a subject for logical analysis, 122
Seventeenth century, *see* Renaissance
Sex, transcendental notions of, denied by Ovid, 19; ascetic idealism a revulsion from, 36 f.
Sex duel, 145, 146, 205; skepticism about love dramatized as, 5; poem reflecting the new interest in, 78; in real life, 121; one-sided in Shakespeare's comedies, 204; comic method formulated by him, 227
Sex superiority, arguments about, 41, 61, 71, 83 f., 110
Sexuality, *see* Sensual love
Shakespeare, 18, 21, 22, 23, 71, 82, 122, 145, 146, 154, 229; type of wit and mockery found in his three love-game comedies, 1 f.; their dramatic method, 2-6; indebtedness to Lyly, 2, 172, 198; their work compared, 3 ff., 172 f., 190, 191, 194,

Index

196, 205, 214; intellectual substance of the comedies, 6-10, 12; significance, 7, 10-17, 223; satire of courtship in *Troilus and Cressida*, 15, 183, 215, 216-22, 224; Ovid's influence, 26-31, 32; traditional antagonism toward love and woman reflected in comedies, 84; Renaissance perplexity reflected in much the same way by Castiglione and, 120; conflict in sonnets, analyzed, 174-84; attitude and method in poetry of Donne and, 180, 182; individual interpretation of amorous thought, 181; spirit of sonnets more related to tragedies than to love-game comedies, 182; nature of relationship between sonnets and comedies, 183, 208, 220, 221; comic use of conflict in other than love-game comedies, 185 ff.; his addition to established pattern of conflict, 185; first play in which reconciliation is given full treatment, 188 f.; first love-game comedy in which quarrel over the nature of love is dramatized for first time in fashion inaugurated by Lyly, 190-98 (*see also Love's Labour's Lost*); character revelation and pastoral setting of second love-game comedy: analysis of the play, 198-207 (*see also As You Like It*); new note of deeper concern with opposed elements of love in third love-game comedy: analysis of the play, 208-16, 220, 221, 232 (*see also Much Ado about Nothing*); audiences interested in more substantial treatments of human passions than those found in earlier comedies, 221; whether he gave love story an intentionally derisive treatment, 222; what is meaningful, historically, in comedies of courtship, 223 ff.; romantic love the right Promethean fire for, 226; whether his comedies dramatize any peculiarly Elizabethan problem, 229; *see also* Love-game comedies

Shaw, George Bernard, 227

Short Title Catalogue, 18

Sidney, Sir Philip, 1, 7, 9, 12, 18, 82, 89, 91, 94, 103, 135, 136, 144, 145, 146, 148, 154, 156, 160*n*, 167*n*, 175, 190, 199, 200, 231; use of Platonic idealism as distinguished from Spenser's, 94; compared with Dante, 95; the "Stella" of his sonnets, 106; as embodied pattern of *The Courtier*, 112*n*; conflict in *Astrophel and Stella*, carried in the direction of realism, 130-32; excellence of its poetry, 130

Silvestris in *Love's Metamorphosis*, 168 ff.

Silvia in *Two Gentlemen of Verona*, 189

Silvius in *As You Like It*, 200 ff.

Sixteenth century, *see* Renaissance

Skepticism about love, dramatized as sex duel, 5; movement of literary taste toward, 135, 136; a check to danger of idealizing love, 226

Sonnets, nature of their fundamental conflict, 68; Elizabethans' attitude expressed in, 95, 107; subject matter, and significance, 123 ff.; introduction of, into English literature: foreign inspiration, 123; Wyatt's treatment of lovers' ideals, 127-30; conflict in Sidney's *Astrophel and Stella*, 130-32, 231; realism of Fulke Greville, 132-35; minor poets, 135-36; satire in Drayton and Marston, 137-41; Donne's solution to lovers' difficulties, 141-44, 147, 180, 182; conflicting ideas in comedy and, 144-47; conflict in Shakespeare's sonnets, 174-84, 208, 220, 221, 229 (*see entries under* Shakespeare); effects of analytic methods employed in studies of, vs. what the author wished to communicate and the meaning of his poetry, 228 f.;

Sonnets (*Continued*)
   mirror held up to contemporary attitudes in, 230
Southampton, Earl of, 106
Spenser, Edmund, 1, 7, 9, 17, 18, 22, 96, 99, 100, 126, 144, 148; attempt to form composite ideal, 10; philosophy and portrayal of love, 89 ff., 126
Spring and the quickened world, 22, 57; the traditional season in medieval romance, 49 ff.
"Stella" of Sidney's sonnets, 106 (*see Astrophel and Stella*)
Stesias in *The Woman in the Moone*, 163 f., 168
Stoll, Elmer Edgar, 230; theories about substance of, and sources for, Lyly, 11; Shakespeare, 12, 13; quoted, 229
Suckling, Sir John, 138
Suppositi, I (Ariosto), 11
Surrey, Henry Howard, Earl of, 125, 127
Sybilla, character in *Sapho and Phao*, 166
Symposium (Plato), 35

Taming of the Shrew, The (Shakespeare), 5, 71, 84, 186, 187
Tarquin in *The Rape of Lucrece*, 29 ff.
Testament of Cresseid (Henryson), 71
Theocritus, 199
Theologians, *see under* Church
Theophrastus, 62
Thrush and the Nightingale, 41
Tibullus, 20
Tillyard, Professor, 128, 147
Tofte, Robert, 135
To Rosemounde (Chaucer), 58, 66
Tottel's Miscellany, 107, 125
Touchstone in *As You Like It*, 201 ff.
Troilus and Cressida (Shakespeare), 15, 183, 224; a satire of courtship: analysis and significance of the play, 215, 216-22

Troilus and Criseyde (Chaucer), 48, 55, 60, 66, 67, 70, 82, 97, 188, 219
Trojan War, play of the, 216
Troubadours, ritual elaborated by, 8, 96; its appeal, 9; concept of courtly love, 32, 41; influence of Ovid, 34; ideals transformed by Dante and others, 89; doctrine of love surviving in sonneteering tradition, 124
Tudor England, change in the position of women, 103 ff.; conduct books, 107 ff.
Twelfth Night (Shakespeare), 6, 7, 14, 99, 185, 186
Two Gentlemen of Verona (Shakespeare), 4, 6, 83, 188

Urbino, courtiers at, in *Il cortegiano*, 112 ff.
Utopia (More), 87

"Valediction, A . . ." (Donne), 142
Valentine in *Two Gentlemen of Verona*, 188 f.
Valla, Lorenzo, 86
Vega, Lope de, 11
Venus, treatment by Ovid and by Shakespeare, contrasted, 27 ff.
Venus and Adonis (Shakespeare), Ovid's influence, 27-29
Vergil, 20
Vernon, Elizabeth, 106
Virgin, the, 43; lyrics in praise of, 89
Virgins produced by marriage, 56
Vita Nuova (Dante), 90, 95
Vives, Juan Luis, 104 f.

Way of the World, The (Congreve), 3, 227
. . . "Wife of Bath's Tale" (Chaucer), 9, 38, 41, 60, 66, 83, 84
Wild-Goose Chase, The (Fletcher), 227
Willye, in Spenser's *Shepherd's Calendar*, 22
Wit and mockery, type found in love-game comedies, 1, 6

Woman in the Moone, The (Lyly), 162-64, 168, 205
"Womans Constancy" (Donne), 142
"Woman's Superiority" (Hoccleve), 71
Women, in ritual of "courtly love," 8; attitude of St. Jerome, 36; of medieval moralists, 37 f.; as pictured in *fabliaux* and goliardic poetry, 39, 53; question of sex superiority, 41, 61, 71, 83 f., 110; a "good" woman defined by Chaucer, 51; popular war of prose tracts for and against, 83 f.; traditional antagonism toward, reflected in Shakespeare's comedies, 84; change in the position of, and attitude toward, 103 ff. *passim;* restrictive medieval attitude toward intellectual life of, 104; discussion of, in *The Courtier*, 113 ff.; Lyly's denunciation, 162
Wyatt, Sir Thomas, 1, 9, 67, 91, 94, 125, 135, 136, 144, 145, 146, 147; shift from ascetic idealism to practicability in lyrics of: first artistic manifestations of the new humanism, 69; introduction of sonneteering tradition into English literature: sources, 123; substratum under artifices of poetry, 124; treatment of lovers' ideals, 127-30
Wyclif, John, 85, 87

Yates, Frances A., 190